POLITICAL
SCIENTISTS
AT
WORK

NEW FRONTIERS IN AMERICAN POLITICS SERIES

L. Harmon Zeigler, Jr., General Editor
University of Oregon

CONGRESS IN CRISIS: POLITICS AND CONGRESSIONAL REFORM
Roger H. Davidson, University of California, Santa Barbara
David M. Kovenock, University of North Carolina
Michael K. O'Leary, Syracuse University

REFORM AND REACTION: CITY POLITICS IN TOLEDO
Jean L. Stinchcombe, University of Michigan

LOBBYING: INTERACTION AND INFLUENCE IN AMERICAN STATE LEGISLATURES
Harmon Zeigler, University of Oregon
Michael A. Baer, University of Kentucky

WHO WILL RULE THE SCHOOLS? A CULTURAL CLASS CRISIS
Robert E. Agger, McMaster University
Marshall N. Goldstein, McMaster University

POLITICAL SCIENTISTS AT WORK
Oliver Walter, University of Wyoming

FORTHCOMING:

THE RULERS AND THE RULED, abridged and revised edition
Rogert E. Agger, McMaster University
Daniel Goldrich, University of Oregon
Bert E. Swanson, Sarah Lawrence College

Duxbury Press, a division of Wadsworth Publishing Company

POLITICAL SCIENTISTS AT WORK

Edited by
OLIVER WALTER
University of Wyoming

Duxbury Press, a division of Wadsworth Publishing Company, Inc.
Belmont, California

Duxbury Press
A Division of Wadsworth Publishing Company, Inc.

© 1971 by Wadsworth Publishing Company, Inc., Belmont California 94002. All rights reserved. No part of this book may be reproduced, stored in a retrieval system, or transcribed, in any form or by any means, electronic, mechanical, photocopying, recording, or otherwise, without the prior written permission of the publisher, Duxbury Press, a division of Wadsworth Publishing Company, Inc., Belmont, California.

ISBN–0–87872–003–0

L. C. Cat. Card No. 77–161980

Printed in the United States of America

1 2 3 4 5 6 7 8 9 10—76 75 74 73 72 71

NEW FRONTIERS IN AMERICAN POLITICS SERIES

Political science is a changing discipline, but the changes that are taking place are not very different from those that took place in other social sciences a good many years ago. Briefly, political scientists are becoming interested in empirical (some would say "causal") theory and are seeking the appropriate methodologies that will enable them to develop reliable descriptions of recurring patterns in political life. The nature of the articles that are published in professional journals and monographs, which are no longer the exclusive property of university presses, attest to the general improvement of the discipline. Scholars are beginning to be a little self-conscious about using the term "behavior" as though it designated a specific and unique "branch" of political science.

Graduate education in political science is reflective of this trend. Most departments of political science require that their students acquire a level of sophistication in statistics and research design that would have been considered extreme as late as ten years ago. Thus, a majority of graduate students, rather than a minority as was formerly the case, begin their teaching careers with an appreciation for the importance of a systematic study of political life.

However, one must question the extent to which undergraduate students are exposed to political science research —as it is being conducted today. After all, very few undergraduate students, even if they are political science majors, go to graduate school; and the proportion of political science students who are aware of new developments in research technique or new explorations of "old" substantive areas is probably unfortunately small. Although each year sees the appearance of more texts that rely heavily upon recently published material, one frequently hears the argument that much of the current research is over the heads of undergraduates and must be distilled and compressed to be useful.

It is the assumption of this series that a fruitful way to introduce students to political science research is to let them read it for themselves. They can see the problem faced by the researcher, judge the validity or logic of the methods, evaluate the extent to which evidence is supportive of the conclusions, and formulate some idea of the nature of social research. There is no reason why the pedagogical assumptions of undergraduate instruction should differ from those of the graduate program. If there are facts of political and social life worth knowing, all students should be made aware of them.

L. Harmon Zeigler, Jr.
Series Editor

University of Oregon

PREFACE

Political Scientists at Work is intended for use in beginning and intermediate political science methodology courses. It describes the actual research of prominent political scientists, which is a contrast to the formal model of research—a very precise, logical, step-by-step process. From hypothesis to conclusion all is neatly ordered. The researcher seems invariably to know where he is going and exactly how to reach this destination.

During the 1967 academic year, a number of graduate students, including myself, were involved in a year-long research project for a methodology course; we saw a discrepancy between this formal model and our actual process. Granted, we were not the most competent researchers; still, very little in our projects went as planned. New hypotheses were continually appearing and the old being discarded; data we had planned to use proved inadequate, and we had to turn our search elsewhere; operationalizations which had initially seemed useful proved inadequate; and so on. But in formal research reports this stumbling about never seemed to be mentioned.

The inadequacy of the formal model was further emphasized by Professor Robert Scott in his class on developing nations. Scott stressed that the researcher can never fully anticipate all the problems he will encounter during the course of a project; he must be able to adapt methods and modify theories if his research is to be successful. Neither methodology text nor journal articles dwell on this aspect.

Political Scientists at Work derived from a collection of talks delivered at the University of Illinois during the

1968 academic year. This series was totally conceived and administered by the political science graduate students of the University of Illinois. For generations, Illinois graduate students had trudged to the weekly departmental seminar. This faculty-sponsored affair was sometimes stimulating but sometimes also soporific—at least judging by some of our most esteemed professors' reponses. Because of dissatisfaction with the program, in spring 1968 the Political Science Graduate Student Association proposed to the faculty that the Association assume responsibility for the series. The Department agreed, at least in part, and consented to fund three speakers with one-hundred-dollar honoraria plus expenses.

The Association assumed that it would be difficult to induce leading political science scholars to come to the cornfields of central Illinois for such a sum. For this reason, ten invitations were extended. Almost immediately we received seven acceptances. Since we had invited such prominent scholars, the Department could hardly refuse to fund the added four and, with only slight hesitation, they agreed. Following this initial success, the series was incrementally expanded to twelve seminars.

A serious problem with past seminars had been lack of an integrated theme. One week the subject would be the politics of oil in Saudi Arabia and the next it would be leadership in B-29 bomber crews. To overcome this deficiency, our series of talks was built around the research process. We asked leading political scientists to decribe how they actually conducted their research. In other words, we were interested in "research autobiographies" and asked speakers to deal not so much with their findings as with the conception, development, and execution of projects. In particular they were asked to consider such questions as why subjects were chosen for study, why various theories and methods were used, and what modifications took place in the subjects, concepts, theories, and methods throughout the study.

Karl Deutsch, Donald Matthews, Harmon Zeigler, Theodore Lowi, Leroy Reiselbach, Harold Guetzkow, Theodore L. Becker, and Pertti Pesonen delivered talks at the University of Illinois, and revised transcripts of their talks are included here. Along the way, Richard L. Merritt and Michael Baer were brought in as collaborators with Karl Deutsch and Harmon Zeigler respectively. Harold Guetzkow found he did not have time to revise his paper for publication; he suggested that we use a paper of his on the same subject delivered at an Ohio State University symposium, "The Process of Model Building in the Behavioral Sciences." Thomas Dye and Heinz Eulau did not participate in the series but agreed, at our request, to contribute to this book.

I wish to express my thanks to all the contributors. As I stated previously, because this was a Graduate Student Association project, it was not possible to provide large honoraria, yet these scholars consented to devote a good deal of time and effort both in delivering the lectures and revising them for publication. Special thanks must go to Harmon Zeigler. His suggestions and his patience made this publication possible. I wish to express gratitude to all my fellow graduate students and to the members of the Central Committee—Dennis Judd, Trudy Bers, and Lynda Carlson —who offered uncomplaining help many times. Especially, I'd like to thank James Zais and Jane Mohraz: James Zais was instrumental in convincing the Department that the Graduate Student Association should control the seminar series, and his constant devotion to the series made my task much easier; Jane Mohraz spent many hours reading the transcripts and made innumerable valuable suggestions both on the substance and style of the book. Further, I wish to thank Karl Johnson, Ira Carmen, and Cal Clark for reading and commenting upon various manuscripts, and Phillip Monypenny, who as departmental head, always thoughtfully considered our requests and suggestions. John H. Kessel, the Ohio State University, reviewed the final manuscript.

Finally, for four exciting years—both intellectually and otherwise—I wish to dedicate this book to the University of Illinois Department of Political Science.

CONTENTS

INTRODUCTION *1*

1 Donald R. Matthews,
   FROM THE SENATE TO SIMULATION *9*

2 Leroy Rieselbach,
   BIOGRAPHY OF A BOOK: *THE ROOT OF ISOLATIONISM* *28*

3 Karl W. Deutsch and Richard L. Merritt,
   DATA IN INTERNATIONAL AND COMPARATIVE POLITICS: THE YALE ARMS CONTROL PROJECT *46*

4 Harmon Zeigler and Michael Baer,
   LOBBYING: IN SEARCH OF A THEORY *74*

5 Theodore J. Lowi,
   THE DEVELOPMENT OF ARENAS OF POWER *85*

6 Pertti Pesonen,
   PICTURING ELECTIONS ABROAD: A STUDY IN FINNISH POLITICS *106*

7 Thomas R. Dye,
   POLITICS, ECONOMICS AND THE PUBLIC: Looking Back *125*

8 Harold Guetzkow,
   INFLUENCES OF MILIEUX ON THE DEVELOPMENT OF A MODEL AND ITS METHODOLOGY IN INTERNATIONAL RELATIONS: AN AUTOBIOGRAPHICAL ESSAY ABOUT A DECADE OF RESEARCH WITH THE INTER-NATION SIMULATION *151*

9   Heinz Eulau,

       THE LEGISLATIVE SYSTEM AND AFTER: ON CLOSING THE MICRO-MACRO GAP   *171*

10   Theodore L. Becker,

       SOME THOUGHTS ABOUT WHY THE SCIENTIFIC STUDY OF JUDICIAL POLITICS HAS BEEN SO DULL   *193*

INTRODUCTION

By far the most prominent, if not the most important, trend in political science during the past twenty years has been the attempt to become scientific. Central to this drive toward science of politics is the effort to build theories with empirically testable propositions. Yet, it is just this emphasis which has led to an often distorted view of the scientific research process itself. If the job of the researcher is to test theoretically derived hypotheses, then he must have both a relatively explicit theory and a set of precise propositions. The research process, then, comes to look something like the following: The researcher develops from existing theory a set of testable hypotheses; next, in a quite mechanical manner, he proceeds to choose an appropriate instrument and tests the hypotheses. It is this model that is implicit in both methodology tests and in journal articles. The straightforward, step-by-step process does have value. For one thing, the logical model of the research process is a convenient way to set forth findings, and for another, it creates the impression among those reading the findings that the researcher is exceedingly systematic. But, as Robert Merton has pointed out, it is a model and therefore does not describe what actually occurs in a successful investigation.[1]

Of course, a political scientist who has carried out any amount of research realizes that the logical model is not a completely accurate description of reality, but this knowledge is often repressed and seldom mentioned. Students setting forth on their first projects would receive little inkling as to the actual process from either methodology

[1] Robert K. Merton, *Social Theory and Social Structure* (New York: Free Press, 1967), p. 103.

texts or formal descriptions of research—a rather odd state of affairs when one considers the stress placed by empiricists upon accurate description.

The logical model hides two essential aspects of research. First, any research involves an almost endless number of choices. Among these are choices of subject, of methods, of how to operationalize important variables, and of the degree of importance to place on different variables. Seldom, if ever, are these choices clear-cut or in any way mechanical, and this is especially true in political science, where our limited theories give little direction. The point is that the success or failure of a project is dependent upon often vague and contradictory choice criteria. Second, the logical model glosses over the continual change in method and theory which is the hallmark of the research process. Certain methods prove ineffective; new ones are chosen. Various explanations do not lead to correct predictions; others are used. And all along the way the researcher's expectations about the nature of the political phenomena undergoes constant change.

In regard to the first aspect, there are, of course, choices dictated by the nature of one's problem. If one is concerned with the behavior of cabinets, he studies cabinets. Further, the approach the researcher employs will sometimes dictate decisions. Obviously, if one believes that it is possible to undertand all of politics by first understanding the group, then surely he will study group behavior. But frequently these choices are not so clear, and even in the above cases they become much less clear as the researcher begins dealing with specifics. Choice criteria become vague and many times have no relationship whatsoever to theory, contrary to what might be implied by the logical model. Numerous instances can be found in the following essays.

Why did Harmon Zeigler and Michael Baer choose to study lobbying in Oregon, North Carolina, Utah, and Massachusetts? Why did Theodore Becker choose judges in Hawaii? Why did Donald Matthews decide on the Senate and Leroy Reiselbach on the House? Certainly the choices were not dictated by initial assumptions. Matthews chose the Senate because it was small and he wished to complete his doctorate. Reiselbach chose House districts because they were more homogeneous, thus lending themselves more easily to a test of his hypotheses. Zeigler and Baer picked the four states because they seemed to provide "maximum dispersion of socioeconomic and cultural variables." One also suspects that Oregon might have been selected because the political scientists held positions at the University of Oregon. Finally, the fact that Becker was teaching in Hawaii at the time may have had something to do with his choice of Hawaiian judges. The point is that choice of subject is seldom predetermined. Research choices can be based upon theoretical imperatives, but they can also be based upon such considerations as time, money, and location, or personal preference, as Theodore Becker so forcefully points out.

The choice of instrument is also crucial to the success of a research project, and just as the subject choice is open to wide discretion, so also is the choice of instrument. In almost every one of the essays, the authors point out instances of such discretion. Richard Merritt and Karl Deutsch relate how there were no "pat formulas about how to identify elites." When the elites were selected, the project directors were also faced with the decision of whether or not to use professional interviewers and highly structured qustionnaires or to use European scholars with open interview schedules. Either choice would result in various costs and benefits; the correct choice was never intuitively obvious.

The Matthews-Prothro study of Negro political participation ran into many of the same dilemmas. On the one hand, a study based on communities would be the best method to examine the influence of political structure, election laws, and racial attitudes on participation rates. On the other hand, such a study would make it impossible to generalize about Negro participation in the entire South. As Matthews points out, this methodological decision was further complicated by the uncertainty of budget size and the need to play "the-more-and-the-faster-you-spend, the-more-you will-probably-get" game. The importance of non-theoretically related choice criteria and the wide choice range is again seen in the Pertti Pesonen study. Because Pesonen wished to study the Finnish electorate over an extended period of time, it was necessary to use a panel design. But the sample size and the location of the study were largely determined by availability of resources.

Another choice is that of operationalization. The means to operationalize concepts may be obvious, but on many occasions they are not; if they are apparent, other constraints may not permit an optimal decision. For instance, Reiselbach points out numerous meanings of isolationism. But he could not simply translate these meanings into testable concepts for the very reason that roll calls in Congress did not allow for such analysis. Rather, he was forced to choose aid and trade as indicators of the isolation variable even though it was obvious that this was somewhat of a distortion of reality.

Thomas Dye in *Politics, Economics and the Public* faced a similar problem. He found that gathering comparable data for all fifty states on even a few variables was extremely difficult and frequently impossible. Thus, the availability of data had much to do with the manner in which key variables were operationalized.

Another set of choices has to do with the selection of relevant variables. Dye also tells how systems theory gave him almost no clue as to which variables were the most relevant to his study. Although he fell back on literature in other areas, to a large degree his final selections were dependent upon his political intuition—a component of the research process not captured by the logical model. Similarly, Harold Guetzkow relates that the choice of relevant variables for the Inter-Nation Simulation was to a large degree quite fortuitous. The lack of international relations theory made the choice unclear; again the selection was dependent upon the political sense of Guetzkow and his associates.

Finally, categorization is part of the research process in which decisions are not always obvious. Any set of categories are abstractions, and there will always be difficulties in fitting all cases into them. It is a rare scheme that does not run into what Theodore Lowi calls "bleeding" across categories. Logically a scheme can seem perfect, but in the real world there are always cases that do not fit. Lowi's agency mission categorization seems quite straightforward, but, as he points out, the difficulty comes when you have agencies with multi-functions.

Thus, the day-to-day choices that the researcher must make do not fit the logical model. They are often not dictated by theory; on the contrary the choices may be forced upon the researcher for strictly non-theoretical reasons. Nor are these decisions mechanical. The decision criteria are often vague or non-existent, and even if the criteria may be well specified, the costs and benefits of various choices may have equal value.

As was mentioned previously, the logical model also hides the changes that occur in formulating theory and method. Method modification, or at least the need for it, is one of the most common features of the research process. It is only the clairvoyant political scientist who can anticipate every problem that will arise when he comes into contact with actual data. The Inter-Nation Simulation (INS) is a good example. Theories of international relations, as previously noted, were of little use in selecting relevant variables or in determining the correct relationships between these variables. Further, little had been done with simulation, and correct procedures were in doubt. INS has been built to a large extent by trial and error. If a variable is causing hang-ups in the simulation, as Guetzkow says, it may simply be thrown out or modified. If certain procedures do not work, they are modified until they do. The point is that these problems could not be anticipated in advance. Therefore, it was only after the simulation was in operation that problems became apparent and could be changed.

Similarly, Matthews and Prothro chose to define participation in terms of a Guttman scale. When the data were analyzed, they found that the scale worked well for whites but that blacks violated a number of Guttman-scale criteria. Thus, the measure had different meaning for the two races. Matthews and Prothro also confronted a problem that all large projects are likely to encounter. The entire project was designed prior to large-scale Negro protest movement in the South. Although Matthews and Prothro undertook a further study, they found it impossible to take into account all changes in modes of participation.

As another case in point, Deutsch and Merritt also encountered a number of unanticipated problems; most importantly, the tendency of the various scholars heading each section of the study to move off in separate directions. This movement was due both to the diverse interests of the participants and to an inadequate communications system. At later stages, a series of conferences had to be set up to overcome these difficulties.

Often, however, these modifications cannot be made during the course of the project. From his earlier research, Theodore Becker has become convinced that those studying the legal system must adopt rather unorthodox research methods. Becker maintains that the study of judicial behavior has not yielded an accurate picture of the legal system simply because academicians are too timid to employ the required methods. His solution: be radical in mind and heart. If accurate portrayals of the legal system are only possible through the use of such techniques as tapping jury rooms and police stations, such methods should be adopted.

It is unfortunate that many political scientists hold such strong commitments to various techniques or methods. As has been pointed out repeatedly, research techniques are instruments. If one instrument does not produce the required results, it should be modified or simply done away with.

Carl Hempel and practically all other modern philosophers of science as well have pointed out that the scientist can never be completely inductive. For every problem needing an explanation, there are an infinite number of possibly relevant facts, and these facts can be classified in innumerable ways. Induction simply does not provide a means to select and order relevant data. This is not to say that the researcher approaches the data with a preconceived and unchanging set of expectations derived from a series of interrelated propositions. Theodore Lowi's essay provides a good example. Lowi worked with data on New York City commissioners. His original expectation was that party recruitment had decreased in importance, and when he tested this hypothesis he discovered that the number of commissioners with party experience had indeed decreased. Yet it was not until he had worked with the data for some time that he made his truly important discovery. It occurred to Lowi that the mission of the agency which the commissioner would be heading might just be of importance. This hypothesis, derived only after working with the data, was confirmed. "Input" agencies experienced almost no decline in party-recruited commissioners, while the remainder all showed quite substantial decreases. To Lowi, "It remains the most remarkable pattern I have ever encountered in my efforts to analyze politics. For me it was something like Keats reading Homer." It is interesting to note that in its early stages the Lowi "Policy Approach" underwent a good many modifications when it came into contact with data, but as it has become more and more complex and precise the addition of modifications has steadily decreased. For Lowi and his students, at least, the "Policy Approach" has reached a stage that Thomas S. Kuhn might label "normal science." In this stage, says Kuhn, the scientist attempts to extend knowledge of the facts that his model displays as particularly relevant; he attempts to increase the fit between facts and the paradigm's predictions; and attempts to further articulate the paradigm itself.[2] Lowi has, in other words, apparently gone beyond the stage where serendipity is likely to occur.

Donald Matthews' Senate study also underwent many changes. He relates that he came to the Senate expecting that social background variables would go far in explaining legislative behavior. After watching the Senate in action and talking to staff members, however, Matthews saw that these variables were of much less importance than the immediate Senate context. His solution was to fall back upon his training in structural-functional sociology. When this was not totally satisfactory, he simply "utilized concepts and hypotheses from the literature on mass communications, voting behavior, and bargaining theory."

Nor did the Zeigler-Baer research go from theory to research to data to conclusion. Symbolic interaction theory was central to the explanation of the researchers' findings. Yet, as they point out, this was not their initial approach. The original expectations simply were not borne out. For instance, Zeigler and Baer originally assumed that interest-group effectiveness was related to such variables as urbanization, industrialization and wealth, and political variables such as party competition and party cohesion. The relationships were not present, and they began searching for new propositions that might help to explain the data. Finally, the solution proved to be symbolic interaction theory.

Pertti Pesonen describes a similar pattern. Initially he used two models to construct his questionnaires. During the project he discarded one of the models largely because of lack of time and resources. Another model—a communications network model—was incorporated after Pesonen heard Lester Milbrath give a visiting lecture—an occurrence that could hardly have been predicted. Indeed, the data had been collected three years prior to the incorporation of this theoretical perspective.

In the course of their research, both Dye and Eulau have become disillusioned with systems theory. Dye's disillusionment came when he attempted to use systems theory with actual data. Although suggesting the existence of three categories of variables —input, political system, and policy outputs—systems theory gave little hint as to the interrelationship of the variables or the

---

[2] Thomas S. Kuhn, *The Structure of Scientific Revolutions* (Chicago: University of Chicago Press, 1962), p. 24.

importance of these variables. In other words, systems theory did not provide a very adequate research map. In the choice of variables, for example, Dye was forced to fall back upon economics and non-system theory in political science. As Becker points out, systems theory—*à la* Easton—can not be considered a research paradigm in Kuhn's sense of the word. Dye's experiences are prime examples. The approach may have pointed him in the right direction, but it gave him very little information on how to reach his destination. Further, if systems theory had been a real paradigm, Dye certainly would not have been so surprised by his findings.

Eulau's disillusionment came when he discovered that systems theory gave no clue as to how to bridge the "micro-macro" gap. In working with the data from the legislative system study, he and his associates wished to talk about the behavior of collectivities using data from individual legislators. The initial theory provided no hint as to the relationship between data at various levels. The "Nomenclature of Unit Properties" expounded here was conceived, then, to fill a void in the initial theory—a void encountered only after substantial data analysis.

Research, then, is not a precise, well-ordered process. One can conclude that it is a process filled with endless decisions made difficult by vague or non-existent choice criteria. It is one which requires constant modification in theory and method. "Research," declares Leroy Reiselbach, "proceeds in a sort of groping fashion in the direction in which you set out, but not without straying from the path regularly and having to change routes on occasion." This would seem to be the rule rather than the exception.

No one would say that the political scientist should not be technically competent nor that he should disregard scientific principles. Technical skill and adherence to sound scientific tenets are certainly prerequisites for any good research, though these are not enough. The political scientist enamored of technique often flies into the void of the trivial and the irrelevant. The political scientist overly concerned with an ideal model of science frequently never gets off the ground. Rather, the successful researcher is one who can think in terms of elegant logical models and yet at the same time can deal with inelegant and inexact data.

1 FROM THE SENATE TO SIMULATION

Donald R. Matthews
The Brookings Institution

The most unpromising way I know to begin an interview with a politician is to ask, "How did you happen to get interested in a political career?" To ask a group of academicians about the genesis of their research is to run the risk of equally windy, self-serving, and unrevealing replies. An academic's capacity for candid and critical self-analysis of his own research activity probably is not much better than that of the politician asked to expound upon how he became a statesman.

Perhaps this is one reason political scientists so rarely talk about how and why they choose to do research on one topic rather than another; how or why they choose between competing theoretical orientations, research designs, and techniques of analysis; how or why their initial plans and ideas alter in the process of research. This is embarrassingly autobiographical stuff that is usually printed in Prefaces and Appendices.

The textbooks on methodology do not say much about these questions either. Ordinarily, they present a highly

---

This is the first publication of Donald R. Matthews' essay. All rights reserved. Permission to reprint must be obtained from the publisher and the author.

schematic and idealized picture of a research process which bears little resemblance to the reality of false starts, muddled thinking, recalcitrant facts, and limited resources with which the researcher is all too familiar. Perhaps the origins of political research projects are so dependent on circumstances and the emotional commitments and intellectual styles of individual researchers that they defy systematic treatment. This does not mean that the early and artistic phases of political science research should not be discussed. For the more research I do—and the longer I try to help students conduct their own research—the more convinced I become that decisions made at the earliest stages of inquiry determine, in large measure, the quality of the end result. Most "bad" research does not have a chance from the beginning. Poorly conceived research sometimes can be salvaged, but most "good" research flows from wise decisions made at the very start.

I doubt that my experiences as a political researcher are worthy of emulation. But I have been at it for twenty years now and think that I have learned a few things about the early phases of research in the process. Even if I have not, perhaps the reader can learn something from my experiences.

Selecting and Defining Topics

I once heard Alex Inkeles jokingly propound what I have since come to call Inkeles's Law: "All research projects take seven years without regard to size."

In my case, The Law roughly applies. My work on *U.S. Senators and Their World*[1] was spread over ten years—interrupted by the demands of a new teaching career, the arrival of children, and an unexpectedly lengthy detour into the general literature on the recruitment of political elites.[2] Despite a superb collaborator, a big and able staff of assistants, and a large budget, *Negroes and the New Southern Politics*[3] took seven years of nearly full-time

---

[1] (Chapel Hill, N.C.: University of North Carolina Press, 1960), 303 pp. Reprinted in paperback by Vintage Books, 1962.
[2] *The Social Background of Political Decision Makers* (Garden City, N.Y.: Doubleday, 1954), 71 pp.
[3] With James W. Prothro (New York: Harcourt, 1966), 551 pp.

work. My current research on decision making by congressmen[4] has been underway three years so far and will take another year or two to complete. My median number of years per project seems to work out to be about seven!

I probably work more slowly than many political researchers. But the banal point I want to make here is that most subjects tend to grow alarmingly once you penetrate any distance into them. Thus, a decision to conduct research on a topic ordinarily involves a commitment of a significant fraction of your total professional career. At least people who work at about my rate have only five or six chances to decide on research topics during their entire professional lifetimes. Obviously these are important decisions.

Such decisions take me a long time. I do a lot of mulling over possible alternatives before I commit myself irrevocably. Usually this process begins a year or so before I complete my current research, and preliminary work on the next project begins before I am entirely out from under the last one. The long leadtime required to raise funds almost forces this mode of operation upon anyone whose research requires substantial financial resources, but I recommend strenuous efforts to restrict this period of conflicting loyalties and divided attention as much as possible. It's not an easy time in which to make the critical early decisions about your next research.

The situation and its practical imperatives have played a large role in my choice of research topics. My work on American senators began while I was a second-year graduate student at Princeton University. I had signed up for a seminar on social stratification in the Sociology Department and was required to write a paper for it. The idea for an analysis of the class backgrounds of American senators emerged during several conferences with Professor Melvin Tumin, who taught the seminar. (I remember that I chose senators rather than House members because there were fewer of

---

[4] The final report on this research has not yet been published. Preliminary reports may be found in S. Ulmer (Ed.), *Political Decision Making* (forthcoming) and "The Decision-Making Approach to the Study of Legislative Behavior" (paper presented at the American Political Science Association Annual Meeting, 1969, mimeo.). Both articles were prepared in collaboration with James A. Stimson.

them.) I enjoyed doing the paper—it was my first experience at quantitative political analysis—and it was well received. So when the time came to choose a dissertation topic I eventually[5] hit upon the idea of enlarging this sociology paper into a dissertation on the recruitment of U.S. Senators.[6] By the time I completed the dissertation, I had invested so many tedious hours collecting data on the backgrounds of senators that it made sense to revise and extend the dissertation into a book. In fact, as a junior member of the Smith College faculty, I had so little time for research that to begin work on an altogether new topic would have postponed my publishing anything so long that I probably would have been fired.

Situational factors affected my choice of a second research topic in quite different ways, but just as profoundly. In 1957 I moved to the University of North Carolina. The most exciting political events in that part of the South at that particular time were the struggles of Negroes to get registered as voters and, once registered, to use their votes effectively. I happened to have located in the midst of fascinating and historic change: why not take advantage of being on the scene? Furthermore I felt—correctly, as it turned out—that it would be relatively easy to obtain a sizeable grant to conduct research on Negro voting in the South. I like to think that this was less a self-interested example of grantsmanship than it first appears. The Department of Political Science at Chapel Hill was in the process of building. North Carolina is a poor state; the financial resources of the University were relatively limited. The only way to build a first-class department was by attracting substantial outside funds. Alexander Heard's large research project on money in politics and Rogert Agger's comparative community studies had had beneficial side effects for the department—primarily research assistantships for graduate students. A large study of Negro politics would have some of the same indirect payoffs. Finally, Fred Cleaveland, the chairman of

[5] My first choice of dissertation topic—a study of Parliamentary control of nationalized industries in Great Britain—was abandoned when my plans failed to elicit sufficient enthusiasm from relevant faculty members or money from foundations. I was awfully discouraged by these rebuffs at the time. Now, of course, I am thankful that I was saved from attempting to carry out an unpromising research plan.

[6] "United States Senators: A Study of the Recruitment of Political Leaders" (Princeton University, unpublished doctoral dissertation, 1953).

the department, and I were most anxious to attract James W. Prothro, a close friend from graduate school days, to Chapel Hill and the department. An opportunity to collaborate on a large, already-funded research project on a subject in which we knew he was interested would substantially strengthen our case.

But these calculations have not been the only considerations entering into my choice of topics for research. A desire for self-education invariably has been a factor. Here I mean something more than a need to satisfy my curiosity about the subjects I study—all researchers try to educate themselves in that sense. In addition, I have self-consciously sought to use research as a means of acquiring new experiences and skills.

My political science training at Princeton in the late 1940s and early fifties was highly traditional, institutional, and non-quantitative. One of the most appealing motives for writing a dissertation on the recruitment of senators was that it would permit me to develop at least some experience and competence at statistical analysis. And one of the major attractions of expanding the dissertation into a book was that it would require my going to Washington to conduct interviews with senators—I'd never spent a day on Capitol Hill or conducted a research interview until I arrived in Washington to carry out the field work for *U.S. Senators*. The Negro political participation study served, among other things, as a way of learning survey research technology. My prior acquaintanceship with this mode of research had been limited to several amateurish exercises with undergraduate students. Having learned a little about the use of computers for data analysis in the course of the Negro study, my current research on decision making by congressmen provides an opportunity to explore the possibilities of computer simulation and the use of computers for model building and model testing. Perhaps the current generation of political scientists—more adequately and appropriately trained than mine—will not need to engage in such constant and strenuous retooling. But the discipline certainly will continue to change; research is the best way to change along with it.

I've always felt that it is a mistake to research only a single subject, or even to specialize in the study of political phenomena at only the elite or only the mass levels. In part this is because I find an occasional drastic change in subject matter and research technique exciting and reinvigorating. (All too often, political scientists spend their careers defending their first book—not many are worth such dreary self-sacrifice.) I also believe that a capacity for the analysis of elite behavior is strengthened by an understanding of mass phenomena and vice versa. If we are ever successfully to link the two, we must be competent at both.

There is an obvious risk of dilettantism in selecting research topics so as to further one's education. But for me this risk is nothing compared to the certainty of boredom and intellectual superannuation if I were to operate any other way.

I am not aware that my own *political values and policy preferences* played any part in my decision to study the behavior of senators or in deciding to conduct my current research on decision making by House members. Both these efforts were, as best I can tell, stimulated by academic concerns combined with the practical imperatives I have already discussed.[7]

But my research on Negro political participation in the South was in large part stimulated by a longstanding personal concern for the plight of the American Negro. One of the primary objectives of the study was to probe the probable effectiveness of various strategies of civil rights reform. The desirability of racial equality was taken for granted; if Prothro and I had not felt strongly about this, the research would not have been done at all.

Nowhere in this discussion of the choice of research subjects have I mentioned a concern for the development of an empirical theory of politics. I do have a keen desire to contribute to a general and reliable political theory but do not feel, realistically, that this has had much impact on my choice of what to study.

Given the present state of political science, a desire to be theoretically revelant still leaves the resarcher much room for maneuver—there are many competing conceptual schemes and theoretical orientations from which to choose and to which useful contributions might be made. Perhaps a few political scientists actually

[7] This is not to say that value and policy implications cannot be read into either work. *U.S. Senators* is sometimes interpreted as a sophisticated defense of the *status quo;* my current work on congressional decision making will be read by some as an indictment of the House, by others as an argument for the collective rationality of the House. I personally believe that both chambers are in need of enlightened change, but my concern in these works has been to contribute to understanding of Congress rather than its reform. Most proposals to reform the Congress have been based on good intentions and massive ignorance of congressional realities.

operate the way the methodology textbooks say we should—by choosing subjects for inquiry in order to test or flesh out concepts and theoretical constructs which they find promising. Except possibly in the case of my current research on congressional decision making, I confess to operating with altogether different priorities. My choice of research topics has been dictated largely by non-theoretical and non-scientific considerations. Then I have utilized, rather empirically and eclectically, those concepts and bits-and-pieces of theory which seem most likely to help me understand the slice of reality I am investigating. Thus, my interest in theory has had less impact on what I have studied than on how I have gone about studying it.

Choosing a Conceptual-Theoretical Orientation

My initial research on senators was done for a seminar in sociology, so it is not surprising that the original theoretical framework of this research was heavily sociological. Talcott Parsons, Robert Merton, Wilbert Moore, and other structural-functional theorists provided most of my intellectual equipment; my particular interest was in the impact of social stratification on the political life-chances of Americans.[8]

In the process of expanding this work into a dissertation and preparing the review of the literature which appeared as *The Social Background of Political Decision Makers,* I gradually realized that political life-chances were not terribly interesting or important to me anymore. By now I thought of myself as a "political behavioralist," and this new and embattled group was self-consciously seeking to differentiate itself from sociologists as well as "traditionalists" in political science.

One of the cardinal tenets of the early behavioralists—Harold Lasswell, V. O. Key, Jr., David Truman, and Richard Synder were especially influential in my case—was that the behavior of political actors was not entirely determined by the laws, rules, and formal-organizational factors which "traditional" political scien-

---

[8] This initial concern is reflected in "United States Senators and the Class Structure," *Public Opinion Quarterly,* 18 (1954), 6–22.

tists usually studied. Stephen K. Bailey's *Congress Makes a Law*[9] brilliantly illustrated that the behavior of congressmen was, at least in part, a result of their own values and predispositions which were, in turn, a product of their total life experiences. I speculated that perhaps a systematic analysis of the relationships between the social backgrounds and career lines of senators and their behavior could prove this point definitively, and this was what I set out to determine in *U.S. Senators*.

After hanging around Capitol Hill for a few weeks—just watching and talking to a few Senate staff members—it was apparent that social background variables did not make as much difference in the behavior of senators as the immediate context within which they lived and worked. Thus, my initial plan to focus exclusively on these background variables was abandoned, and I decided to describe and explain the patterns of senatorial behavior I saw, using any kind of independent variables I could find to account for them.

Congress is a confusing place, especially when you have never been there before. I didn't get much help from the political science literature. Bailey, Ralph Huitt, Lewis Dexter, Bertram Gross, and a few other behaviorally-oriented political scientists had arrived ahead of me, but most of their research had not yet appeared in print. Thus, the literature on legislative behavior was sparse indeed. So, I fell back on my training in structural-functional sociology to provide the theoretical perspective I so badly needed. When this intellectual apparatus did not seem to help penetrate the thicket, I utilized concepts and hypotheses from the literature on mass communications, voting behavior, and bargaining theory. Thus, I ended up studying senators in a quite different way than I had intended.

It is relatively easy to alter the focus of your research when a lonely scholar. It is largely out of the question when directing a sizeable organization in sample survey research. Here you are forced to decide what hypotheses you wish to test in the process of designing the study. This makes for rigorous work. But survey research is limited in two ways: first, it is almost impossible to ask meaningful questions when we know little about the subject; second, it is extremely difficult to modify the instrument even though conditions may change in the midst of research. Jim Pro-

---

[9] (New York: Columbia University Press, 1950.)

thro's and my experiences in conducting the Negro political participation study may illustrate these points.

From the beginning, the basic question Jim Prothro and I were interested in was the relative importance of political versus demographic variables in explaining the extremely low rate of black participation in Southern politics. There were two reasons for this preoccupation. In the early '60s, political scientists were still fighting Paul Lazarsfeld and *The People's Choice*[10] brand of social determinism which characterized so much early electoral research. Angus Campbell, Phillip Converse, Warren Miller, and Donald Stokes in *The American Voter*[11] had recently made significant progress in introducing political variables into the analysis of voting and political participation. We wanted to push this line of research much further, stressing community-level political variables which the Michigan team had not stressed extensively in their work.

Our interest in the impact of demographic versus political variables was also stimulated by our concern about civil rights policy. The Eisenhower and Kennedy Administrations championed a "do-it-yourself" theory of civil rights reform: give Southern Negroes the vote and let them vote themselves equality. This presupposed that it would be possible to vastly increase the size of the Negro electorate in the South through federal legislation and Administration action and that this black vote would have an impact on policy outcomes. But Southern Negroes were poor, undereducated, and alienated. Groups like this are unlikely candidates for active citizenship, without regard to their skin color. To what extent were the pitifully low rates of Negro political participation the result of their position at the bottom of the social and economic heap? Or was the low rate of Negro participation the result of overt and direct discrimination in electoral laws and their administration, the absence of qualified Negro leadership and sympathetic white candidates, and other political factors? The answers to these questions seemed to have obvious and important implications for public policy.[12]

---

[10] (New York: Columbia University Press, 1948.)

[11] (New York: Wiley, 1960.)

[12] Our first effort to answer these questions was "Social and Economic Factors and Negro Voter Registration in the South," *American Political Science Review*, 57 (1963), 24–44, and "Political Factors and Negro Voter Registration in the South," *ibid.*, 355–367. This extensive analysis of ag-

As our data analysis progressed, so did history. Both demonstrated that Negro voter registration, at least, could be very substantially increased by legal pressures from the federal government. This resulted in a shift in our attention toward the problem of policy outputs: Once Negroes are voting in substantial numbers, will they be able to force additional changes in public policy favorable to their interests? This, of course, is a far more difficult problem to analyze with any precision. Negro political participation—which we had been able to measure in our survey—becomes an independent variable rather than the dependent one; the dependent variable becomes public policies, extremely difficult to measure and about which our survey was silent. We did the best we could under the circumstances, but we would have designed a different type of study if we had known in advance that Negro voter registration would increase as rapidly as it did.

History confounded us in another way. The Negro protest movement began with the first student "sit-in" in Greensboro, N.C., while our survey was in the field. It was too late for us to redesign the study to take this development into account. We were able, however, to raise sufficient additional funds to conduct a previously unplanned sample survey of black college students in the South in order to probe the factors which triggered the early student protesters into action. But a whole new arsenal of political and quasi-political tactics—sit-ins, freedom rides, marches, mass protests, riots—were developed and popularized in the course of a few months. At the time we designed the study, Southern politics was electoral politics; by the time we completed our analysis five years later, Southern politics was a rather different game in which "political participation" had taken on new and broader meanings. We were unable to give these new modes of participation in the political process the attention they deserved.

The role of theory in my current research on decision making by congressmen can be dispensed with quickly, since this research more closely follows the textbook model of how research ought to be carried on than anything I have done before. Much of the credit for this methodological purity rightly belongs to my young

---

gregate data was conducted prior to our sample survey. Imposing methodological problems were encountered in carrying out this substudy, but I shall not discuss them here.

collaborator, James A. Stimson, who was brought up in the exacting traditions of scientific research which those of us well over thirty have learned only imperfectly through years of trial and error. But, since some of the critical decisions about the study were made before he joined me, a portion of the credit is rightly mine as well.

The basic hypothesis of our research is that members of the House of Representatives normally make up their minds how to vote on ordinary roll calls on the basis of cues provided by other members rather than on the basis of their own independent evaluation of the merits of legislative proposals. This is not an altogether new idea: references to legislators taking cues from one another are frequently encountered in the literature, including, of all places, *U.S. Senators and Their World*.[13] What is new about our hypothesis is that we argue that cue taking is the *normal* process of decision for House members and that decisions made in this way are more likely to be rational (or nearly so) than if members normally followed a different decision rule.

This hypothesis had two sources, and I doubt that I would have chosen to do research on it if both had not been present. First, I had observed cue giving and cue taking in the Senate many years ago. Second, I read the literature on rational decision making[14] and had the opportunity to discuss it with my colleague at the Center for Advanced Study in the Behavioral Sciences in 1964–1965. Gradually I began to fuse these two experiences in my own thinking.

How do congressmen, I asked myself, make such a large number of decisions on complex, specific, and technical policy proposals in a wide range of subject areas in such a limited amount of time? In terms of Congress as a whole the answer was the specialization provided by the committee system. Whether or not individual decision making involved a similar type of specialization had never been considered. The literature on congressional roll-call voting is silent on this question, too, settling for correlations between assumed independent variables (e.g., constituency characteristics, party membership) and the congressman's vote, without concern

[13] *Op. cit.*, pp. 251–254.
[14] Particularly influential for me were A. Downs, *An Economic Theory of Democracy* (New York: Harper, 1957) and D. Braybrook and C. Lindbloom, *A Strategy of Decision* (New York: Free Press, 1963).

for intervening processes. This reminded me of *The People's Choice* stage of electoral research, when moderate correlation between the demographic attributes of individuals and their vote was considered an adequate explanation of electoral choice. Perhaps research on legislative decision making would benefit from adopting the strategy of *The American Voter* by concentrating on the *process* of decision making without too much concern for ultimate causes.

Thinking about the process of decision making by congressmen quickly leads to the conclusion that congressmen must have worked out ways to make reasonably acceptable decisions on the basis of very little information and without the investment of much time. What is the most plausible low-information decision rule for a harried congressman? We believe that it is cue taking, and we are currently trying to prove (or disprove) the point. Our method of pursuing this task is described in the next portion of this paper.

Which Research Method?

Research topics and research methods are so interrelated that a decision on the first often determines the second. Of course these decisions are not invariably made in that order. A good many political scientists, once they have mastered a demanding and esoteric research technique, tend to investigate only topics susceptible to this kind of analysis. Either way—and a good argument can be made for both procedures—options about research methods are often limited. Nonetheless, the way in which these limited choices are made can have a substantial impact on the quality of research.

I had gone to Washington to conduct personal interviews with members of the United States Senate, but the kind of interviews I would carry out and how my interviewees were to be selected remained undecided at the time I arrived. Within a few weeks I had decided in favor of relatively unstructured interviews and against attempting to interview a representative sample of senators.

No doubt these decisions were influenced by my realization that conducting structured interviews with a sample of senator-respondents would be far more difficult and time-consuming than the kind of interviewing program I ultimately launched. But I was also aware that I still did not know what the relevant and interesting questions about senatorial behavior were; to lock myself into a standard interview seemed most unwise under these circumstances. I was also worried about how much "openness" I could expect from the senators. If some proved to be far more cooperative than others, then tabulating responses and generalizing from these to the universe of all senators seemed a dubious procedure.

There were obvious dangers and disadvantages to proceeding as I did. One was that I might end up talking only to those senators most easily accessible to academic researchers—a small set of ex-eggheads and Northern Democrats with quite unrepresentative views about the Senate and public policy. I therefore made especially strenuous efforts to reach conservative Republicans and Southern Democrats. The people I talked to were viewed as informants, not respondents; I asked them about other members as I asked them about themselves. This, too, I hoped would guard distortions resulting from not interviewing a representative sample. Finally, I sought to check as many of the impressions I took away from the interviews as I could by quantitative analysis of the formal record of the Senate. I am by no means satisfied with what I was able to do along this line, but I remain convinced that it was worth the effort (and that a lot more effort should be expended in this direction in the future).

If I were to do this study over again, would I make these same decisions? In the mid-1950s, confronted with a choice between following rigorous methods or developing new insights, I think I grabbed the right horn of the dilemma. In 1970, given the sizeable advances we have made in understanding Congress in the intervening years, we no longer need to choose between the two.

The Negro political participation study posed so many complex problems of research design and method that it is impossible to remember them all. Two decisions Prothro and I made on these matters still stand out in my mind as especially critical, so I shall confine my comments to them.

The first of these was our definition of the dependent variable. Most prior research on the problem had focused on Negro voting (and non-voting) in the South. Our original thinking was almost exclusively about this mode of participation too. But as our plans developed and became more concrete, we became increasingly interested in other forms of civic participation as well. Eventually we decided to study the general phenomenon of Negro political participation, not just voting and non-voting.

This decision presented us with a tough problem of operational definition. Eventually we "solved" it—at least to our satisfaction—with a Guttman-type cumulative scale of political participation. Political participation, when this approach is adopted, becomes a continuum along which people can be arrayed according to the most demanding form of participation in which they engaged. Per-

TABLE 1

Political Participation

None	Talk Politics	Talk Politics	Talk Politics	Talk Politics
(Type I)	(Type II)	+ Vote (Type III)	+ Vote + Participate in Campaigns (Type IV)	+ Vote + Participate in Campaigns + Belong to Political Group (Type V)

sons who engage in rare and demanding forms of participation (say, running for public office or belonging to a political organization) also are supposed to participate in the less demanding ways (such as voting or talking politics) as shown in Table 1.

Our white respondents fit this pattern well; for them, participation in the political life of the region did, in fact, have the cumulative aspect that scaling theory says it does. The same scale, however, did not work as well for the blacks in our sample. A significant minority of them were active at quite high levels (Types IV and V in the above diagram) but had never voted! Moreover, while most whites fell near the center of the scale in a bell-shaped curve, there was a large pile-up of minimally active Negroes at Type II, a deep valley at Type III, and a smaller peak of Negroes at Type IV. Obviously, voting was more "difficult" for Negroes than whites if many Negro non-voters were otherwise political activists. Whites who displayed any political activity at all usually voted, but that was not true among Southern Negroes. Thus, by examining the relationships between different kinds of participation within the two races we were able to show the vastly different meanings of the act of voting for Southern Negroes and whites. A large portion of our book was devoted to explaining these racial differences.

This method of defining and measuring political participation had drawbacks. Given the large differences between the two races, no single measure of political participation worked equally well for blacks and whites; certainly ours did not. But if different definitions of "political participation" were used for the two races, comparisons across race lines could not be made. We felt it essential to make such comparisons. So we made the plausible assumption—which was buttressed by subsequent analysis—that the pattern for Southern whites was "normal" and used the political participation scale as the measure of our dependent variable for blacks as well as whites.

We felt—and still feel—that this sacrifice in statistical purity was more than offset by our ability to make intraracial comparisons and to point out the different relationships between the same modes of participation within each race. Not all of our reviewers agreed.

The second dilemma we faced was straight out of the methodology textbooks: Was the study to be primarily descriptive or analytic in emphasis? At the time our research was in the planning stage, no sample survey of Southern Negro opinion ever had been done, and the Southern Negro component of nationwide samples was too small to permit reliable inferences being drawn from them. We felt, therefore, more than the usual need to fully describe our subject. How many Southern Negroes actually voted? How many participated in political life in other ways? How do Southern Negroes feel about politics? What did they want? Ignorance about such elementary matters was overwhelming, and public policy was being made on the basis of guesses about answers to questions we could provide, within known limits of accuracy, by means of a South-wide sample survey.

On the other hand, as political scientists (and as reformers, too), we had quite analytic interests, focusing on the relative impact of politico-legal versus socioeconomic variables on Negro participation rates. If the study were to emphasize this question, a region-wide sample survey probably was not the best way to go about it. Negro participation rates seemed to vary widely from community to community, apparently in response to differences in political structure, electoral laws and their administration, white racial attitudes, the adequacy of Negro leadership, and other community variables. In a normal nation-wide sample survey, there are too few respondents in each community to come to grips with these local variations. A series of community studies seemed the better way to satisfy our analytic and theoretical concerns. But, of course, a research design of this sort would not permit us to make descriptive generalizations about all Southern Negroes.

An added complication was uncertainty about the size of the budget. Our funds were drawn from a large Rockefeller Foundation grant to the Institute for Research in Social Science at the University of North Carolina to support a series of studies on "The Changing Position of the Negro in the American South." Our project was only one of a number that IRSS planned to support from the grant, and no firm allocation of funds among these projects had been made. Our share of the grant apparently depended upon how fast we, as compared to the other researchers, could spend the money. This kind of "the-more-and-the-faster-you-spend, the more-you-will-probably get" game is not conducive to lengthy deliberations over research design.

Finally, in the course of a marathon conference with Warren Miller of Michigan's Survey Research Center (to whom we had decided to contract out the field work), we came up with a compromise design which would permit us to conduct both a Southwide sample survey and a series of community studies at a cost which did not exceed our guess as to the ultimate budget for the project. The trick was to select communities for intensive analysis from among SRC's primary sampling units. By oversampling in these PSUs, we would end up with community samples as well as a Southwide sample, a large number of interviews being counted in both. This plan permitted us both to explore community-based variables in considerable depth and to generalize about all Southern Negroes from a single study.

My cue-taking hypothesis about decision making by House members might have been explored in a variety of ways. However, the possibility of testing the idea by means of a computer simulation occurred to me very early in the game, and no other approach was seriously considered until after a computer model had been developed.

While I remained unimpressed by most efforts at simulation in political science research, congressional decision making seemed like an unusually promising area in which to give it a try. Roll-call votes are recorded and reoccurring events, and they require members to make a hundred or more public decisions about issues of some importance and visibility each year. Most roll calls in Congress are fairly controversial, and the number of near-unanimous "hurrah" votes is relatively small. If a model of decision making by congressmen could be developed which would predict individual votes, the model would have to make at last 50,000 unique predictions each session. By comparing the predictions made by the model with how the votes were actually cast, it should be possible to determine the extent to which the cue-taking hypothesis held true.

It was at about this point in my thinking that a first-year graduate student named James Stimson was routinely assigned to me as a part-time research assistant. We talked about my ideas on congressional decision making for hours. He then began work on a computer program which, we both hoped, would embody some of them in operational form. This proved to be an extremely valuable learning experience for both of us. The necessities of computer programming forced a new level of logic and precision in our thinking about decision making. Assumptions of which we were only faintly aware jumped out into full view. And the task of defining terms operationally served as a sober reminder of the large gap which remains between theory expressed in the English language and any operational model. Somewhere in this process Stimson became no longer just a research assistant but a full and equal collaborator whose substantive and theoretical contributions to the enterprise were as important as his technical proficiency as a programmer.

About a year after starting on the program, Stimson came up with a primitive version of the model which worked. Its accuracy in post-dicting actual votes was astounding—between eighty-five and ninety percent of all votes cast by all members on all issues were correct! Alternately "giddy with success" and convinced that "something must be wrong somewhere," we spent months checking the model for circularity, experimenting with different operational definitions, examining the relatively few errors of prediction, running the simulation for different years, and so on. All of this checking and fiddling resulted in a number of refinements to the model but failed to significantly change its awesome batting average. We began to *think* that we "had something."

But what? Our simulation not only predicts the votes of members of the House of Representatives but purports to do this by reproducing, in simplified form, the process by which members make up their minds. Success at prediction does not prove that our model of the process is correct; it's possible to be right for the wrong reasons. But our disturbing accuracy at prediction certainly lends greater plausibility to our hypothesis than it had before.

There were still problems and doubts to be resolved. The data on which we base our simulation are the past votes of cue givers and cue takers; associations between the two are assumed to represent responses of the latter to the former. But the votes of cue givers and cue takers might be highly correlated in the absence of communication between the two. Moreover, other more conventional hypotheses about congressional voting—for example, that members "vote their districts" or are motivated by ideological concerns—will often result in predictions very similar to those of our model. How, then, are we to know which model of the decision process is correct? Obviously the time had arrived for us to go to Washington to talk to members about their voting.

The winter and spring of 1969 were spent conducting interviews with a random sample of one hundred members of the House of Representatives. Since a clear hypothesis was to be tested, standardized questions were a necessity whether the members liked it or not—and many of them did not. And our primary concern—how often members cast a "yea" or "nay" vote on the basis of very little information and what they do when confronted with such a situation—was potentially quite threatening to congressional ego and institutional pride. We therefore devoted a great deal of thought and effort to creating an interview situation conducive to candid responses. This seems to have paid off: our response rate was high, we encountered little overt hostility, and all but a handful of members talked freely and openly about a cue-giving and cue-taking system in the House.

This system as described by the members themselves is a great deal more complex than our computer model. This we expected, even desired. All scientific models are oversimplifications of reality —hopefully, creative simplifications which focus attention upon only the "important" and "strategic" elements of the total situation. But the congruence between our model and the members' descriptions of their normal decision making process was substantial. Now we *know* we "have something." How useful that "something" will be in subsequent political science research remains to be seen.

Some Concluding Comments

I do not intend to denigrate technical research competence; far from it. I've had to struggle long and hard to develop the methodological capabilities I have. Compared to the awesome proficiencies of the products of today's best graduate schools, my technical skills are modest; but compared to what I was taught twenty years ago they are impressive, indeed. Unless political science dies, it will continue to change rapidly. Political scientists trained in the 1970s will be pretty lousy tehnicians by 1990 unless they devote much of their time to reeducating themselves. Research, I have found, is the best way to do that.

But a second theme implicit in this discussion is that technical proficiency is not enough. There is an art to good political science research—an instinctive understanding of things political—a gift for asking the right questions, at the right time, in the right way —a knack for resolving the practical problems of the research enterprise in efficient and creative ways—and, I wish I knew what else. A small handful of political scientists have been masters of this art; the rest of us do the best we can with what we have. Perhaps by sharing our research experiences, we can enlarge that small handful.

2 BIOGRAPHY OF A BOOK: THE ROOTS OF ISOLATIONISM

Leroy Rieselbach
Indiana University

I was told that these seminars, reflecting student interest, would focus on the problems involved in designing and conducting research rather than on the substantive findings that the projects generated. Following this line, I will survey, briefly, some of the issues I faced over a period of years in beginning a doctoral dissertation and in carrying it through to final publication, in the form of *The Roots of Isolationism*.[1] The first stage of this process, the dissertation phase, is a problem of continuing interest to graduate students and, as such, worth discussing. In any case, I thought I would present a kind of biography of one particular book.

Antecedents of the Project

I ought to say first that I seriously doubt that there exists, in fact, anything that can be taken seriously as a

---

This is the first publication of Leroy Rieselbach's essay. All rights reserved. Permission to reprint must be obtained from the publisher and the author.

logic of discovery. At least, when I reconstruct the genesis of my interest in the general issue of Congress and foreign policy and in the more specific question of the correlates of roll-call voting on international issues it seems highly idiosyncratic. In any event, my choice of a thesis topic illustrates the place of values, of normative considerations, in decisions about what to study.

I grew up in Milwaukee, Wisconsin. Joseph McCarthy was the state's junior senator at the time I was becoming aware of politics, and I heard a lot of discussion, much of it sympathetic, about him, what he was supposedly trying to do, and how he was going about doing it. It was not uncommon in those days to hear it argued that McCarthyism, the attempt to find disloyalty in high places and to attribute undesirable foreign policy outcomes to Communist influence, was a product of a particular region of the country or a phenomenon fostered by particular ethnic groups.

I carried these notions, and some interest in their truth or falsity, around with me for many years. As a graduate student, I encountered in seminars and elsewhere some of the literature on Congress, especially on roll-call voting, and my interest in such issues was renewed. Duncan MacRae's *Dimensions of Congressional Voting* was particularly influential in this connection.[2] About this same time, I was steered to papers by George Belknap and Charles Farris which illustrated the utility of Guttman-scale analysis for treating legislators' roll-call votes.[3] These methods were combined with my earlier concern with the Midwest and the attitudes of its residents toward foreign policy. I began to focus my attention on some hypotheses relating constituency characteristics of legislators and their voting behavior in Congress.

During this same period, I had the opportunity—in truth I had little choice—to try my hand at writing seminar papers. If I may be permitted to put in a plug for the Yale Political Science Department, one thing that is required there is an early start on research and writing. While such projects are not always successful—though a surprisingly large number are—the effort to test,

---

[1] (Indianapolis: Bobbs-Merrill, 1966.)

[2] (Berkeley, Calif.: University of California Press, 1959.)

[3] George M. Belknap, "A Method for Analyzing Legislative Behavior," *Midwest Journal of Political Science*, 2 (1958), 377–402, and Charles D. Farris, "A Method of Determining Ideological Groupings in the Congress," *Journal of Politics*, 20 (1958), 308–338.

even in a preliminary way, specific propositions enables the student to become familiar with problems of data collection and analysis. As a result, when a dissertation project begins to take shape, the fear of dealing with data and employing quantitative techniques is greatly reduced. This is not to say that thesis research is always excellent, but merely to suggest that at Yale some of the mistakes which dissertation writers commonly make have been made earlier in the preparation of seminar papers. It seems reasonable to attribute, in part at least, the large number of Yale dissertations which are eventually published to the considerable research experience given to students in New Haven *prior* to their undertaking a thesis.

In my own case, during my first year I did a roll-call study of congressional foreign policy decisions, seeking to relate party, region, ruralism, and ethnicity to "isolationist" voting in the House of Representatives. Moreover, one of the things about the MacRae book and David Truman's *The Congressional Party*[4]—which came out about the same time—that troubled me was that each dealt with a single, two-year Congress, raising a question about whether the findings were peculiar to that historical period or, in fact, were more general in nature. So, I wanted to build a longitudinal dimension into my analysis. For reasons which I cannot now recall, I decided to work with two three-year periods, one prior to World War II in order to capture what I could of the prewar isolationist sentiment in Congress and the second, 1949–1952, to cover the McCarthy era. I soon discovered that there was a serious problem with a three-year period: elections intervened, changing the identities of the representatives and shifting some districts to the opposition political party. I quickly came to realize why the single Congress, meeting during a two-year period, was the appropriate unit of analysis in this type of study.

This study had employed percentage measures of isolationism, and I came to recognize the difficulties inherent in this sort of index—e.g., the fact that two congressmen may wind up with the same index score but take contrary stands on many, even all, of the roll calls on which the index is based. During my second year as a graduate student, I undertook to learn something about alternative ways to treat roll-call votes, and I wrote a seminar paper

[4] (New York: Wiley, 1959.)

that explored, using voting data from the United Nations General Assembly, the relative merits of a variety of quantitative techniques, such as cluster-bloc analysis, various indices of cohesion and likeness, and Guttman-scaling procedures. The result of this exercise was to give me some knowledge of what methods were available and for what purposes each might be useful.

In short, the necessity to begin doing research early in my graduate career provided an opportunity to get some methodological problems resolved in my own mind.[5] This meant that when I began to think about designing a dissertation project, I had some experience with the most appropriate *modes* of data collection, management, and analysis; I had made certain common mistakes and wouldn't make them again.

Planning and Writing a Dissertation

When I reached the dissertation-writing stage, my decision was to apply some of the methods with which I had experimented to my long-standing interest in the determinants of foreign policy voting in Congress. To begin with, there was the need to move from this general formulation of the problem to some specific hypotheses capable of being tested empirically. This task was made easier by the requirement of following the Yale custom of starting a dissertation with a chapter reviewing the literature and placing the general problem in some sort of meaningful context. Thus, I read everything I could get a hold of on legislative voting and on the question of American posture toward the rest of the world; there was, I recall, a good deal less on these topics than I expected to find. I put together a propositional inventory, specifying a number of hypotheses, some of which had been around, untested, for some time. This inventory of propositions appears in the book, as in the first chapter, in substantially the same form in which it was prepared for the dissertation.

Specifically, there seemed to be three catgories of variables

---

[5] For the results of these efforts, see my "The Basis of Isolationist Behavior," *Public Opinion Quarterly*, 24 (1960), 645–657, and "Quantitative Techniques for Studying Voting Behavior in the U.N. General Assembly," *International Organization*, 14 (1960), 291–306.

which potentially might be related to roll-call voting. After discarding several alternative formulations, I chose to call the first cluster "social background characteristics," referring to the position in the social structure occupied by a representative prior to his service in Congress: his religious preference, his occupation, and so on. The second set, called "political attributes," included the electoral competitiveness of the congressman's district, his committee assignments in the House, his seniority, and of course his party affiliation. Finally, there was a third set of variables, the "constituency factors," which included the region, socioeconomic status, ethnicity, educational level, and the like, of the districts. Each cluster of factors—social background, political attributes, and constituency—appeared to suggest possible correlates of foreign policy voting in Congress.

There was also a fourth category which intrigued me—something which might be called "personal" or "psychological characteristics." It seems eminently reasonable to believe that the actions of legislators, like those of private citizens,[6] will reflect their personalities. Yet, short of the unlikely introduction in the House of a resolution that all "sex criminals should be publically whipped, or worse," I had no way of assessing these attributes among congressmen. The ordinary graduate student does not have the resources to spend very much time in Washington interviewing; at least, nobody came running to offer me the money required to ascertain the legislators' personality characteristics. So I immediately abandoned this category, although I still think it would be well worth investigating. Thus, I was left with the three classes of variables enumerated above.

There was also the problem of the dependent variable, voting on foreign policy issues, or isolationism-internationalism, as I came to call it. Defining isolationism, in the broadest sense, as the desire to limit or reduce American involvement in or commitment to the rest of the world solves only part of the problem. Isolationism, clearly, may not be a unidimensional phenomenon; in fact, it probably is not. It may have a geographical focus; people, including lawmakers, may favor involvement in one area ("Asia

---

[6] For evidence that isolationist sentiments are related to personality traits, see Herbert McClosky, "Personality and Attitude Correlates of Foreign Policy Orientation," in James N. Rosenau (Ed.), *Domestic Sources of Foreign Policy* (New York: Free Press, 1967), pp. 51–109.

firsters," for instance) but aloofness from another. It may also revolve around substantive considerations; one group may prefer military commitment but resist economic ties; another may hold the reverse perspective. The issue, of course, is how to capture these various possibilities. The answer was provided by the available roll-call votes; the sorts of questions put to a vote in Congress simply do not allow for analysis of these complexities of the isolationist phenomenon. Thus the constraints imposed by the nature of roll-call votes forced me to define isolationism in terms of foreign aid and foreign trade. Both aid and trade seemed to require an American choice as to whether or not to commit this country's economic resources abroad.

A second criterion led to the same choice of issues to investigate. As previously noted, I wanted to generate findings which could not be challenged as mere artifacts of examining a single Congress; my seminar paper experiments convinced me of the utility of longitudinal analysis. These earlier efforts also led to the conclusion that it would be desirable to cover a period beginning before World War II so that the controversies concerning the Neutrality Laws of the 1930s and the extension of the Selective Service System could be included. Foreign aid and reciprocal trade were issues with extended histories and which came to a vote repeatedly during the period under consideration. The only problem here was with a measure of foreign aid for the prewar era. The aid program, as we commonly conceive of it, is a postwar development, and I needed some equivalent issue from the earlier period. The compromise I settled on, after looking over the roll calls, was to use the 76th Congress (1939–1940), which debated the repeal of the arms embargo provisions of the Neutrality Laws. This issue is, in a sense, comparable to foreign aid of the post-1945 era, for in each case Congress had to decide whether to make American money and goods available to other nations in furtherance of the national interest.[7]

Having established aid and trade as the issues to be studied,

[7] In submitting an article using these data, I did encounter the criticism that the arms embargo repeal was not entirely comparable to the postwar aid programs. I then examined the passage of the Lend-Lease Act (77th Congress, 1941) and found similar voting alignments on the two topics. See "The Demography of the Congressional Vote on Foreign Aid, 1939–1958," *American Political Science Review*, 58 (1964), 577–588.

the next question concerned which Congresses to examine. Ideally, of course, one should look at all of them, but as I was willing to get my degree before producing the definitive study of congressional isolationism, I was amenable to the argument advanced by my thesis committee that I sample the Congresses. The limitations of studies like MacRae's and Truman's provided the rationale for selecting the specific Congresses. Findings from a single two-year period might reflect, among other things, the nature of the relationship between the White House and Capitol Hill, the status of the legislative party as majority or minority, and whether or not the party had a President in the White House. I decided on controlling for this factor so that whatever findings I came up with would be independent of changes in the party balance and control of the Presidency. The 76th Congress, mentioned earlier, was, of course, in the Roosevelt era and saw the Democrats in the White House with a legislative majority. I then chose the 80th Congress (Democratic President, Republican congressional majority), the 83rd (GOP chief executive and legislative majority), and the 85th (Republican President, Democratic Congress). The argument here was that, given the obvious importance of the executive in foreign policy making, findings which persisted across these four Congresses ought to have more validity than propositions generated from examination of any single Congress.

Thus, I had winnowed the project down to an examination of some relationships between three sets of attributes of congressmen and legislative voting on aid and trade bills in four Congresses. For instance, I hypothesized, on the basis of the literature, that the representatives of rural Midwestern districts should be more opposed to aid and trade than lawmakers elected in urban and East Coast constituencies. Similarly, I suspected that legislators chosen in marginal districts would be less willing to take extreme stands—either pro- or anti-aid or trade—than those from safe seats. I wound up with about ten or so additional hypotheses of this type which I wanted to test.

I should add, to digress for a moment, that when I submitted my original dissertation prospectus, it contained several other things that I intended to do as a part of my study. For one thing, I wanted to look at both houses of Congress. This goal was abandoned for two reasons. First, because House districts are generally more homogeneous than whole states, analysis of the lower chamber offers a better opportunity to assess the relationship between constituency characteristics and legislative voting than would a focus on the Senate, using states as the basis for categorizing constituencies. Second, from a much more practical point of view, studying both chambers would extend the time needed to finish the thesis considerably. This second concern also led quickly to the scrapping of an original intention to try, using Gallup and other poll data, to get at the correspondence between constituency opinion and legislators' positions. I believe—and my subsequent experience on doctoral committees confirms this judgment—that political science graduate students far more often tackle problems too broad to manage. Seldom do they seek out minute topics of trivial import.

The more difficult decisions came in moving from these general hypotheses to more specific ones, complete with operational definitions of the variables. Previous experience helped out here as well. I had had enough difficulty with percentage measures to see their weaknesses clearly. For one thing, it is difficult to tell if each set of rolls selected in some *a priori* fashion really "taps" the same dimension; the researcher must rely on his intuition or some "face validity" criterion. Second, there is the possibility of gross distortion in the scores. A simple case of this would be a set of ten roll calls on which Congressman A votes "yea" on numbers one through five and "nay" on numbers six through ten and thus scores fifty percent on the measure derived from these votes. Congressman B votes "nay" on the first five and "yea" on the second five and also scores fifty percent. In an ordinary analysis, these two men would almost certainly be lumped in the same category despite the fact that they disagreed on every roll call which underlies the index. How frequently such a situation occurs in this type of research is not clear, but I did know that there were ways to avoid these problems.

One way was to use the Guttman scaling procedures. The cumulative property of the Guttman scale provides clear gains over the percentage index. The acceptable scale, with its maximum of ten percent inconsistent (or erroneous) responses is at least *prima facie* evidence of unidimensionality; if the votes fall into an acceptable pattern, it is at least highly probable that the representatives perceive the roll calls as part of some particular set. Likewise, the assigning of scale scores establishes a rank order, from strongly favorable to strongly opposed on the set of votes, which ensures that legislators having the same rank have the same or nearly identical voting records; thus the problem, noted above, of similar scores masking dissimilar vote patterns is averted.[8] In short, relying on my previous research exposure, I began to apply Guttman-scale procedures to the aid and trade roll calls in my four Congresses.

With reference to the dependent variables, one other problem should be mentioned: comparability across Congresses. In order to be able to talk about developments with regard to isolationism over time, it would be useful to have some feeling that the scale derived for, say, the 76th Congress was measuring the same sort of thing as the scales employed for the 80th and subsequent Congresses. The only way I could see to handle this issue was to omit votes on items, like an amendment to the reciprocal trade bill dealing specifically with the rate of duty on cotton or hemp from the Far East, which would be unlikely to recur at other times. Excluding such items as these meant that the scales actually developed included votes—those on final passage, recommittal motions, or acceptance of a conference report—which posed the question for the legislators in general terms, in effect requiring that they pass judgment on the program in final form after all the details of that year's bill had been worked out. In one sense then, at this general level, each scale gets at the congressional decision of whether or not to have an aid (or trade) bill in a particular Congress.

Even so, it is difficult to argue persuasively that the scales are strictly comparable. The first draft of my dissertation included some absolute comparisons—e.g., Republican isolationism fell by so many percent from one time period to the next. A number of persons raised questions about this on the grounds of the inappropriateness of these comparisons, and I felt compelled in the final version to make relative rather than absolute statements. That is, I wound up making statements of this sort: the magnitude of the differences between the parties, or between the representatives from particular regions, declined from one Congress to the next. Thus, I could say that while in the 76th Congress the

---

[8] On scaling roll calls, see MacRae, the Belknap and Farris papers, and Lee Anderson, Meredith W. Watts, Jr., and Allen R. Wilcox, *Legislative Roll-Call Analysis* (Evanston, Ill.: Northwestern University Press, 1966), ch. 6.

isolationists were all Republicans, by the 83rd and 85th Congresses members of both parties voted against foreign aid in roughly equal proportions. I did not have to argue for perfect comparability if the analysis was limited to this sort of relative statement. This rationale did permit some gains from the longitudinal perspective while averting several possible errors in interpretation of the data.[9]

The final major set of decisions in the research design stage of the project pertained to the measures of the independent variables. Recall that there were three types of factors involved here— background characteristics of the congressmen, their political attributes, and the constituencies they represented. Most of the data for the first two categories were readily available in the *Congressional Directory*, the *Biographical Directory of the American Congress, 1774–1949*, and the many invaluable publications of the *Congressional Quarterly*. These sources were culled for information about the legislators' prior occupations, previous political experience, committee assignment, and so on. Election data, including figures on special elections, are in the *America Votes* volumes. Religious affiliation was the most difficult to ascertain, especially for the earlier Congresses, because church preference was often not included in the legislative biographies. The Library of Congress graciously supplied some data here, but some remained fugitive. For the most part, however, I was able to gather the needed information, and while there were some missing data, they were, on the whole, unlikely to bias the analysis.

The largest, and most time-consuming, problems were the choice of indices for the House districts and the collection of these data. I began with the notion that I would follow precedent wherever I could, and this led me immediately to Duncan MacRae's *Dimensions of Congressional Voting*. MacRae used occupational data from the Census to construct measures of ruralism and socio-economic status for the constituencies. The proportion of the male work force engaged in farming and farm-related activities was the index of the former, while the proportion in managerial, professional, and technical jobs constituted the status index. These

---

[9] Some attention has, more recently, been paid to this problem of comparability. See Aage R. Clausen, "Measurement Identity in the Longitudinal Analysis of Legislative Voting," *American Political Science Review*, 61 (1967), 1020–1035.

data, for the 81st Congress, which appeared in an Appendix to the MacRae volume, also were appropriate for the 80th, which I used in my sample. Professor MacRae most generously made available calculations of these measures for the districts in the post-1950 reapportionment period, thus reducing my work to generating the figures for the very few districts which were altered during the 1950s. However, I had to make these calculations for the 76th Congress *de novo*, using the 1940 Census and following MacRae's ground rules.

For two other indices—educational level and ethnicity—however, I was on my own, though the decisions were not too difficult. With respect to education, I concluded that a simple percentage measure—the proportion of the total population with some college training—would suffice. On ethnicity, my hypothesis focused on a presumed relation, specified in the writings of Samuel Lubell,[10] between German and Irish background and isolationist sentiment. The German-American, according to this line of reasoning, suffered an emotional conflict stemming from loyalties divided between his ancestral land (that from which he or his forebears had emigrated) and his newly adopted homeland. Isolationism, with its non-involvement goals, provided a convenient way out of this conflict. There was a sharp drop in the Democratic vote for President in counties heavily populated by those of German origin. As the conflict between the U.S. and Germany developed between 1936 and 1940, this provided the evidence for the proposition. The Irish-American, on the other hand, disliked the British for the obvious historical reasons and chose isolationism in preference to Anglo-American alliance. By extension, representatives of districts with heavy contingents of German- and Irish-Americans could be expected to vote against "entangling" aid and trade policies. Because accurate estimates of the ethnic composition of congressional districts are most difficult to get, I settled for the percentage of the population born in Germany or Ireland as an index of district ethnicity on the (perhaps dubious) assumption that newly arrived immigrants would settle where there were sizeable communities of their fellow countrymen.

If the selection of indices was not overly complicated, the col-

---

[10] *The Future of American Politics*, 3rd Ed., rev. (New York: Harper, 1965), ch. 7, and *The Revolt of the Moderates* (New York: Harper, 1956), ch. 3.

lection of the data was time-consuming and burdensome. For most constituencies, the indices were calculated by summing the population and index data for the counties making up the district and dividing one figure by the other. Though hardly intellectually challenging, these operations took some time. Unfortunately about one-fourth of the districts did not follow county lines. For these, it was necessary to overlay constituency and census tract maps, discover which tracts and other census units fell in each district, and add the various figures for all these units. Moreover, it was difficult to find district boundary maps, especially for the 1939–1940 congressional districts; I managed to get the necessary maps only after a barrage of letter writing and phone calls (at my own expense). The whole process of generating these district data took more than six months and constituted the largest problem of the research.[11]

Once the design was completed and the data collected,[12] the card punching and analysis were relatively straightforward. One problem, which happily no longer exists, was the limited capacity of the available computers of that day. Violating strict statistical assumptions, I decided to follow precedent and treat the Guttman-scale scores as interval rather than ordinal data and to run product-moment correlations against several quantitative independent variables, such as electoral margin and various constituency characteristics. To do so required a computer program which would handle missing data, since some items for some legislators—religious affiliation, for example—were not available. While we take the ready availability of such programs for granted today, they did not exist or did not work easily then. I still have a most vivid memory of sitting in front of an IBM 650, from midnight to four A.M., watching my data cards read at a rate of two per minute by the machine, which almost literally gulped one down and digested it before moving on to the next card. It took four hours to do a

[11] Much of this sort of constituency data is available for the 1960s in the *Congressional District Data Books* and the supplements to them (Washington, D.C.: Government Printing Office, 1962–1967). But to build a longitudinal dimension, extending back into the 1950s or earlier, into research may require mapping operations of the sort described here.

[12] Throughout the entire process, I got substantial quantities of advice, much of it useful, from my faculty thesis committee and, equally important, from my fellow students. Informal conversation in which ideas about design and data collection could be tried out on others proved most helpful.

simple 15 × 15 or 17 × 17 Personian correlation matrix. The remaining analysis entailed a variety of cross-tabulations which I did, over many months, on a counter-sorter.

A second problem of this phase of the research was how to achieve the necessary controls, especially for the influence of the constituency factors. To have confidence in any relationships discovered required some assurance that they were not artifacts of party, region, or other district attributes. These last, however, were not randomly distributed across the country. For example, to take the ethnic hypothesis described earlier, when the Irish came to this country, they tended to settle in the cities. There are very few rural districts with significant numbers of Irish-Americans residing in them. As a result, it was difficult to determine whether the internationalism (not isolationism, as hypothesized!) found among the representatives of Irish districts was an urban or truly an Irish-related phenomenon. Or was it peculiar to the East Coast, for most of the heavily Irish districts were in New England? (The German-Americans were, from my point of view, a bit more considerate, having settled in both urban and rural areas and in several regions of the country.) In any event, these skewed distributions caused some difficulties in analysis and interpretation. The controls I could use left something to be desired; frequently I could find only one or two regions in which there were sufficient numbers of the relevant kinds of constituency to permit meaningful comparisons; often I could control for urbanism or ruralism, but not for both. Such difficulties took time to iron out.

These various problems were not encountered in any identifiable pattern. I did not anticipate all of them in advance; many of them were pointed out to me as I went along, as I wrote draft chapters. Some criticisms, in fact, took me quite by surprise. The result is that research proceeds, in a sort of groping fashion, in the direction in which you set out, but not without straying from the path regularly and even having to change routes on occasion. Perhaps others can write a clear master plan which they follow to the letter. If so, I'm happy for them; but I was unable to do it so neatly, and I haven't improved much in this regard in subsequent research efforts. Things do not always go as expected—the unexpected occurs—and you ought not be depressed when this happens; you should be prepared to push ahead, to adjust the design or procedures, until you find an acceptable solution.

From Dissertation to Book

It is, of course, a satisfying experience to find that a piece of work is not only adequate to obtain a degree—for which the project was initially undertaken—but also is publishable, at least in the view of one set of editors and reviewers, in book form. Two general comments are in order in this connection. First, while the transition from dissertation to book is tedious in many respects and takes a good while to make, nonetheless it affords an opportunity to rethink some of the ideas which guided the initial research and to reanalyze old data or collect new data. In the present case, I did a little of all these things. I tried, for example, to cast my findings in a broader frame of reference; specifically, I advanced a paradigm of congressional voting, in which my data and those of Miller and Stokes[13] seemed to fit together. The paradigm pictured, in very broad outlines, a set of factors related to the legislator's voting decisions. Thus, I replaced the final thesis chapter with a new last chapter of, hopefully, more general theoretical import.

Moreover, I got a chance to check out the persistence of my findings in a later Congress. The 1960 election restored the Democrats to office. They gained control of both the White House and Capitol Hill. Thus, in a sense, the situation had come full cycle, for this same political configuration had characterized the 76th Congress, the first in my sample. During this interval between completion of the thesis and publication, I was extremely fortunate to get a grant from The Study of Congress, sponsored by the American Political Science Association and supported by the Carnegie Corporation, which enabled me to test all the propositions advanced in the dissertation in the 88th Congress. These data permitted me to append a postscript to the published book, updating the findings to a point closer in time to the date of publication.

Second, in addition to the opportunity to improve the quality

[13] Warren E. Miller and Donald E. Stokes, ''Constituency Influence in Congress,'' *American Political Science Review*, 57 (1963), 45–57. See also the reanalysis of the Miller-Stokes data by Charles F. Cnudde and Donald J. McCrone, ''The Linkage between Constituency Attitudes and Congressional Voting Behavior,'' *American Political Science Review*, 60 (1966), 66–72.

of the manuscript, publication introduced me to the problems of "commercialism." It is not unreasonable for publishers to put out books in the hope of selling them, but this means that they will view matters from a somewhat different perspective. My dissertation, as the earlier discussion indicates, was to a great extent an exercise in hypothesis-testing, in exploring the correlates of roll-call voting in Congress. My editors suggested that I try to give the data broader relevance by drawing from them their implications for the general issue of foreign-policy formulation. I chose to focus on the problem of Presidential leadership in policy making, and, thus, in rewriting the thesis I attempted to infer what my findings might mean from the strategic perspective of a President seeking to mobilize legislative backing for his aid and trade programs. In other words, the data remain the same, but in the book they are explicated from a point of view absent from the dissertation.

The Last Word: The Reviewers

When a book hits print, after some seven years of work in the present case, all of the choices made in the conception, design, execution, and analysis of the project are there in cold black and white, and there is a certain anxiety about how those to whom the book is addressed will receive it. What will the reviewers say? The reactions will indicate how satisfactory the whole range of decisions made in carrying out a piece of research has been. There have been three reviews of the book. Two of them, while hardly raves, are, I believe, on balance generally favorable; at least I have been willing to have others read these reviews.

In the light of the discussion here, it seems more appropriate to discuss the third, the least favorable, review. The lesson is clear: no matter what choices you make, regardless of the rationale underlying these decisions, someone is likely to feel that you have exercised poor judgment. This review, by an historian named Melvin Small,[14] was not entirely negative. He says, "the volume offers an impressive amount of empirical data which enriches our under-

---

[14] "Democracy and Foreign Policy: A Review," *Journal of Conflict Resolutions*, 12 (1968), 249–257, at 250–252.

standing of recent American history," and that it "supplements and, in many respects, surpasses more intuitive standard works" in the field. But it suffers from "crippling" weaknesses, mainly, it seems, from a failure to be thorough enough. For one thing, "by selecting only one Congress from the thirties, and that one an extraordinary one, he may describe isolationism during the decade inaccurately." More "depression Congresses" should have been studied; my rationale for selecting four Congresses over a twenty-year period (1939–1958), while not explicitly rejected, apparently was not persuasive.

A perceived second fault is the restriction of the study to aid and trade voting, as dependent variables, which causes the book to ignore "indicators which may better reflect congressional attitudes about foreign policy." Examination of roll calls on internal security bills, or perhaps on military matters, would have been helpful in this regard. Third, "an examination of *Senate* roll calls on treaties and diplomatic appointments would be more useful. . . ." as a supplement to aid and trade voting. In short, there is a narrowing or winnowing process by which specific projects take form, a process which leads to a focus on some features of a general problem at the cost of excluding some of the things which might be done; and in the view of this reviewer at least, the reduction of the project to manageable proportions was accomplished at excessive cost. Now, I do not for a moment deny that data on other issues, in other Congresses, or in other chambers would add to our store of knowledge, but I do wonder whether it is realistic to hope that one piece of research can provide all the answers.

Not all of the criticism reflected this wish that I had written a different book; some was most appropriate. Small and another reviewer, for instance, pointed to difficulties inherent in the choice of isolationist-internationalist terminology. I alluded to the definitional problem at the outset and employed an operational definition of these factors based on votes for or against restricting American overseas involvements. But this is not entirely satisfactory in trying to explain the behavior of, say, Senator William Fulbright, who became disenchanted with military adventures and bilateral aid agreements. This suggests the need to explore the possibility that different types of isolationism exist; for example, one kind might include opposition to the commitment of military forces abroad while accepting humanitarian contacts such as foreign aid. There might, in fact, if one employs a simple military-humanitarian dichotomy, be four types: a "pure" isolationism, opposing both forms of contact; a military isolationism, rejecting the use of the armed forces to defend other lands; a humanitarian (or economic) isolationism, denying the utility of aid and trade programs; and a "pure" internationalism, favoring both military and humanitarian contacts with the nations of the world.

Another suggestion of considerable merit involves the mode of analysis I employed. Most of the relationships presented in the book are bivariate ones, associations between some independent variable and roll-call position, with one or, at most, two controls added. This data treatment does not answer the question of how much of the variance in roll-call position the set of independent variables employed accounts for. As one reviewer suggested, and quite rightly, the use of multi-variate—specifically, multiple regression—techniques could have shed light on this issue. In sum, the reviews provide not only reaction to what has been done but also suggestions about what might profitably be done next.

Conclusion

At the obvious risk of generalizing from a single case ($N = 1$), I might point out a number of threads that run through this highly personal, and perhaps idiosyncratic, narrative. These morals, if I may call them that, can be set out by way of a conclusion.

1. Research is not likely to proceed according to a fixed plan. Study of the philosophy of science and stress on research design will sensitize the student to the issues he may have to confront, but such efforts will not provide all the answers. The best advice, perhaps, is to be prepared for the unexpected.

2. The transition from a theoretically interesting idea to a manageable research project requires choice and compromise; the scholar cannot do all that he deems worth doing. He must eliminate features of his proposal to which he assigns lower priority; he must state his hypotheses in a form which facilitates testing; he must devise adequate measures of the variables from available data; he must anticipate, and be ready to adjust to, criticism of his work. In short, he must seek to design a project which is both

feasible and likely to produce meaningful results, to steer a course between the impossible and the trivial.

3. Research skills develop cumulatively, and the sooner the student begins to acquire them the more quickly he will reach the point where his ability to conduct significant research is not inhibited by a lack of experience or an unfamiliarity with appropriate methodological techniques.

4. Research projects will take longer than expected to complete. Even within the narrowing of focus, study design, data collection, preparation, and analysis, interpretation of the results and the writing of text will consume more time than anticipated.

When all is said and done, some will surely think you have not made your choices wisely or well; but with a little luck enough people will find your work sufficiently useful to justify its having been undertaken in the first place.

3 DATA IN INTERNATIONAL AND COMPARATIVE POLITICS: THE YALE ARMS CONTROL PROJECT

Karl W. Deutsch
Harvard University

Richard L. Merritt
University of Illinois

There is a common line of interest that connects many of the different projects political scientists have been working on in recent years. It is the shift toward the use of verifiable, empirical data. We cannot have fruitful political research without insight, nor can we have it without experience, nor without the ability to recognize the phenomena that are occurring in politics and in society. It is impossible to count phenomena unless we recognize them first. The acts of insight and recognition, the operations of observation and description, precede all else. But if we do not want to remain the prisoners of the infinitely varied personalities, preferences, and biases of different observers, we must try, as in other fields of science, to increase the scientific components of our work—that is, to use evidence that can be reproduced, checked, and verified impersonally.

This is the first publication of Karl W. Deutsch and Richard L. Merritt's essay. All rights reserved. Permission to reprint must be obtained from the publisher and the authors.

The Greek philosopher Heraclitus said that when men dream, each dreamer inhabits a private world of his own, but when men are awake, they are all looking at the real world, with real buildings in it and real doors in the buildings. To be awake is to share a world in common with other people. A scientist is inevitably and necessarily a dreamer part of his life, just as the poet or artist is. From time to time he has to think or speculate, to recognize or surmise patterns in his data or in the world around him. In these moments he is closer to the poet and the artist than he is to the hard-boiled "man of science." But, having had his vision, his idea, his hunch, or his insight, he must then get down to the task of gathering and analyzing the data that can test the viability of his insights and his surmises. These data must speak not only to him but also to anyone else who has had appropriate training. Only in this way can data be shared with others, both across space from one researcher to another and across time, and only in this way can they contribute to the steadily growing body of cumulative knowledge.

We are now engaged in the transition and transformation of political science. This is true not in the sense of introducing a radically new kind of thinking. Since the day Aristotle sent his research assistants out to collect some 128 constitutions of Greek city-states we have had a combination of the insight of alert political scientists and efforts to gather comparable data. What is changing are the proportions. We are still getting some ideas—and, indeed, as in any other field of social science, we could do with a good many more of them. But what we are also trying to do now is to get more effective use of data to test the tenability of the surmises, the propositions, and the folk beliefs we have about politics.

Using Data for Studying Politics

Our focus in the study of politics is most generally the capabilities of governments, the loads upon them, and the consequences, such as stability or instability, of the mix of capabilities and loads. When we ask what the gross capabilities of governments are—that is, what they can do—both domestically and in international relations, we may begin by asking what particular governments are in fact doing and how well they are doing it.

Capabilities

One useful indicator of a government's capabilities is the extent to which it controls the country's wealth. How much of the Gross National Product can the government collect in revenues and disburse for whatever purposes the government and the men who run it see fit? There are countries in which government officials can collect only a very small fraction of the national income—and that only at ports of entry! In others they can collect taxes in the interior as well. Some countries tax every commercial transaction, but not individual consumers.[1] The Internal Revenue Service can collect taxes from every income earner in the United States. What is more, it can do so reasonably efficiently, at the cost of checking only one income tax return in twenty. In cross-national perspective, it turns out that underdeveloped countries collect as taxes between ten and eighteen percent of the Gross National Product, whereas the figure for developed countries lies between thirty and fifty percent, and the public sector is larger still in Communist countries.[2]

A related indicator, suggesting the extent to which the central government dominates the organized political life of a country, is the percentage of total governmental revenues at all levels that the central government gets. This figure is roughly sixty percent in Switzerland, seventy-two percent in England, seventy-five percent in Sweden, and one hundred percent in France.[3] (The French have tried to spotlight the little government money that does not go through Paris but, officially at least, all expenditures of the French state are supposed to go through some authority of the central government.) A person's attitude toward centralization may cause him to be pleased or dismayed by any particular figure. The point here

---

[1] Merle Kling, "Taxes on the 'External' Sector: An Index of Political Behavior in Latin America?" *The Midwest Journal of Political Science*, 3, 2 (May 1959), 127–150.

[2] Some recent data are given in Karl W. Deutsch, *Politics and Government: How People Decide Their Fate* (Boston: Houghton Mifflin, 1970), pp. 3–4, 6–7. See also Frederic L. Pryor, *Public Expenditures in Communist and Capitalist Nations* (London: Allen and Unwin, 1968).

[3] From data in Bruce M. Russett, Hayward R. Alker, Jr., Karl W. Deutsch, and Harold D. Lasswell, *World Handbook of Political and Social Indicators* (New Haven and London: Yale University Press, 1964), pp. 56–68.

is rather that such an indicator does tell us something about how much governments can spread out decision making or how strongly they can concentrate it.

Other data indicate the capability of governments to provide their citizens with certain standards of living: life expectancy, literacy, percentage of young people enrolled in institutions of secondary and higher education, the number of doctors and hospital beds, the share of crimes followed by prosecutions, the distribution of weath and other values, and economic growth. In all these respects, governments perform very differently in different countries. They may even perform differently for different individuals within the same country. In the United States, it costs you one-tenth of your life expectancy if you are born as a black: white female babies born in 1967 had a life expectancy of seventy-five years and black female babies only sixty-eight years—a differential of almost ten percent.[4] When a black's life expectancy is as good as that of his white neighbor, we may be a great deal closer to racial justice than we are now. In the meantime, ten percent or seven years of a person's life is a serious amount of inequality to contemplate. And the same is true of the income differential of forty percent between whites and blacks in the United States of the early 1960s. If we recall that this differential declined roughly one percent per year from 1940 to 1960, then it still means that, at this rate, it will take until the end of the century to make incomes reasonably equal among the races in the United States.

These are but a few of the numerous indicators of governmental capacity available to political scientists today. They also provide a basis for estimating the limits of a government's capabilities, what it could *not* do even if it were to try. Besides merely being indicators of capabilities, however, these data may also give us an idea of the loads placed upon government. Determining what different population groups within a country actually receive may also suggest which of these population groups are likely to be contented or discontented. Which governments are likely to be popular and among which groups, in which regions, and under what conditions?

---

[4] U.S. Bureau of the Census, *Statistical Abstract of the United States, 1969*, 90th Ed. (Washington, D.C.: Government Printing Office, 1969), p. 54.

Goals and Other Loads

The demands made by relevant portions of a population comprise an important desideratum for governments. What tasks do governments impose upon themselves? What are the goals of the elites and other politically relevant strata in a country? What goals underlie the demands of mass opinion? In short, what are the value configurations that predominate in a society, and how have these value configurations changed over time?

Less than a century ago racial supremacy was a fervently professed political value in almost all of Western Europe and America. To talk about racial supremacy in those days was to utter a commonplace. Today, by way of contrast, there are few places left in the world—the Union of South Africa, Rhodesia, and perhaps parts of the United States—where a government could get an electoral majority even among a minority of the population for a policy of outright racial supremacy. That hangovers from an era of racism continue to plague us in the United States today is indicated clearly by the life expectancy and income data cited earlier. By the same token, however, school attendance has become more equal. Too many black children by now have been taught too often that "We hold these Truths to be self-evident, that all Men are created equal . . ." for them to ignore any longer the injustices of their environment. Such a change in basic values, however slow in coming for blacks and whites alike, had a profound effect upon American politics in the 1960s.

Similarly, few political writers and, what was more important, politicians in power in the 1890s and 1900s disputed the value of colonies and empires. Today colonies are something for a few *aficionados* and collectors. Portugal, the poorest country in Europe except for Albania and Turkey, is one of these. And even here the value of its colonial territories and their colonial status is questionable: Angola and Mozambique rank 140th and 141st, respectively, among 141 cases in a computer analysis of forty-five indicators of national performance; so far as we know, they are the two worst-governed packages of real estate on earth. They are nonetheless the last of the great colonies once scattered across the face of the globe. Colonialism has truly become a leftover institution for politically-backward countries—even though it still causes a great deal of human suffering.

Just as values and value configurations change, so do perceptions. Most of the people of the world probably perceived war—up to and including all-out warfare calling for the total mobilization of national resources and manpower—as a legitimate and practicable means to pursue policy as late as the early 1940s. Hiroshima brought about important changes in the image of war. Today there are doubtless few who would consider an all-out atomic war practicable, and many question the legitimacy of any war whatsoever. This shift in perceptions in response to a dramatic technological development points to an important avenue of research: In what circumstances, and to what extent and in what ways, do external events change images about politics?

A review of the empirical literature on the formation of and changes in attitudes suggests some findings relevant to the issues that governments must face.[5] First, images tend to be fairly stable. Generally, no more than a tenth of a population changes its images in response to an external event. The disgust of the French electorate in the late spring of 1968 over the actions of some of the more extreme students, for instance, seems to have changed their voting habits by a mere three percent (albeit under an electoral system that substantially magnified the effects of this shift).[6] Small changes in images tend to be cancelled out by the effects of subsequent events. Second, the occurrence of a very dramatic event can change the images of up to thirty and even forty percent of a population, if the mass media abundantly report the event and if all governments and major authority figures endorse the reports as being true. After Pearl Harbor, for instance, about forty percent of the American public changed their view of the Japanese. Third, the cumulative effect of events is the most powerful agent for changing images. Viewed within a time span of five to ten years, changes are slow, but over twenty or thirty years everything changes remarkably fast. Our emotions and sentiments race ahead of the actual changes in the world of day-to-day politics, but our imagination lags behind. It takes a generation's time for more fundamental perceptual changes to take place. This fact might

---

[5] For a fuller discussion see Karl W. Deutsch and Richard L. Merritt, "Effects of Events on National and International Images," in Herbert C. Kelman (Ed.), *International Behavior: A Social-Psychological Analysis* (New York: Holt, 1965), pp. 132–187.

[6] From data in Karl W. Deutsch, *Politics and Government*, p. 348.

suggest a limitation of the human mind, or simply of the thinking of the man in the street—but it might also be useful information for political scientists interested in policy formation. Most short-run changes take longer than expected and will be smaller than expected, but many long-run changes will be bigger and come faster than expected.

Still another type of load upon a political decision system comes from the outside. When Admiral Perry appeared in Japan in 1853, Japan was confronted with a demand: the necessity either to develop itself very quickly into a modern power or else to become a colony. The China of Mao Tse-tung faced a similar challenge from the Soviet Union in the late 1950s and early 1960s: to accept at the very least the hegemony of the USSR or to push hard for its own self-assertion. The aggressive behavior of a reckless neighbor, population growth rates that shift power relationships among states asymmetrically, the growing gap between the wealthier industrialized states and the poorer lands of the Third World, the pollution of man's environment—all constitute loads imposed from the outside upon the decision-making systems of states, albeit with varying degrees of immediacy and intensity.

Governmental Decision Making

The way in which a government decides to use its capabilities to meet the demands or loads upon it depends upon its decision-making capacity. Such steering facilities rest upon the perception of a country's capabilities and goals, its facilities for reallocating resources to meet the goals, and, above all, communication processes that signal back to the decision makers how well or how poorly they are doing. Steering facilities are crucial to effective government. If the automobile industry in Detroit were to design a more powerful car than ever before but were to eliminate the reverse gear or reduce the size of the windshield, this car would be a menace on the road (besides being difficult to park). And yet there are writers and governments who design foreign policies of this sort.

Increasing the elephantine characteristics of a state's national power at the cost of reducing its capabilities for intelligence—international perception, responsiveness and self-control, ability to forecast events—is, in effect, to turn the state into a machine that can get itself and its occupants into very serious trouble. Soviet tanks rolling into Czechoslovakia in August 1968 gave a very impressive demonstration of the qualities of Russian hardware: practically no tank conked out on the road. At the same time, however, they impressively demonstrated the poverty of Soviet intelligence, for many of the Soviet decision makers evidently really thought that their actions foiled an American- or West German-inspired plot to take over Czechoslovakia—a plot that did not exist. They were apparently living in a perceptual world in which big powers can still make war with impunity upon their smaller allies (and, of course, they are not the only ones living in this dreamlike world!). Such blind persistence in following outmoded policies can lead to a decline in decision-making capacities that greatly increases the risks for the survival of a country. By way of contrast, nineteenth-century Japan and twentieth-century Communist China adapted well to the necessity to modernize in a deadly hurry; and in many respects the American government has been able to meet the growing demands for legal equality made by the tenth of our population that is black.

The majority of governments in the history of the world have sooner or later failed to live up to the demands made upon them. Just as, for every living species known to biologists there are eleven species that have died out, so, too, for each of the approximately 140 governments in the world today there are several which perished in time past. Some, of course, survive remarkably well. But it bears noting that, although we like to think of the United States as a young country, it in fact has the oldest continuous political regime now operating in the world. Every other country has had more drastic political and constitutional changes in the last 180 years than the United States.

The ability of a government to endure for a long time depends upon its responsiveness to demands—new loads or inputs as well as new trends and critical phases in present loads. One indicator of this endurance is the stability of personnel. On the one hand we are interested in government personnel, those who actually participate in the making of governmental decisions. On the other hand we must pay attention to the stability of elite groupings. The French and Latin American republics, for instance, are well known for great instability of top government personnel but high stability of top elites. The colonels leading governments were quite often overthrown, but they were overthrown with monotonous regularity by other colonels who came from the same land-owning strata in Latin American society. (More recently, more of them have been coming from the small-town middle classes.) Other related indicators include the stability of regimes, social systems (including such aspects as property ownership), nationality, and sovereignty. For each of these we can get quantitative estimates of changes over time in each of the roughly 140 countries of the world; and from these indicators we can begin to get some notion of patterns of cross-national stability, as well as the correlates of stability.

These examples are intended to be illustrative rather than exhaustive of the types of quantitative indicators available for studying the capabilities, loads, and decision-making capacities of governments.[7] There are, of course, many different strategies for gathering and analyzing appropriate data. And each encounters its own theoretical questions, organizational issues, and limitations on data gathering. One such strategy was adopted by the Yale Political Data Program, initiated in 1962 in conjunction with Harold D. Lasswell and Bruce M. Russett, and currently completing its second major data-analysis project.[8] It has concentrated on a limited number of variables—such as demographic data and rates of change, economic indicators (Gross National Product, Gini indices of the inequality of income and land distribution), such political indicators as the stability of governments, and psy-

[7] For more detailed suggestions, see Karl W. Deutsch, "Toward an Inventory of Basic Trends and Patterns in Comparative and International Politics," *The American Political Science Review*, 54, 1 (March 1960), 34–57, Karl W. Deutsch, "Social Mobilization and Political Development," *The American Political Science Review*, 55, 3 (September 1961), 493–514, and Karl W. Deutsch, "The Theoretical Basis of Data Programs," in Richard L. Merritt and Stein Rokkan (Eds.), *Comparing Nations: The Use of Quantitative Data in Cross-National Research* (New Haven and London: Yale University Press, 1966), pp. 27–55.

[8] On organizational problems and solutions of the Yale Political Data Program, see Karl W. Deutsch, Harold D. Lasswell, Richard L. Merritt, and Bruce M. Russett, "The Yale Political Data Program," in *ibid.*, pp. 81–94, and Bruce M. Russett, "The Yale Political Data Program: Experience and Prospects," in *ibid.*, pp. 95–107. See also Russett, Alker, Deutsch, and Lasswell, *World Handbook of Political and Social Indicators*, and Michael C. Hudson and Charles L. Taylor, *World Handbook of Political and Social Indicators*, 2nd Ed. (New Haven and London: Yale University Press, forthcoming in 1971).

chological variables such as the degree of achievement orientation in a national society—for a large number of countries.

Some Questions of Research Design

Data programs of this type, and more broadly the use of data for testing theories, raise four general problems. First, they raise the question of *system levels:* How many levels of the political system—from world politics, alliance systems, and the decisions of a nation-state down to the level of intranational regions, larger interest groups and political parties, smaller groups, cliques, or families, down to particular individuals in key positions, or even down to some critical component of their personalities—must we take into account if we are to understand adequately the probability of some political outcome?[9] How much, on the average, do events at each level contribute to the outcome, and what is the contribution of interactions across two levels or more? In particular, it may also be important to find out whether regularities of political behavior which hold across countries—such as the curvilinear relation between per capita income and amounts of civil violence (which tends to be high in countries with incomes between $150 and $500 per capita, but low in very poor and very rich nations)[10]—holds equally well across different districts within the same nation.

A second group of questions centers on the *domain* of our research. Should we compare a few countries or many? Should we concentrate on countries from a particular region, culture, ideology, or level of industrial development?

Third is the set of problems dealing with the *depth in time* which we choose for our investigation. Shall we be content with studying short-run changes over, let us say, up to five years at

---

[9] For a brief discussion of system levels, see Deutsch, *Politics and Government*, pp. 125–129.
[10] See Russett, Alker, Deutsch, and Lasswell, *World Handbook of Political and Social Indicators*, pp. 306–307. See also Ted Gurr, with Charles Ruttenberg, *The Conditions of Civil Violence: First Tests of a Causal Model* (Princeton, N.J.: Princeton University, Center of International Studies, Research Monograph No. 28, April 1967), p. 67.

most, or shall we insist on adding some background information about relevant quantitative and qualitative changes over several decades or even centuries? How far back in time do we have to go if we are to understand the dynamics, strengths and weaknesses, and effects on politics of, say, the British class system?

A fourth set of choices must be made about the *levels of accuracy*—and conversely, the margins of error—which we must expect to find in our data, even after we have done our best to make them as accurate and reliable as their nature, and our time and resources, will let us make them. There is a *law of permissible error* which connects the margin of error remaining in the data with the margin of error acceptable for the making of the specific decision for which the data are to be used. It is thus quite possible that some moderately error-riddled set of data may be accurate enough to decide some research problems or policy questions, but not precise enough to decide some others. If this is so, then some decisions about data acquisition, data quality, and efforts to remove inaccuracies should be made in advance, in the light of the theoretical or practical questions that the research project is intended to help decide.

Thus far, all these questions have been put rather abstractly. The discussion of at least one particular research project may help to make clear how we have tried to translate these abstract principles into practice. The research that we shall discuss—the Yale Arms Control Project—exemplifies the strategy of concentrating more in depth on comparable data for a smaller set of rather similar states.

The Yale Arms Control Project

The Yale Arms Control project focused explicitly upon the interrelated questions of arms control and movements toward Western European unity. Organized at the suggestion and with the financial support of the United States Arms Control and Disarmament Agency, it used a variety of indicators to investigate such topics as the likelihood of further steps toward European unity, probable developments in the domestic politics of France and West Germany, and specific issues of arms control and defense, such as the proposed multi-lateral force (MLF) for the members of the North Atlantic Treaty Organization (NATO). It was begun in early 1964, performed the bulk of its research during the summer and fall of this year, and reported its findings in early 1966.

Many aspects of the Yale Arms Control Project deserve attention from the point of view of the sociology of political science knowledge. This brief summary will look at only four of these aspects: the formulation of the problem for research; organizational questions, as reflected in the staffing and personnel problems we encountered; research design; and the evaluation and continuation of the project. It will stress the practical aspects of carrying out the project rather than discussing the findings emerging from it. These findings are discussed in great detail elsewhere.[11]

Problem Formulation

For many years we and several of our colleagues have concentrated our attention upon problems of large-scale political

[11] For a summary, see Karl W. Deutsch, "Integration and Arms Control in the European Political Environment," *The American Political Science Review*, 55, 2 (June 1966), 354–365. The main findings are in Karl W. Deutsch, Lewis J. Edinger, Roy C. Macridis, and Richard L. Merritt, *France, Germany and the Western Alliance: A Study of Elite Attitudes on European Integration and World Politics* (New York: Scribner's, 1967), and Karl W. Deutsch, *Arms Control and the Atlantic Alliance: Europe Faces Coming Policy Decisions* (New York, London, and Sydney: Wiley, 1967). Other studies from the project include J. Zvi Namenwirth and Thomas J. Brewer, "Elite Editorial Comment on the European and Atlantic Communities in Four Countries," in Philip J. Stone, Dexter C. Dunphy, Marshall S. Smith, and Daniel M. Ogilvie (Eds.), *The General Inquirer: A Computer Approach to Content Analysis* (Cambridge, Mass., and London: M.I.T. Press, 1966), pp. 401–427, Bruce M. Russett and Carolyn C. Cooper, *Arms Control in Europe: Proposals and Political Constraints* (Denver: University of Denver, Monograph Series in World Affairs, 4, 2, 1967), Richard L. Merritt and Donald J. Puchala (Eds.), *Western European Perspectives on International Affairs: Public Opinion Studies and Evaluations* (New York: Praeger, 1968), Richard L. Merritt and Ellen B. Pirro, "Press Attitudes to Arms Control in Four Countries, 1946–1963" (New Haven: Yale University, Political Science Research Library, mimeo., 1966, publication forthcoming in 1971), and Donald J. Puchala, "European Political Integration: Progress and Prospects" (New Haven: Yale University, Political Science Research Library, mimeo., 1966, publication forthcoming in 1971). The questions used in the elite interviews and the distribution of responses are in Karl W. Deutsch, Lewis J. Edinger, Roy C. Macridis, Richard L. Merritt, and Helga Voss-Eckermann, "French and German Elite Responses, 1964: Codebook and Data" (New Haven: Yale University, Political Science Research Library, mimeo., 1966).

community formation. A subject of particular interest—intrinsically, because of its political relevance to today's world, but also scientifically, since its relative degree of failure or success remains an open question inviting a variety of analytic and prognostic research approaches—is the postwar movement aimed at economic and political unity in Western Europe. The suggestion of the Arms Control and Disarmament Agency that we undertake an empirical study of arms control and political integration in Western Europe was therefore a welcome one, giving us the opportunity to test some of our notions about political integration as well as our tools for studying such processes.

In viewing the research problem initially, we outlined three types of questions that interested us:[12]

> 1. Are nation-states and national policies in Western Europe, and particularly in France and West Germany, being superseded by supranational loyalties, interests, and institutions? If so, in what respects and to what extent?
> 2. What are the implications of recent nationalistic and/or supranational currents in European politics, and again particularly in France and West Germany, on the acceptability of various proposals for arms control or disarmament which are relevant to the interests and policies of the United States?
> 3. What are the most important trends in the domestic politics of France and West Germany, especially with respect to the continued stability of these governments? How do these trends impinge upon French and West German foreign policy?

The emphasis on France and West Germany stemmed from our belief that they are the keys to the success or failure of unifying movements, that their agreement on any set of policies would significantly enhance the probability that those policies would be adopted by the entire Western European community, and that their inability to agree on any of them would doubtless doom the proposals to failure. This is, of course, an assumption that could bear further examination.

Determining in a general sense how best to get answers to these questions led us into a serious consideration of the interplay between theory and method in the social sciences. Our review of the

---

[12] Deutsch, Edinger, Macridis, and Merritt, *France, Germany and the Western Alliance*, p. vii.

literature revealed that purely analytic studies had not brought us very far down the path toward concrete indications of trends in European unification. If one prominent statesman or scholar were to say that Europe was moving rapidly toward political integration, or that the West Germans seriously desired MLF, and another equally prominent individual were to assert roughly the opposite, then how could we choose between these contradictory but perhaps equally plausible prognoses? Moving political science from the art of persuasive writing to an empirically-based discipline clearly demanded impersonal and verifiable data to test our notions about perceptions and behavior.

Our review of these past writings on European unity also suggested that the difficulty with some empirical studies of these highly significant questions was an overreliance upon single indicators or methodologies. Western European public opinion, for instance, generally supported the idea of further steps toward unity, while being less of one mind when it came to specific plans whose implications were spelled out in some detail. This fact by itself was interesting. But how indicative was public opinion of the attitudes and behaviors of the policy-making and communication elites? Similarly, would knowing the distribution of elite attitudes tell us much about infrastructural developments, such as trade? Just as with the need for empirically verifiable indicators, it seemed clear that it would be important to use a multiplicity of indicators. Such a multiple-indicator approach could provide a built-in set of reliability checks on the usefulness of any single indicator, besides presenting the possibility that mutual verifiability would enhance the strength of conclusions to be drawn from them.

Our decision, then, was to approach the three main questions we had asked from the multiple-indicator point of view. We brought to bear on our topic every empirical research technique then in our methodological arsenal: systematic interviews with elite groupings in France and West Germany; limited public opinion surveys, together with extensive secondary analysis (particularly using factor analysis) of surveys previously conducted; a computerized content analysis, using the General Inquirer system, of prestige newspapers in France, West Germany, the United Kingdom, and the United States; a hand content analysis of a wide variety of newspapers and other publications from these four countries, focusing upon their attitudes toward ten specific arms control events ranging from the Baruch Plan of 1946 to the nuclear test ban of 1963; an analysis of flows of trade, migration, mail, and student exchange among the countries of the western alliance, using the "relative acceptance" model developed by I. Richard Savage and Karl W. Deutsch;[13] and a propositional analysis of arms control proposals in the postwar years. Each project was conceived separately, but within a common framework. Our intent was to determine the contribution that each could make to the study of European unification and to match them against each other as a form of reliability control.

Organization: Staffing and Communications

A multiple-indicator approach requires a variety of skills and an amount of research time that are beyond what an individual scholar can provide. Hence a crucial aspect of the Yale Arms Control Project was assembling an appropriate research team. On the one hand, we needed researchers with an intimate knowledge of European politics and an abiding interest in problems of European unification. Where historical and area knowledge, empathy, and "understanding" are absent, the mechanical application of research methodologies to an intellectual problem is all too likely to lead to sterile research results. The task, then, was to find first-rate scholars with broad political and historical interests. On the other hand, this type of knowledge, empathy, and understanding is by itself not enough. The successful completion of the project required scholars competent in the newer research methodologies of the social sciences, preferably people who themselves had had first-hand experience in the application of empirical research techniques to politically relevant problems. Finally, and on the very practical level, there was the question of finding scholars who had both the inclination and time to participate in the project. The time between our acceptance of the research proposal and the projected beginning of the field work was short, thereby placing even more constraints upon the availability of potentially interested collaborators.

[13] I. Richard Savage and Karl W. Deutsch, "A Statistical Model of the Gross Analysis of Transaction Flows," *Econometrica*, 28, 4 (1960), 551–572. See also

That we were successful in recruiting a team of scholars who fulfilled these demanding criteria augured well for the project itself. The final staffing included six principal investigators in charge of various aspects of the research, six other scholars who helped to conduct the elite interviews in France and West Germany, six consultants who attended working conferences from time to time and reviewed drafts of manuscripts, and a dozen research assistants (one of whom ultimately became a major investigator). With only a couple of exceptions these were people who either had been born and raised in Europe, receiving their advanced training in political science in the United States, or else had spent some years living and performing research in Europe on problems related to integration. All senior researchers, however, worked only part-time on the project, or at most full-time for only a few summer months, and, since the project had to be started right away, still had to complete during the same period some earlier research commitments.

Successful recruitment notwithstanding, several organizational problems emerged. The most immediate of these was less a problem than an opportunity: reorganizing the entire project somewhat to take into account the special interests and skills of the principal investigators. This was more true with respect to the projected elite interviews than with other parts of the project, for the simple reason that the preparation, conduct, and analysis of the interviews required the greatest amount of intellectual effort and organizational coordination. A series of lengthy conferences held at Trumbull College of Yale University, attended by as many of the staff (including consultants) as could be present, ironed out the questionnaires and general procedures to be followed.

More difficult was the problem of creating and maintaining adequate communication among the members of the research team. The facts that the principal investigators were working at three different universities (and one of them spending the entire year abroad), and that the interviewing was performed by a total of eight men in a relatively short period of time, merely complicated the normal communication problems encountered in project

---

Puchala, "European Political Integration," and Hayward R. Alker, Jr., and Donald J. Puchala, "Trends in Economic Partnership: The North Atlantic Area, 1928–1963," in J. David Singer (Ed.), *Quantitative International Politics: Insights and Evidence* (New York: Free Press, 1968), pp. 287–316.

research. The failure of the project's administrative office to send timely information to people in the field caused unnecessary anxieties. In some cases, such as when the administrative director engaged an interviewer without consulting the supervising principal investigator, these communication failures caused outright friction. Retrospectively, it would seem to have been preferable to stress intragroup communication at the cost of economizing, even if it had meant flooding the participants in the project with research memoranda.

Third, although each of the principal investigators was knowledgeable about some advanced research methodologies, none was thoroughly familiar with the advantages and limitations of all of them. This is to be expected in any large-scale research project, and indeed it is precisely this specialization and division of labor that forms the basis for good project research. But in this case, too, the insufficient flow of communication failed to fill the methodology gap. The consequence was that each separate part of the research project moved increasingly in its own direction, knowing little about the problems and preliminary findings of the other parts. At a later stage, to be sure, a set of conferences enabled the participants to learn what the others had been doing and gave the principal investigators the material needed for drafting the project's final reports. It was nonetheless clear that fuller information at an earlier stage would have improved both the research operation and the substantive findings of the project.

Finally, there was the problem of dispersed interests. Simultaneous with his work on this project, each of the principal investigators continued to carry a major teaching load at his university and in addition was conducting other significant research in more or less related fields. The effect of this was twofold. On the positive side, it kept the budget low and gave a broader focus to the Yale Arms Control Project, since each researcher could bring in findings and ideas from his other research. Less positively, however, it meant that other interests distracted the researcher from devoting his full attention to the multifarious aspects of the task at hand. This at once exacerbated and was exacerbated by the communication problems mentioned earlier.

To be sure, these various organizational issues did not pose insuperable problems. Considerable integrative work in the final phase of the project, together with the fact mentioned at the outset—that the principal investigators were well suited to their tasks and were relatively homogeneous in their backgrounds, training, and research interests, besides having a lively interest in the research topic—meant that we could substantially overcome the communication problems and centrifugal tendencies encountered during the research phase. In fact, it could be argued that this centrifugal tendency is an important characteristic of a large variety of common endeavors, successful as well as unsuccessful, and that the difference between success and failure in group projects may lie in the good will of the participants and the exercise of at least a modicum of direction (or some other coordinative mechanism) during their research phases.

Research Design

Turning our general formulation of the topics that interested us into a design for empirical research posed a variety of questions, less or more difficult to resolve according to the type of methodology used. It is tempting to discuss the intricacies and implications of all these intellectual and technical decisions: the standardization of public opinion data for factor analysis; validation of the "relative acceptance" analysis of trade and other communication flows among nations; the selection of publications for content analysis; the construction of a General Inquirer dictionary for the computerized content analysis. In each case the main publications stemming from the project treat these issues in some detail.[14] Here we shall simply refer to some of the questions encountered in our interviews with French and West German elites. The reason for this is twofold: first, the elite-interview project posed particularly thorny issues in designing empirical research; and, second, as noted earlier, it was this part of the project which occupied the bulk of our research time and energy.[15]

The starting point of any study of elites is the question of their value: why are we interested in national elites in the first place? Our response was based on a wide range of reading and thinking

[14] See footnote 11 above.
[15] For a more general discussion of the uses and limitations of elite studies, see Richard L. Merritt, *Systematic Approaches to Comparative Politics* (Chicago: Rand McNally, 1970).

about political phenomena. It seemed clear that elites play an extremely important role in national decision making—even if it is not always possible to specify in complete detail the nature and attributes of that role. On the one hand, various elites participate directly in the decision-making process. They raise questions of national and foreign policy, initiate legislation, issue decrees, interpret laws, decide among competing points of view, implement legislative and other decisions, and select the key personnel to fulfill these various functions. If we would understand a nation's politics, therefore, we must look directly at those who participate in decision making. On the other hand, elite studies can probe the perspectives of an entire stratum of people. Depending upon the degree of homogeneity among elite groupings, a general study, using systematic means for selecting individual elite members and securing data about them, would tell us something about the values and perceptions that go into the decision-making process. Neither of these arguments for elite studies is to deny the importance of other factors. And it is for precisely this reason that we also examined public opinion, press attitudes, and underlying trends in the economic and social spheres.

Identifying the relevant French and West German elites was a challenge. There are no handbooks giving pat formulas about how to identify elites, just as there is no general acceptance of any notion of who the elites of a country might be. At each stage, therefore, we had to invest, adapt, and justify to ourselves the steps we took. After consulting numerous scholars who had written extensively about elites (including Harold D. Lasswell, Robert A. Dahl, Carl J. Friedrich, Wendell Bell, Erwin K. Scheuch, and Juan J. Linz in the United States, and leading scholars in France and West Germany) and relying particularly upon our own past experience,[16] we adopted a mixed strategy. We first listed the general *fields of competence* which we wanted represented: political, military, mass media and intellectual, civil service, and business

---

[16] Karl W. Deutsch and Lewis J. Edinger, *Germany Rejoins the Powers: Mass Opinion, Interest Groups, and Elites in Contemporary German Foreign Policy* (Palo Alto, Calif.: Stanford University Press, 1959), Lewis J. Edinger, "Post-Totalitarian Leadership: Elites in the German Federal Republic," *The American Political Science Review*, 54, 1 (March 1960), 58–82; and Lewis J. Edinger, "Continuity and Change in the Background of German Decision Makers," *The Western Political Quarterly*, 14, 1 (March 1961), 17–36.

elites, plus a sixth category of labor leaders, professionals, and others. Second, we specified the level of *positions* we were interested in, such as the top civil servants in key ministries, the chairmen of relevant parliamentary committees, the chief editors of major newspapers, and the like. Third, we wrote to a large number of colleagues and other experts in the two countries, asking for the names of prominent people in their special fields of competence whom we should interview—people who in the *judgment of expert informants* were important in decision-making processes, fairly representative of their elite grouping as a whole, and likely to be informed about national and international politics. We combined the lists and supplemented them with names selected from official or other handbooks listing occupants of elite positions.

The final lists was comprised of 441 French and 650 West German leaders. The next stage was one of self-selection. We wrote to each person on our lists to request an interview, receiving positive responses from almost half of the French and three-quarters of the Germans. Finally, to winnow down the possible respondents to the number of people whom, given our time constraints, we could in fact interview, we adopted quotas for each of the six groupings that interested us and ranked the potential candidates according to their prominence in the eyes of those who had earlier recommended them to us. Unfortunately, we had neither the time nor resources to examine the characteristics of those whom we did not interview. Our feeling was nonetheless that our procedure had produced a fairly representative and otherwise excellent set of 147 French and 173 West German respondents.

In all we prepared three questionnaires for these respondents.[17] The most extensive and, for our immediate research goals, most important, sought to find out what views they held on (1) domestic affairs, (2) foreign policy and international relations, (3) European integration and alliances, and (4) arms, arms control, and disarmament. Designing such a questionnaire raised at the outset the question of research strategy. One approach would have been

[17] The open-end interview schedule appears in Deutsch, Edinger, Macridis, and Merritt, *France, Germany, and the Western Alliance,* pp. 303–311. The manifest attitude, latent attitude, and biographical data questionnaires, together with the distribution of responses, are to be found in Deutsch, Edinger, Macridis, Merritt, and Voss-Eckermann, ''French and German Elite Responses, 1964: Codebook and Data.''

to prepare a list of closed-end questions. The collective experience of our co-workers and consultants, however, counseled against this approach.[18] Our elite respondents, we felt, would feel frustrated by any efforts to force their answers into narrow boxes, and resentful that we would treat them simply as single and perhaps not very unique voices in a mass. Moreover, it was clear that such a procedure would cost us the rich and valuable information that these leaders could give us from their own varied experiences. Another approach would have recorded on tape the responses to open-end questions.[19] We rejected this approach, too, rightly or wrongly suspecting that the presence of microphones and tape recorders would inhibit the openness of the respondents.[20]

The procedure we finally adopted represented a compromise. Our interviewers followed the open-end technique during the interviews themselves—asking broad questions, seeking to get clarifications of responses, requesting information on specific points, and withal making notes about the interview on specially prepared forms. Immediately after the interview they were to retire to a quiet spot and, with the help of their notes, reconstruct the discussion. This meant in practice answering a very lengthy series of detailed (closed-end) questions about each point that they were supposed to have covered in the interview. Subtleties, modifications, and other points were to be recorded on tape for later use, after their transcription, at the analytic stage.

The procedure placed a great burden on the eight interviewers.

[18] See Daniel Lerner, "Interviewing Frenchmen," *The American Journal of Sociology*, 62, 2 (September 1956), 187–194. For a report of a project that successfully used closed-end questionnaires in interviewing elites, see William H. Hunt, Wilder W. Crane, and John C. Wahlke, "Interviewing Political Elites in Cross-Cultural Comparative Research," *The American Journal of Sociology*, 70, 1 (July 1964), 59–68.

[19] Our Yale colleague, James David Barber, had used this technique successfully in his interviews with Connecticut legislators: *The Lawmakers: Recruitment and Adaptation to Legislative Life* (New Haven and London: Yale University Press, 1965).

[20] There was also a technical consideration: Granted the increased accuracy of the taped interviews, they would have required elaborate content analyzing procedures for processing. Faced with limited time and resources, we chose in effect to have our interviewers code the information received in the interview (as will be described below). For a different strategy, see Frank Bonilla and Jose A. Silva Michelena (Eds.), *The Politics of Change in Venezuela: A Strategy of Research on Social Policy* (Cambridge, Mass., and London: M.I.T. Press, 1969).

It was for precisely this reason that we chose to ask professional scholars to perform the interviews, rather than relying upon the trained but anonymous interviewers that a commercial surveying firm could provide. The latter would doubtless have produced more standardized, and hence in a sense more reliable, data. But they would not have had the fingertip feeling for European and international politics that we felt was necessary for asking and interpreting information given by some of the most influential people in the Europe of the mid-1960s. Using professional political scientists (and in one case an historian) had the distinct advantage of bringing knowledgeable partners for discussion to the interviews. It also meant, however, that they were not trained in the conduct of systematic interviews (although, of course, each had a long record of other types of political interviewing). This in turn meant that the data emerging from the interviews as a whole tended to be more idiosyncratic than would have been desirable.[21] The net effect was nonetheless positive: the increased understanding these men brought to their task more than made up for any loss in completely comparable data.

A second questionnaire aimed at biographical information about the respondents. We anticipated that our research assistants in Paris and Cologne could prepare much of this from published biographical directories. The interviewers could then fill the gaps during their discussions with the respondents. As it turned out, the administrative task of scheduling interviews and keeping track of interviewers occupied an inordinate amount of the assistants' time, leaving little for the biographical spadework. A consequence was that, despite the best efforts of our assistants and interviewers, the biographical data questionnaires were useful only for the most basic types of information. In retrospect, it is clear that getting relatively complete biographical data on the 320 French and German leaders we interviewed would have been a research project in itself.

The most innovative questionnaire focused on the latent aspects of the respondents' perspectives. Prepared mainly by Edinger and Scheuch, it sought to provide means by which interviewers could

[21] Unpublished research performed in early 1968 at the University of Illinois by William R. Klecka suggests that more attention should be paid to the possibility of interviewer bias in this and other elite studies.

estimate the respondents' degree of information about, involvement with, and perceived influence on the political matters that interested us. Reliable estimates of these dimensions, correlated with data about the respondents' personal histories and manifest perspectives, could make a significant contribution to the study of political belief systems. Our approach was simple enough: a series of seven-point scales along which the interviewer could score the respondent on such questions as the saliency of the four major categories of issues, his emotional involvement (affect) with them, the firmness of his opinions and receptivity to new information (cloture). sensitivity to the views of others, and tough-mindedness.

The latent attitude questionnaire was only partially successful. On the one hand, it did provide some insights into the political perspectives of the people we interviewed. As we reported earlier,[22]

> Taking together the ratings on efficacy and anxiety, tough-mindedness and alienation . . . , it appears that a significant proportion of French leaders feel tough-minded but ineffective and anxious in dealing with their own countrymen and, to a lesser extent, with their international environment. In West Germany, this tough-minded but frustrated group is smaller, and its remaining frustrations seem to be less in the domestic than in the foreign field.

A quick review of subsequent French and West German politics suggests that these moods were borne out in practice: the absence of sweeping changes in French foreign policy, even after the May 1968 disturbances, the 1969 resignation of President de Gaulle, and the subsequent election of Georges Pompidou; and the reorientation of German foreign policy under the Brandt government.

But, on the other hand, the latent attitude data we gathered did not provide us with the basis for making broad generalizations about the interrelationships of elite perspectives. The major reason for this was simply the difficulty in equating the perceptions of the eight interviewers, in turn no doubt due as much to insufficient discussion among project members about the scales themselves and their application as well as to insufficient pretesting in

---

[22] Deutsch, Edinger, Macridis, and Merritt, *France, Germany and the Western Alliance*, p. 257.

the field. Such problems notwithstanding, our research staff felt that this type of instrument deserved further exploration.

Project Evaluation and Continuation

The research design for the Yale Arms Control Project by and large produced a wide variety of interesting information on arms control and integration in the Western European environment. The research reports, all unclassified, went into the scholarly literature as well as government files. And yet a nagging question persists: How can we estimate the project's actual impact upon the scholarly and official community?

One way to measure impact, of course, is to look at the project's reception by various audiences. Since the primary sponsor was the United States Arms Control and Disarmament Agency, it was to this agency that we submitted our initial reports. Generally speaking, the reaction of the ACDA's project evaluation officers was one of interest and constructive criticism. Unfamiliar research methodologies, such as the computerized procedures for General Inquirer content analysis, appeared to some as less relevant than those, such as interviews, that by now are part of the intellectual equipment of most politically interested people in academia and government. More unsettling was the possibility that our research —painstakingly conducted over the course of two years—would simply end up as one more heap of partially read and generally unheeded papers filling up some government official's filing case. And, of course, there is no way of knowing exactly how much impact our research had on policy-making processes. Subsequent assurances were encouraging: the comment by a highly-placed ambassador, for instance, that our report was the "most useful" that ACDA had received from any university, or the claim of a well-informed Washington columnist that our findings (not identified by authorship but unmistakably described in his column) about the low priority that West European elites placed on a multilateral force (MLF) contributed to the Kennedy Administration's abandonment of the program. But such assurances are in no way a substitute for the thoroughgoing evaluation and critique necessary if policy scientists are to perform work at once intellectually respectable and useful to the government.

Evaluation is slower yet in the academic marketplace of ideas, brief book reviews in scholarly journals notwithstanding. It may be some years before the project's intellectual underpinnings, research techniques, and findings meet the scrutiny they need.[23] Only then, perhaps, will we find out what the scholarly impact of the project was. It may be comforting to add that, in this sense, our experience is not atypical of a broader issue of information exchange in political science.

Still another way to check the impact of a study is to see what new research it spawns. On the one hand, to be sure, each of the principal investigators is continuing his own research on problems related to arms control and integration in the Western European environment. To this extent there is intellectual continuity. But, on the other hand, many of the questions the project raised remain unanswered today.[24] Contractual deadlines did not give us the time we needed during the analysis stage to make the most out of our manifold findings. This was particularly true with respect to their theoretic relevance for the study of politics. Similarly, as noted earlier, the centrifugal tendencies of the principal investigators meant an early abandonment of some possibly fruitful avenues of research, such as improvements in means for assessing latent attitude structures of elite respondents.

It would therefore be useful to undertake a retrospective but searching examination of the impact of the Yale Arms Control Project. Indeed, perhaps most large-scale research projects should include plans for subsequent self-evaluation sessions. In this particular case it would be helpful to get information about the project's reception by the scholarly community interested in ideas and research methodologies; its usefulness for those in government who supported the research; the research gaps it filled and later efforts to fill the others; the new research it generated; the accuracy and relevance of its policy implications. Such an undertak-

[23] Some beginnings have been made. See Lewis J. Edinger and Donald D. Searing, ''Social Background in Elite Analysis: A Methodological Inquiry,'' *The American Political Science Review*, 61, 2 (June 1967), 411–415, and Roger W. Cobb and Charles Elder, *International Community: A Regional and Global Study* (New York: Holt, 1970).

[24] Models for such review studies of projects include Robert K. Merton and Paul F. Lazarsfeld (Eds.), *Continuities in Social Research: Studies in the Scope and Method of The American Soldier* (Glencoe, Ill.: Free Press, 1950), and Richard Christie and Marie Jahoda (Eds.), *Studies in the Scope and Method of The Authoritarian Personality* (Glencoe, Ill.: Free Press, 1954).

ing would not be merely of intrinsic interest. It would also tell us a great deal about the sociology of political science—how political scientists go about their work and, especially, how they can improve the intellectual and organizational aspects of their future projects.

Conclusions

Our brief survey of the data problems and our closer look at the experiences of one larger data-based project—the Yale Arms Control Project—suggest several conclusions.

First, data-based research on problems relevant to policy is practicable. It can lead to substantial and usable results within eighteen to twenty-four months from the start of a project, with findings that stand the test of subsequent political developments.

Second, the costs of such research can be relatively modest: between one and two man-years for senior investigators, two to four man-years of assistants' or students' time; if undertaken at a university where some faculty members and some doctoral candidates or other students, undergraduates or graduates, care to give some of their time, the irreducible budget without computer content analysis but with university overhead may be about $85,000 over a two-year period, or about $110,000 if computer content analysis is included. If one government agency, private foundation, or university is not willing to support on this scale a research project that might produce findings inconvenient to this sponsor, then another agency, foundation, or organization with a different outlook or interest may be willing to do so. If no sponsor can be found, a highly motivated group of faculty and students could organize to carry through the project on a voluntary basis, without loss of quality.

Third, writings about research methodology, or about the philosophy of social science, will gain greatly in usefulness, as well as credibility, if they are undertaken by authors who also have had first-hand personal experience in conducting successfully at least one major data-based research project.

Fourth, quick policy research requires further testing in unhurried follow-ups. Sponsors, as well as some academic investigators, often are impressed with the urgency of getting quick results to be used in some pressing policy decision. Once the main findings, relevant to this particular decision, have been extracted from the data, both sponsors and investigators may lose interest in searching for further possible findings in the data, or in testing, retesting, and refining the first apparent facts or relationships that emerged from the early stages of the analysis. This tendency is dangerous for policy, and it can be disastrous for the growth of social science. The greater the pressure for speed, the greater will be the risks of error which we may have to accept for the time being, but also the greater will be the need for later, unhurried rechecking of the first quick results. The speed required for first aid must be balanced somewhat by greater care in later observations, test series, and sometimes post mortems, if the quick, practical application of currently available knowledge is not to degenerate. Any major data-based research project, therefore, should include explicit provisions in its research design, as well as in its budget, for eventual careful retesting, cross-checking, and follow-up of its earlier findings. Where such budgetary provisions cannot be obtained from the original sponsor, universities should set aside some amounts from the overhead costs of the project—or charge frankly a higher percentage of overhead—to make sure that university standards of testing and verifying the research results will be maintained.

Fifth, in addition to thus continuing or rounding out an ongoing research project beyond the immediate policy interest of its sponsor, provisions should be made for a subsequent critique and evaluation of the work and its results, perhaps three or five years after the conclusion of the original work, and perhaps in collaboration with another independent team of scholars. Just as in the surgical practice of good hospitals there are "tissue committees" to evaluate the surgeon's diagnosis in the light of the evidence of the organs and tissues removed in the operation, so there should be research evaluation committees to check on the confirmation or disconfirmation of policy research findings in the light of the data used at the time, as well as in the light of subsequent developments.

Sixth, to make these suggestions practical, more elaborate provisions should be made for administration and internal communication at all stages of the project, for the preservation, storage, and retrieval of all data, and for the recording of all relevant decisions about research design and methods at all stages of the work. At the end of the project, findings, data, interview protocols, and test instruments should be stored at a suitable and central archive, such as the Inter-University Consortium for Political Research at Ann Arbor, Michigan. These materials should then be made available from there to all qualified scholars for secondary analysis (subject only to such safeguards as may be needed to protect the anonymity of the original respondents, where such protection is required).

Together, these six recommendations might go some way to help data-based social science research to reduce the probability of cumulative error and to increase the chances for the cumulative growth of usable and dependable knowledge.

4 LOBBYING: IN SEARCH OF A THEORY

Harmon Zeigler
University of Oregon

Michael Baer
University of Kentucky

A rather important aspect of this essay is not just to discuss the substantive subject, but rather to trace the development of the project in the mind of the authors. The idea for this study actually began several years back when one of the authors of *Lobbying*[1] wrote *Interest Groups in American Society*,[2] which was begun as an attempt to apply Bentley's and Truman's theories of American politics. It ended up instead as a departure from traditional group theory. Although the first portion of *Interest Groups* sounds very much like traditional group theory, the last part, in which the author began to deal with empirical

---

This is the first publication of Harmon Zeigler and Michael Baer's essay. All rights reserved. Permission to reprint must be obtained from the publisher and the authors.

[1] Harmon Zeigler and Michael Baer, *Lobbying Interaction and Influence in American State Legislatures* (Belmont, Calif.: Wadsworth, 1969).

[2] Harmon Zeigler, *Interest Groups in American Society* (Englewood Cliffs, N.J.: Prentice-Hall, 1964).

problems, is not at all similar to the theory set forth in the *Process of Government*[3] and the *Governmental Process*.[4]

This was the beginning of a drifting away, almost a declaration of independence from traditional group theory. In the writing of *Interest Groups,* the author concluded that we need a more precise frame of reference than is possible with traditional group theory. His ideas were further developed when in 1963 he wrote an essay on interest groups in state politics, which ultimately wound up as a protest against the way interest group politics had been treated in the past.[5] In this particular essay the departure from traditional group theory was complete. There was no mention made of Bentley and Truman; yet even considering the relative absence of data, new ideas began to emerge. Following this essay, we concluded that more data was needed to further the study of interest groups. There had already been a plethora of case studies of interest groups; thus what was needed was more systematic research.

An application was submitted for a grant to study lobbying at the state legislative level. The Department of Health, Education, and Welfare funded this study of interactions between legislators and lobbyists. The basic question we hoped to answer is one that might appear almost trite; however, it had not been previously answered. It was simply, "what would happen if there were no lobbyists?" We wanted to know if anything really different would take place in a state legislature if lobbyists suddenly went home. This was the type of question that seemed to us quite reasonable as a start, especially since most of the case studies of "interest groups in action" began with the assumption that they were studying something important. The case studies thus were beginning with a premise that had never been directly established.

Interestingly enough, by the time we began to work on this study some work had been completed on the United States Congress. In particular, Lester Milbrath's book, *The Washington Lobbyists*,[6] suggested that interest groups really weren't very important. Mil-

---

[3] Arthur F. Bentley, *The Process of Government* (Chicago: University of Chicago Press, 1908).

[4] David Truman, *The Governmental Process* (New York: Knopf, 1951).

[5] Harmon Zeigler, "Interest Groups in the States," in Herbert Jacob and Kenneth N. Vines (Eds.), *Politics in the American States* (Boston: Little, Brown, 1965), pp. 101–147.

[6] Lester Milbrath, *The Washington Lobbyists* (Chicago: Rand McNally, 1963).

brath implied that most legislation would have been the same whether or not interest groups had been around to lobby.

Now, the ultimate goal is not to study one specific legislative system, but rather to develop a systematic and comparative analysis of the effect as well as the process of lobbying. The task of trying to discover what lobbyists accomplish obviously had to be done on a comparative basis. A single lobbying group in a single state might be highly influential, but one could not generalize to the overall impact of lobbying from this single study. This, in fact, is where case studies have failed in the past. Much as one might ask about the effect of a party system, we can inquire about the impact of an interest group system. Interest groups may or may not be integrated into the decision-making process of a political unit, but certainly the more integrated the groups and their representatives are, the more likely they are to be effective. With a comparative study in mind, we selected four states to study: Oregon, Massachusetts, North Carolina, and Utah. These states were selected to provide the maximum dispersion of socioeconomic and cultural variables. In addition, they were from four different regions of the country.

One of the more immediate discoveries of the study was that state legislators, no matter where they are from, do not like anyone coming in and inquiring about their relationship with lobbyists. It turns out that while we were investigating Massachusetts, Massachusetts was investigating us. If you read through the records of the Massachusetts General Court you will find the following bill:

> Ordered, That a special committee, to consist of five members of the House of Representatives to be designated by the Speaker thereof, is hereby authorized and directed to make an investigation and study of the reasons for the interviews of elected officials presently being conducted for the University of Oregon Institute of Community Study, the person in charge of the interviews, the source of financial backing for such interviews, and take any other action which it deems necessary and proper in carrying out the purpose of this committee.
>
> Said committee shall be provided with quarters in the state house or elsewhere, may hold hearings, may travel within the Commonwealth and may expend for clerical or other services and for expenses such sums as may be appropriated therefor.
>
> Said committee shall report to the General Court the results of its investigation and study by filing the same with the clerk of the

house of representatives on or before the last Wednesday of March in the current year.[7] (HB 3176, March 1966)

The discussion with the committee chairman revealed a number of reasons for such an investigation. First, the committee chairman felt it was possible that this study could be a "Republican plot" to reconstitute the Republican majority in Massachusetts. He felt it was quite possible that some of the questions, particularly those having to do with bribes and threats, may have been planted in the questionnaire by the Republican Governor of Massachusetts, through his contact with Governor Hatfield, also a Republican, of Oregon; and also through another Republican, Arthur Fleming, President of the University of Oregon and a member of the Political Science Department at the University. The committee chairman also indicated that some committee members felt the material gathered might be used in the upcoming political campaigns.

Other pitfalls into which we fell in Massachusetts might serve as a warning to future researchers, although it is probably impossible for any research project to avoid every possible area of trouble. The committee chairman pointed out that some legislators were disturbed with our failure to hire a Massachusetts interviewing firm and with our (intentional) failure to explain the details of our study to the Speaker of the House and President of the Senate. They were also disturbed that each respondent was not given a full explanation of affiliations and connections of the research center sponsoring the project; the chairman indicated that the project could have been sponsored by any number of interest groups. Finally, it appears that the Massachusetts legislators were somewhat afraid that results of our surveys might reach the Massachusetts Crime Commission, which had recently been investigating and reporting on activities of Massachusetts politicians.[8]

We had to convince the legislature that our study was not involved with the Republican Party nor was it in any other way involved in a conspiracy concerning either the Crime Commission or the Democrats. Judging from the number of responses that we eventually obtained, it appears that the legislators were finally convinced (eighty-seven percent).[9] All this, however, does make a

[7] Massachusetts General Court, House Bill Number 3176 (March 1966).

[8] Personal interview with committee chairman (April 1966).

[9] Eighty-seven percent of the Massachusetts legislators allowed the complete interview to be administered.

point. When we later concluded that the Massachusetts lobbyists are not very effective, one of the reasons appeared to be that no one in Massachusetts trusts anyone else.

Once a grant had been obtained and states selected for the project, an interview schedule was prepared and pretested in Colorado and Arizona. Through the pretest, we learned that legislators and lobbyists were more sensitive than larger, random samples of people. One must be especially careful in phrasing questions, and particularly in broaching controversial topics or areas. For example, it would be very useful to utilize a portion of Edwards' Personal Preference schedule to relate the personality structure of lobbyists to their interaction. However, after attempting to administer the schedule in the pretest, it was removed from the interviews. We found that legislators were very reluctant to answer those questions which touched upon extremely personal matters. We learned quickly not to ask questions of this nature.

After pretesting the schedule in Colorado and Arizona, a final version was developed that was then administered by professional interviewers in each of the four states—Massachusetts, North Carolina, Oregon, and Utah. Well over ninety percent of the legislators and registered lobbyists in these states were interviewed. In addition to the survey instruments, three of the states were visited by at least one of the authors. We interviewed four or five legislators and lobbyists in each state in an attempt to gather background information, personal observations, and personal impressions. In most of these in-depth interviews, we tried to interview knowledgeable, influential persons as indicated by the original interview schedules. The interviews were tape-recorded and ran from one to four hours in length. We sought to amplify the information derived from the more structured instruments and to acquaint ourselves with the politics of the states. The in-depth interviews were extremely helpful in aiding the interpretation of the interview schedules when we began writing about the roles and effects of the lobbyists.

The first question we wanted to ask both legislators and lobbyists was: "what does lobbying accomplish?" It is quite difficult to ask this kind of question and get a candid answer. In fact, the trouble with survey research is the necessity of asking blunt questions. Partially for this reason, what has been done in the past to measure the effects of lobbyists has been very meager. First, there has been the case study, which generally assumes that lobbyists have some effects. Another technique has been to ask legislators how effective lobbyists are. Wahlke, Eulau, Buchanan, and Ferguson tried this in their study of Tennessee, Ohio, New Jersey, and California.[10] This method alone can lead to some serious problems because of the norms attributed to the role of the legislators. Assertion of independence is very important; therefore, legislators are not likely to be totally honest about the influence of interest groups. In addition, other research has indicated that many legislators do not even know who the lobbyists are.[11] Garceau and Silverman found that more than one-third of the legislators in Vermont could not identify the lobbyists of the most important interest groups.[12]

To circumvent this problem we administered, to both legislators and lobbyists, a Guttman scale which measured the influence of lobbyists. The assumption was that the legislators would underestimate and that the lobbyists would overestimate the influence of interest groups on political decisions. The scale consisted of three questions which ranged from the relatively weak to the relatively strong.

> "Some people are more influenced by lobbyists than others. Thinking of yourself, how often have you been influenced by a lobbyist to the extent that you began to question your position on an issue or bill?"
>
> "Can you recall being influenced by a lobbyist to the extent of changing your opinion on an issue so that your opinion was not as far from the lobbyist's position as it was initially?"
>
> "How often have you been influenced by a lobbyist to the extent of coming to agree with his position on an issue or a bill?"

The weak form of the question measures only a moderate form of influence in which the lobbyist successfully penetrates the mind and creates the possibility of another alternative. It doesn't imply anything about the resolution of the conflict. Indeed, it might be resolved in the initial way, but nevertheless, the legislator has

[10] John Wahlke, Heinz Eulau, William Buchanan, and Leroy Ferguson, *The Legislative System* (New York: Wiley, 1962).

[11] Oliver Garceau and Corinne Silverman, "A Pressure Group and the Pressured: A Case Report," *American Political Science Review*, 43 (September 1954), 672–691.

[12] *Ibid.*, 685.

become aware of an alternative that didn't exist in his mind before. The successful lobbyist is, of course, one who can convince the legislator to modify his views in a manner consistent with the interest group's position. The set of questions formed a scale, and by examining the answers of both legislators and lobbyists we reached some conclusions about the relative strength of interest groups in these states. We found that Oregon has the most effective lobbying system, followed by Utah, with Massachusetts and North Carolina bringing up the rear.

Our first thought was to determine if something about the state's socioeconomic and cultural patterns contributed to the strength or weakness of interest groups. This would follow from the earlier work Zeigler had done in which he had linked the strength of interest groups with urbanization, industrialization, and wealth, as well as the political variables party competition and party cohesion.[13]

Although one cannot draw definite generalization from four states we did *not* find that these relationships existed in the four states of our sample. We were left with the conclusion that system variables and interest group strength are not really related. Therefore, we searched for other possible explanations of strength and came up with two. The first had to do with the characteristics of the group itself, a notion which was quite compatible with traditional interest group theory. The group with high prestige would be likely to influence more legislators. Secondly, we thought that the *interaction situation* itself might explain the strength that an interest group possesses. Interaction theory would lead us to argue that the skills of the lobbyist determine whether or not an interest group has a strong or weak position in the political system of a state. Both the group characteristics and the interaction situation were considered as two categories of explanatory variables.

The authors were considering these theoretical approaches when two things happened. First, Heinz Eulau spent two or three days discussing the data which had been collected and offered extremely rewarding suggestions. Second, the authors were heavily exposed to symbolic interaction theories of social psychology. As a result of this exposure to symbolic interaction theories and the conversations with Eulau, we regrouped our thinking and began to

---

[13] Zeigler, "Interest Groups in the States," p. 1B ff.

write our study with symbolic interaction as the basis of the theory.

Eulau had pointed out something very interesting that had led to consideration of the symbolic interaction theory. He observed that, although there was nothing especially remarkable in the socioeconomic characteristics of the states we were considering, there was one characteristic that we had not explored—one we had not even noticed. This characteristic was output—what the state legislatures actually did. Eulau noted that states like California, Oregon, and Utah had a very strong interest-group system and a relatively large public expenditure per capita. Conversely, weak lobby states like Tennessee, Ohio, and North Carolina spend relatively small amounts at the state level. There is one obvious explanation for the strength of lobbyists in Oregon and their weakness in Massachusetts. There is more to do at the state level in Oregon than there is in Massachusetts because the state level is where the money is being spent.[14] This is a simple but excellent explanation of the way to begin to explain the strength of lobbying in the states: one reason that there are strong interest groups is because there is good reason to be strong. Of course, this alone is not a satisfactory explanation, but it did make us begin to think further about reasons for variance in the rates of interactions between legislators and lobbyists. So this simple explanation led us into the interaction theory *per se*.

We should make it clear that we cannot lay any claims for adhering to the textbook method of conducting research. Frankly, the final theory did not come first. It came after we had played with the data for some time and found that it could not be analyzed properly on the basis of an earlier communications model which we initially used. Our interview had originally been developed out of a series of hunches based primarily upon communications theory. We were concerned with identifying the communicators and the types of communication in the legislative arena.

We now were looking at the same information, but in a framework of interaction theory. By interaction we mean that legislators "emit behavior in each other's presence, they create products for each other, or they communicate with each other."[15] The product they create can either be attributed to the interaction it-

[14] Zeigler and Baer, *Lobbying Interaction and Influence in American State Legislatures*, p. 37.

[15] John W. Thibaut and Harold H. Kelley, *The Social Psychology of Groups* (New York: Wiley, 1961), p. 10.

self or it may be the result of an interaction. Interaction theory asks, why do lobbyists interact with legislators? And why do legislators interact with lobbyists? At this point we get into the question of products and resources.

A lobbyist must interact with a legislator, for it is the legislator who has the authority to make a decision. The lobbyist, on the other hand, cannot vote; so the legislator has an initial advantage in the distribution of resources. The job of the lobbyist is to exchange his unique resources for that vote. This exchange of resources is the basis of legislator-lobbyist interaction. In this interaction, each person's behavior can influence the behavior of the other person. It is not a one-way exchange but a reciprocal interaction, since both parties can be influenced.

The goal of the lobbyist is to create goods which the legislator finds desirable. This does not mean that the lobbyist can say, "Here is $10,000, please hand me your vote." This would be a perfectly legitimate exchange system if it were successful, but because legislators respond to other pressures against bribery it is not successful. For one thing, it is too risky. Besides that, no one has the kind of money that bribery would require. To obtain enough votes would be a very expensive and a very inefficient way of creating a continuing exchange between two people.

The lobbyist can create two types of "useful" goods. He can offer to abstain from politically threatening activity, or he can offer to engage in beneficial activity. Typical threatening activity would be to assert, "We will defeat you at the polls." This kind of action is not really efficient either, because both the legislators and the lobbyists (at least the more experienced ones) know that the votes cannot be delivered or withheld on command. Even those interests which have large memberships do not have control over their members, as Schattschneider pointed out in his book several years ago.[16] Therefore, even those lobbyists with the potential resource of large numbers of voters are reluctant to commit that resource because of its instability. In any case, threatening communications arouse fear, and fear-arousing communication usually produces the least reliable conversion from one point to another.

This narrows the resources of the lobbyists to the second type

---

[16] E. E. Schattschneider, *The Semi-Sovereign People* (New York: Holt, 1960), p. 47 ff.

of goods he has to offer, those of a benevolent nature. This is where the lobbyist can show whatever skill he has. He has *information* to exchange, and information is a commodity very much in demand, especially at the state level. State legislators, if they have any staff at all, generally have inadequate research facilities. In addition, there is a high turnover in state legislatures; thus, many of the legislators themselves are unfamiliar with the vagaries of the legislative way of life. Under these conditions information is at a premium. Basically the legislator needs two types of information: gossip about voting coalitions and technical data. Therefore, we suspected that skilled lobbyists were those who had a reputation for correctly estimating the size of various coalitions. Likewise, skilled lobbyists need to establish a reputation for technical expertise.

Information, therefore, becomes the crucial commodity in the legislator-lobbyist exchange. This means that the legislator participating in the exchange must recognize the lobbyist as a reliable source of information. The lobbyist has to establish his integrity, which is one of his big problems, since legislators are sensitive to electoral pressures and our political culture defines the lobbyist's role as a marginal one. It is always easier for information to be transmitted from an executive agency of the government to the legislature, because in this case there is a legitimate government institution providing the information. Lobbyists can overcome this marginality by consistently reliable performance, thus demonstrating that they are experts in the field that they represent. Just as symbolic interaction theory would have predicted, we found that when a legislator feels a lobbyist is reliable and competent, he is more likely to interact with him.

We have used the phrase "symbolic interaction theory" but thus far have spoken only of interaction. The use of the term "symbolic" involves images of both self and other. Symbolic interaction theory postulates that interaction is composed of the image of oneself, image of the other, and your image of the other's image of you. Except for studies of national images, this approach has been neglected in political research. We sought to identify these three images during our data collection. We tried to obtain the lobbyists' self-conception, the lobbyists' conception of the legislators, and the lobbyists' conception of the legislators' conception of them. We collected similar data for the legislators. Our basic hypothesis was that the more congruent the images of the legislator and lobbyist, the more successful the interaction would be. When the lobbyist and legislator have implicitly agreed upon their images, their interaction will proceed smoothly since each of them knows what to expect from the other. When they do not have congruent expectations, the interaction might be disastrous. We found that continued interaction could not really get off the ground until conceptions were congruent and satisfactory.

So that these hypotheses could be tested, we measured each respondent's image of self and other by using a thermometer scale. We showed the respondent a picture of a thermometer and asked him to indicate his feelings toward each group. Strong positive feelings were indicated by a "temperature" approaching one hundred degrees, neutral feelings were indicated by fifty degrees, and negative by degrees close to zero on the thermometer. This seems to be a fairly efficient way of obtaining a generalized feeling of warmth toward the other. We found, as the theory had suggested, that as interaction increases so does the thermometer score. Even more significantly, as interaction increases the difference between the legislator's feeling toward the lobbyist and the lobbyist's perception of this feeling diminishes. Therefore, among the high interaction groups, the lobbyists are really quite accurate in their estimate of what the legislator thinks of them. This is one important estimate of influence. For if a lobbyist is successful in his estimate of the legislator's view of him, he is likely to succeed in his lobbying effort since his expectations approach reality.

Perhaps in conclusion we should note that in spite of all the congruence of conceptions which was found in the states with higher interaction rates, the lobbyist's self-image remains one of persuader while the legislator's image of the lobbyist's role is one of informer. In any given interaction, the lobbyist will tend to think of it as persuasive communication, while the legislator will view it as an informative communication. Ironically, this perception on the part of the legislator is to the advantage of the lobbyist, because overtly persuasive communication is less efficient than subvertly persuasive communication. Thus, we found that the lobbyist is frequently able to convey his persuasive communication successfully to the legislator in spite of his images of himself and his job.

5 THE DEVELOPMENT OF ARENAS OF POWER

Theodore J. Lowi
University of Chicago

The *Arenas of Power* framework and the whole Policy Analysis Approach are rooted in my work on New York City, beginning in the late 1950s. I was studying the background and recruitment patterns at the top of the political patronage in the administrative system of New York government. My cutting-off point was the "cabinet level." There is no such thing as an official cabinet in New York government, but between 1898 and 1959 there were 1200 commissions at that level of government. It is amazing how much you can do with data drawn from people in those positions.

The most intriguing thing was simply to ask what the changes have been over sixty years in what seem to be the dominant patterns of representation. One of the obvious questions was about the state of the party in a town that was known for machine politics. In the diagrams, P+ represents the proportion of commissioners who had held high party positions prior to appointment. By high party position I meant noticeable, recognizable functionary posi-

---

This is the first publication of Theodore J. Lowi's essay. All rights reserved. Permission to reprint must be obtained from the publisher and the author.

tions, including a regular designation as a candidate for an elective post, a position as delegate to some convention, membership in some important party committee, and, most importantly, the holding of such party posts as Assembly District Leader, Election District Leader, and the like. Only the obvious and outstanding ones were counted, and thus the "Party Recruitment" designation is a fairly restrictive and pure category.

I presumed that party had something to do with the recruitment of commissioners to government. Party-recruited commissioners are to be distinguished from those who may have become important

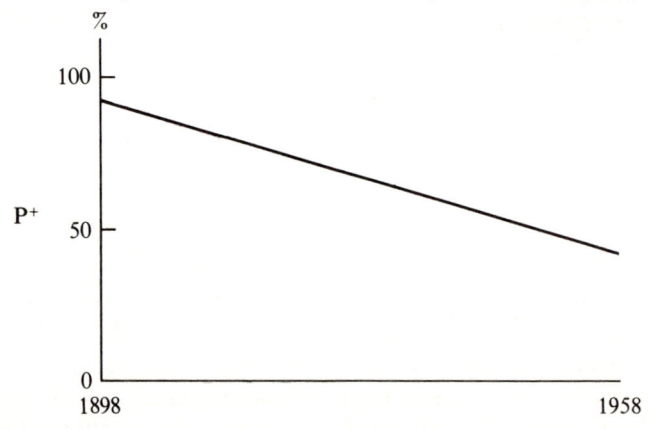

Diagram 1. Party recruitment of the top patronage in New York City—1898–1958. Percent party-recruited (P^+) commissioners, total cabinet-level.

party functionaries after appointment, or from those who never did perform any major party functions before, during, or after appointment.

Diagram 1 gives a picture of the history of party recruitment between 1898 and 1958. Some interesting quirks in the actual trend line have been ignored in order to give the overall secular trend, which is a line extending downward from a high of over ninety percent party-recruited to a low at the end of the Wagner Administration of around forty-five percent. Actually, among those appointees on whom I had information, one hundred percent were party-recruited. But only about ninety-two percent had sufficient biographies, with eight percent not ascertained either on this or other characteristics. I thus felt warranted in saying, as I did in

At the Pleasure of the Mayor,[1] that at the turn of the century the party system held a "monopoly of access" in New York. By 1958, the monopoly had obviously been broken.

It is possible to get a tremendous amount of professional mileage out of this pattern alone, and I do so in the book. I speak at length of the decline of party and the rise of pluralism, and I felt then, and feel now, warranted to consider the case that way. It is not the entire story, but it is a *bona fide* part of the story. When one important institution declines in its function as a recruitment channel, other institutions, especially in large cities, are standing by to take up the slack. In my background data, I have ample evidence for the degree and character of the pluralistic patterns that developed in the city. Parties came to compete for access to government on a more or less equal basis with other important institutions. An argument about the pluralistic city is well grounded in such findings as those on Diagram 1.

However, it was inevitable that I would take further steps, and one of the most compelling ones resulted from my awareness that I was dealing with a public administrative process. I had been fairly well grounded in these aspects of the political science literature, for which I am very grateful to Wallace Sayre, Herbert Kaufman, and James Fesler. I now asked myself the simple question of whether or not it makes a difference if commissioners are in fact serving in administrative agencies. I felt it might make a difference if one commissioner were appointed to the Department of Sanitation rather than to the Department of Health, and so on and so forth. How different would the pattern on Diagram 1 have been if one introduced the possibility of variation according to some public administration factors? In a straight pluralistic approach, the variation we would get could be simply taken as evidence for the "multi-nuclear" system; that gives us a good jargon word, and it does, admittedly, capture a certain reality. But is that enough? Is there not another lesson? Could there be an explicable, predictable, institutionalized pattern to this variation, or are we left in the lurch with the question-begging notion of the "interplay of forces" among the "multi-nucleated power centers"?

To take the next step, then, it was necessary to use a simple and

[1] (New York: Free Press, 1964.)

conventional definition of "agency." It comes right out of the public administration literature, and I had the help of the aforementioned colleagues, plus Dahl at Yale and Truman and Neustadt, who were unusually helpful to someone who had no official connection at Columbia.

The first thing you come up with in this dimension is, of course, a distinction between line agencies and staff agencies—or better yet, line agencies and overhead agencies. Overhead agencies, as you know, deal almost exclusively with other governmental agencies. Line agencies are characterized by their *non*-governmental, outside clientele. But the literature and common sense suggest a little bit more than that. It is pretty obvious that we ought to distinguish *among* line agencies, between those that deal in services and welfare on the one hand and those that deal with regulation and property protection on the other.

That gives us three categories of agencies—overhead, services and welfare, and regulation-property protection. Then I identified a fourth, which I called "input agencies" for lack of a better term. These are simply the taxing and assessing agencies.

The types are pretty clear in the abstract. Problems did arise in fitting the agencies into these categories. Fortunately, the answer was quite simple. Most local agencies tend to be in my terms unifunctional in the sense that overwhelmingly their outputs fit into one category or another. I simply discussed the activities of a few "multi-functional" agencies with my colleagues and a few experts in order to get some kind of consensus on their predominate function. For example, the Department of Markets turned out to be pretty clearly a regulatory department even though it does perform a good many services. The City Planning Commission is overwhelmingly an overhead agency even though it does operate out in the field as a regulatory agency regarding zoning. For some purposes it might be better to deal with agencies as bi- or multi-functional, but for purposes of analyzing the recruitment data this was not possible.

Following this classification we get four groupings of agencies and, therefore, four stacks of personnel and personnel-background data. It is now easy to control for the mission of the agency in any other kind of analysis. This is precisely what I did in Diagram 2, where I controlled for type of agency while looking at the overall history of party recruitment. I could have presented four trend lines, because some differences among all four agencies are interesting. But fortunately it is not necessary to complicate the analysis that much because the general trends in party recruitment are fairly common for three of the four types, so much so that for these purposes I can make the point with only two trend lines. The first trend line is the percent of all commissioners party-recruited in all line agencies and the overhead agencies. The second line is the percent party-recruited among all the commissioners who served in the input agencies.

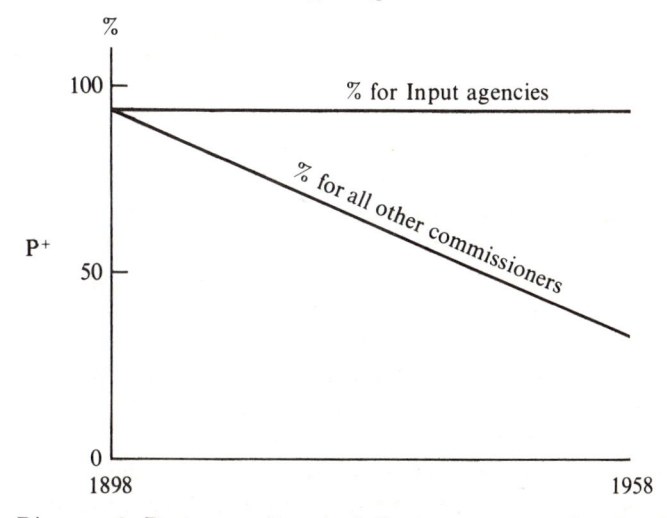

Diagram 2. Party recruitment of the top patronage in New York City—1898–1958. Percent party-recruited (P^+) commissioners, comparing heads of input agencies with heads of all other agencies.

When this control is performed the trend line for the three sets of agencies taken together declines from something over ninety percent of the total population at the turn of century (or, virtually one hundred percent on whom the information could be obtained) down to about thirty-five percent of the total in the Wagner administration. Again it looks like a solid case for the argument that party monopoly was replaced by pluralistic competition. But then look at the second line. It remains the most remarkable pattern I have ever encountered in my efforts to analyze politics. For me it was something like Keats reading Homer.

The differences are so clear, so systematic, so repetitive. In each and every instance, for each and every mayor, party was the overwhelmingly dominant recruitment pattern in the one set of agencies and not so in all the others. Take the LaGuardia period of twelve years duration as the best example. Generally his appointments were made strictly on a non-party basis; very often a party leader was disqualified for holding office even if he also possessed the appropriate technical qualifications to a very high degree. Yet, in the input agencies, LaGuardia made straight machine appointments. Thus, while party was losing its grip dramatically on most governmental agencies, it seemed to be holding fast to its monopoly in this one group of agencies. Such dramatic findings as these require elaborate explanation. And this is what I have been trying to provide in the decade since I first encountered the pattern. So, this is where the whole policy approach to politics began for me. And, quite obviously, the line of analysis, the line of argument, has to be grounded in policy and policy distinctions.

From this point on the decision had to be made as to what to do about this discovery. In my New York book, I do talk to a certain extent about this pattern. I spent a good bit of time speculating on what kind of politics seems to be associated or could possibly attach itself to each of these kinds of agencies or how this could in turn explain the observed differences in my statistics. And in the New York study there wasn't just a party difference that had to be accounted for. Let me merely mention some of the other characteristics, without unduly complicating this part of the story. One of the most important characteristics was something I called "job-oriented skills." This refers to individuals who had a history, or career, or an advanced degree in, the technology of the given agency—not just any skills, but those which were related precisely to the technology of the agency over which the man was appointed to serve. A tax lawyer in the Tax Department would possess job-oriented skill, but an ordinary lawyer, who might have many skills, would not be catalogued as job-oriented in the Tax Department. Another characteristic was professional status, which was defined by membership in a professional society, the publication of a notable article or book, or something of this sort. Another characteristic was bureaucratic recruitment, referring to those who spent most of their careers in a single large bureaucracy. Another was prominence in some economic interest group. Still another— and a very important one indeed—was tenure. This I defined as the length of service of a commissioner as a proportion of the

The Development of Arenas of Power

length of service of his appointing mayor. These ranged from a fraction of a percent, where the commissioner simply could not compete with the head of the kitchen, to a thousand percent in the extreme case of Robert Moses, who was appointed by a succession of mayors who went the way of all political flesh while Robert Moses went on and on.

There are still other interesting characteristics that could be thrown in, but the point would remain the same. With each of these characteristics, there is an interesting and significant pattern of variation among all four of the types of agencies. For example, while job-oriented skills are today fairly highly distributed among all agencies, there is considerable difference in proportion just as there is between the two sets of line agencies. But when you add to that the fact that skilled persons in the regulatory agencies tended to be from the professions, while skilled persons in the service and welfare agencies tended to be from out of the bureaucracies, you start getting something interesting. Likewise with the tenure characteristic. Actually, months of continuous service were on the average quite high among commissioners in the inputs agencies and were fairly low among regulatory commissioners. Tenure was not too much higher than that for welfare and services commissioners, but then another factor intervenes, a characteristic I failed to mention above. This is simply the raw pattern of reappointment, the fact of being held over by a new administration. Interestingly enough, service and welfare commissioners were reappointed at very high rates, while regulatory commissioners were not. This already begins to suggest an interesting political pattern, in which it is much more difficult for regulatory commissioners to establish supportive relations with their clientele than it is for service and welfare commissioners to do so.

In any case, you can start adding up the very considerable differences among the distributions of these and other recruitment characteristics. Then you face the agonizing problem of formulating a set of statements consistent with these variations and at the same time politically plausible and theoretically significant and parsimonious. It would be easy to give a plausible underlying rationale for any one set of findings. And that has all too often happened in scientific political science. What we then get is the *sense* of theory without any real theory building. Each of the generalizations based upon a single set of findings is too *ad hoc* and uncumulative. *Ad hoc* explanations for individual findings or confirmed hypotheses may sound good on their face, but when one accumulates them on the assumption that they all belong to a single level of analysis, one can easily find himself with 300, 400, perhaps 500 percent explanatory value. For myself, I would rather hold to a single line of analysis, a single vocabulary, a single explanatory standpoint, and settle for seventy or eighty percent explanatory value. Somehow I get a feeling that that is better theory. Eventually I will want to talk about variations in political patterns in behaviors in Congress, among committees, among bureaucracies, and so on. I wanted a means of avoiding an explanation of the power of the Appropriations Committee grounded in sociological theories, an explanation of the Education and Welfare Committee founded in ideology and share attitudes, and an explanation for observed block structures in Congress based upon the psychology of perception or of attitudes, and so on and so on.

But in addition to the search for a single level of analysis, in order to avoid the problems just mentioned, I also wanted the level of analysis that seemed to me to get closest to the timeless and unchanging core of the political system. I do not know if I have found it, but I am satisfied that I am fairly close to it in the policy dimension. Thus, I have sought my explanation for these New York statistics and for a large variety of other political phenomena by invoking closure around the policy dimension and variables to be constructed out of that dimension. It started with a very simple statement about the importance of mission to the reality of the administrative agency. It spread from that to an insistence that mission will in some way or another determine every other unit and relationship in the political process. To my knowledge, this set of steps has never been taken in political science. But I say that not merely to be boastful; I say it in order to solicit your sympathy for the weaknesses in what I consider such a novel effort.

Turning from New York City to the political system in general requires some reformulation of the categories but no real change in the manner of approach. It was good that I switched to the federal level, because this new, larger, and different context forced me to formulate appropriate abstractions for the four categories, which continued to remain quite empirical in my own mind as long as I stuck to New York City. Nonetheless, I never did depart from the policy-politics nexus that I had formulated on a speculative basis in trying to make sense of the variations in the New York City statistics. And I have never departed very far from the original distinctions I made between the political context of the regulatory agencies and the political context of the service and welfare agencies in New York. But I have elaborated and improved upon them, adding appropriate theoretical concepts for the other "arenas of power." However, I have never departed much from the original notion that the regulatory agencies live in a context of pluralistic politics, as described in great detail by Truman, Dahl, and others. But in contrast, the services and welfare agencies in New York (and everywhere else) live in a context of class politics. This is best described by contemporary Marxist students of community decision making.

Here, of course, broke open the whole business. The purpose became one of *beginning* with *a priori* and formalistic descriptions of the policy involved and moving from that to a predictive statement about the politics associated with it. In face of the possibility of many important exceptions, all of the statements in the analysis take that form. This is the way the system of analysis has been closed off. Every pattern, every dimension and unit of political activity must be dealt with in the same words and in the same direction. Things that cannot be dealt with this way are either irrelevant (for example, psychological patterns, individual decision making, the value schedules of individuals, etc.) or are undeveloped aspects of the reality that are simply not yet incorporated into the analysis.

All of this was, of course, developing during that period when the community power structure research and controversy were formulated. I had been an early and enthusiastic part of that movement. In fact one of my early seminars with Robert Dahl at Yale was a study of Guilford, Connecticut. The study was inconclusive but may have had much to do with whetting Dahl's appetite for more of the same. I was also very much in sympathy with Dahl's later formulation of a response to the Hunter approach to whole communities. To me, Dahl's argument that biases were built into power structure research on whole communities was completely unassailable. By the time he was arguing for control according to "issue area" I was becoming familiar with New York

City where it would be impossible to generalize about power structures.

On the other hand, there was something missing in this approach, and I think I was able to find it precisely because my own research exposed me pretty exclusively to the administrative sphere. Using the concept of issues as the means of identifying "power for what," meant too much of a commitment to ephemeral aspects of politics. An issue could be something as recent as yesterday's newspaper, and it could be something that could not repeat itself ever again. Thus, while it implied a proper principle of analysis, the notion of issue itself would not do the job. I discussed this problem at some length in my original published formulation in *World Politics*.[2] So, the problem with issues analysis is that there is no theoretical basis underlying it. One somehow had to provide a characterization of the issues, and that meant that already we would be abandoning the notion of an issue area as a control. Without that characterization, there would be no way within the confines of the research on issues to explain what one might find. Each issue could provide a rich case for data, but there had to be some way of determining what each case exemplified. Without that characterization, which *must* be *a priori*, the researchers in this area were left with highly systematized empirical results that could be generalized only in the most abstract and *ad hoc* manner. It was out of this (as I feel, at least) that pluralism became increasingly ideological in political science. Multiples of issues produced multiples of names of activists with incomplete repetition of names, and that in turn would just as inevitably reveal plural power patterns as the Hunter approach would turn up integrated power patterns. More abstraction was required, but it did not have to be the abstraction of the neo-Marxist. I felt, and continue to feel, that that abstraction should emerge out of something more permanent than issues but should at the same time capture the spirit behind Dahl's choice of issue. Exposure to the work of administrative agencies made the turn to formal policies a relatively natural process. These spelled out the purposes for which administrative agencies were organized, and these were the things for which they were responsible and for which they were given their primary resources. These were also the things around

---

[2] Theodore J. Lowi, "American Business, Public Policy, Case Studies, and Political Theory," *World Politics*, 6, 4 (1964), 677–715.

which most active people defined and stated their own objectives, and these were likely to be the most determinative—in one way or another—of strategies and tactics.

It was only a short step from reformulation. That reformulation was as follows: Each statute states a policy of the government in the sense that it is, for better or worse, an intention to use the coercive powers of government in a certain way and not in other ways. Each is in one way or another, therefore, a function of government. Properly categorized and defined, these are the basic and fundamental functions that motivate the political system and all of its parts. Thus, these same outputs should set the limits on the motivation of persons and institutions within the system.

Different people might perceive each function differently at a given point in time, but ultimately if these people are rational they should come to operate in comparable ways for each function despite differences in perception. This is a particularly handy formulation, because in the real world it is next to impossible to learn precisely what a person's motivations and objectives are, and when we multiply that difficulty by the number of people whose motivations we would have to learn in order to use them in a predictive way, it becomes clear that any *a priori* device for stating what the motivation is becomes extremely efficient. Moreover, I am not so much concerned with the precise measurement of each person's motivation as I am to present the logic of the analysis. Fundamentally my only interest is in the ultimate connection between a given set of policies and an outcome in a set of measurable political relationships, regardless of whatever motivations might have intervened. Those established relationships *are* the power structure and the political process.

So, for these reasons, my political analysis really starts with an exercise in jurisprudence. In order to carry out this phase of the work, I spent a year in Washington reading statutes. My real education began with the reading of a thousand pages of agriculture statutes. I have been reading statutes and analyzing them ever since. Part of the fallout from that work was my recently published *The End of Liberalism*,[3] which largely resulted from my indignation with the horrible draftsmanship I encountered and the poor results that flow from such draftsmanship.

In an important sense, I was interviewing these statutes. I was

---

[3] (New York: Norton, 1959.)

interviewing them just as surely as one can interview individuals in depth. To a degree data are better dead than alive, because a person can distort, alter, and just plain lie in an interview, whereas if the thing is official, printed, and public, it is there and remains the same until an official change is made in it.

One of the first things I discovered, other than my sense of how little real law is in the statutes, was the high degree of variability within each of the conventionally designated subject matter areas. There is no "agriculture policy." And there was no reason to believe that there was a single "politics of agriculture." But there were distinctions that cut through the conventional subject matter area, and I began to feel confirmation that my abstract distinctions were going to prove meaningful.

Thus, there turned out to be two directions one can take from this approach. The first consists in sticking with jurisprudence and talking about laws, their proper classification, and the more or less substantive aspects of public policy. This I continue to do, and I consider *The End of Liberalism* such an exercise. I also consider the first three or four chapters in my forthcoming *Arenas of Power* to be the jurisprudence preliminaries for the second direction one can take. That direction is, of course, the more conventionally considered political scientist's direction, which is to analyze the political process. I have tried to catalog public policies through use of statutes and to reduce them to a manageable number in a manner that tends to reflect the basic functions of the state. Once that classification is established, the scheme ought to cut across conventional subject matter classifications of policies and ought to reveal meaningful and very real political processes. I further wanted to break down conventional subject matter categories without doing any damage to existing institutional realities. That is to say, the actual operating agencies, those of the bureau level, ought to cumulate within my policy categories. The analysis was to be based upon abstract categorizations but without destroying real world institutions and other units.

American history turned out to be a good way to check on the extent to which I could view my categories as real things rather than merely abstract constructs. A reading of public policy history at the federal level convinced me that, to a very large degree, the distinctions I was making were not merely theoretically plausible and statistically distinct but also historically confirmed. The first decade of the Republic was, of course, preoccupied with fleshing out the Constitution. Thus, it comprises an exceptional period, one that I can deal with but not here because it overly complicates matters. Suffice it to say that this was a Constitutional or "constituent" period. Following that, however, the pattern is clear as well as easy to handle.

For nearly a century, the output of the Federal government was overwhelmingly one of supporting the coastal trade and merchant marine, the building of post offices and post roads, subsidies for other kinds of internal improvements, the development and protection of inventions and patents, and matters of this sort. The most important addition following this first block of policies was, of course, land disposal, beginning with giveaways to the Continental soldiers. During this period, most of the really coercive policies were associated with the states. This observation helps to identify the common dimension underlying all of the federal policies of that period. The word I coined for these policies was *distribution*. Although not completely adequate, it does imply the important characteristic of this category, i.e., the capacity of all of these policies for disaggregation. That is to say, each of these policies produces an output that can be broken up into smaller and smaller items, with each item capable of being dispensed with in isolation and without regard to disposal of other items. This means that in the short run it was possible for government to use these resources as though they were unlimited. The tariff is another good example. When we began our tariffs in the 1830s and 1840s, there were a scant few hundred schedules. This spread to over 150,000 schedules by 1930, according to Schattschneider. What we were doing obviously was breaking up the field into a larger and larger number of smaller and smaller categories, so small that in fact many of the categories, again according to Schattschneider, contained only one business. Obviously what the policy makers were doing was responding to conflict by breaking up the parts further and further in order to accommodate a larger and larger number of persons. This is the sort of thing one can do with any kind of resource. For some of these we reserve the term pork barrel, and taken seriously we can use pork barrel synonymously with distribution, or we can conceive of distribution as patronage, if that term be understood not merely as patronage in jobs, but patronage in the old sense of "to patronize."

This is definitely the way things were at the federal level until the Civil War, and so much was this the case that it took many years after the Civil War to alter in any important way the mix of federal policy outputs. In any case, the government went through some kind of Constitutional revolution during the 1880s, and that revolution amounted to a certain type of expansion in the power of the federal government. We associate it with the response to the famous Wabash case, and the policies that inaugurate this new period are the Interstate Commerce Act and the Sherman Anti-Trust Act. But these were only the beginning of a turn of events which deeply altered the relationship between the federal government and the private sector. The distinctive thing about the policies initiated with ICC and Sherman is that the federal government began to use coercion directly upon conduct rather than continuing its attempt to influence through husbanding and expanding alternatives, as in the case of distributive policies. To influence conduct by providing money and services is a type of coercion, but the coercion is relatively remote, and usually there is a considerable distance between those who are benefited and those who are deprived as a result of a given distributive policy. Something different is happening here, and the term regulation seems to capture it very well. Regulatory policy is in essence a statement that some item or action is harmful in and of itself. Or it can be a statement about some preferred future state of affairs toward which a person's conduct must be aimed. This addition of more direct and immediate coercion changes the character of the policies in an absolutely fundamental way. And it is this sort of distinction that is completely missed in the new studies of public policy where the "policy" is a subject matter designation measured usually by budget allocations. Some insights might be gained from these kinds of studies, but they are not policy studies and have almost nothing to do with policy.

In any case, once you make the distinction between distributive and regulative policies, certain political differences are obviously to be expected. And indeed we find in American history two distinctly different phases of politics. The distributive period was one of extraordinary political stability. In fact, the political institutions at the federal level were markedly stable even in the face of the turmoil over abolition. The federal system contrasted tremendously with the states, which were noted for their radicalism, their social movements, and their instability, largely because the states were doing all the regulating and the federal government was doing only distributive work. Further, the period was one in which party politics came to the fore. This was true because parties could deal with government as though no authoritative choices were being made at all. Parties were able to build nationally without getting involved in any ideological and profound conflict-of-interest disputes.

Turn now to the politics associated with the regulatory period beginning in the late nineteenth century. I am not concerned here with cause and effect, but only with association. The politics associated with this new kind of government was distinctly different from the politics of the earlier period. For one thing, it was much less stable. For another, it was a politics in which political parties suffered greatly. Party organization and discipline went into a decline from which they never recovered. Further, it is a time when a significantly large number of revisions in rules and procedures in Congress emerge, along with a large number of demands for expansion of the system of representation. In my opinion, this very expansion of regulatory politics is what explains the ultimate success of the administrative reform movement.

Distributive policies do not disappear with the emergence of regulative policies. Similarly, neither of these policies disappears or even declines as another type of policy emerges. As a matter of fact there is expansion of all types of policies from the Wilson period to the present. But a third type of policy was beginning even as early as regulative policies. These policies were not important in numbers or amount of budget until much later. Policies that I refer to as "redistributive" policies were being demanded by the same labor and agriculture movements that were demanding regulation. The demand of farmers for inflation as a matter of policy was a demand for a redistributive policy. Liberalization of the coinage of silver was a redistributive policy. The first income tax, modest as it was, was an example of a redistributive policy. The most important first federal effort of redistribution—of course since the 1790s—was the Federal Reserve System. From that time forth there were several monetary and fiscal efforts, most of which would fall into the category of redistribution. Again, I am not entirely happy with the word. I use it because it is a good "tion" word, and also because it does suggest most of the common elements that bind these various policies together. Another term for it would be "system manipulation," which was the term I urged upon Randall Ripley in the organization of his reader in public policy. In any case, redistribution refers to all those public policies whose basic instruments imply an attempt to coerce very directly (just as much as regulation is an attempt to coerce very directly), but express their coercion not directly upon the individual but indirectly upon his environment. That is to say, the attempt is to influence conduct by manipulating the *environment of conduct*. An example might be policies in the fiscal and monetary field, especially after the founding of the Council of Economic Advisors. These policies are indeed coercive. But they weren't like regulation. Nobody was saying "Get off the grass." Instead people were being influenced by small changes in the discount rate or by slight manipulations of the income structure.

Now it is true in a very important sense that everything government does is redistributive. People would be doing something different with their money if government was not fighting a war or supporting the merchant marine, or building supersonic transports, or regulating grain exchanges. It is also true that everything government does is regulative, in the sense that its very existence and its activities deeply expand or contract the alternatives of every citizen in some way or another. But to say that all government is regulative and all government is redistributive is only to define government. Such insistence is an admission, of course, that the conservatives were right. They have always argued something that liberals like to overlook, namely that there was no way to avoid the coercive powers of government, however beneficient we might think a certain policy may be. But this definition wipes out important distinctions. That is to say, why should we be prevented from distinguishing among *types* of coercion in the short run, even if in the long run coercion is coercion is coercion? This short-run distinction among types of coercion is what I am trying to establish here as the politically significant basis for analyzing both policies and political process.

Having anticipated one of the more common questions about my distinctions, let me turn briefly to the completion of my historical review. Just as I had speculated on the politics of the services and welfare agencies in New York, so a quick review of history of redistributive issues suggested a much more pronounced class of ideological politics than that which had been associated with other types of policies and other periods. The early efforts to get the original redistributive policies in the late nineteenth century and in the Wilson period were associated with some of the more spectacular class-based social movements in our history. More recently, there have been very few case studies of policy making in this area; but most of them confirm the class or "power elite" nature of this kind of policy making. Most of the cases cited by C. Wright Mills in favor of his power elite notion were not so much "key" decisions as they were domestic[4] redistributive decisions—this is also true with the cases used by Henry S. Kariel in his *The Decline of American Pluralism*.[5] I identify these various patterns in my *World Politics* article, and since that time I have

TABLE 1

Impact of Governmental Process

Coercion

		Immediate	*Remote*
Specificity	High	Regulative	Distributive
	Low	Redistributive	Constituent

had nothing but strong confirmation in the data. It was on the basis of this kind of material that I suggested in that first article that there are three general theories of power in America competing for dominance, that each was wrong about two-thirds of the time, and that each approached scientific precision and high predictive power when the limits of its applicability were established.

Thus, from a statistical perspective in New York and a historical perspective at the national level, there is enough to suggest a real basis for the abstract and jurisprudential distinctions made among public policies as a starting point for empirical political analysis. Distributive policies were characterized by high specificity of impact and low command or remoteness of the coercive factor. Politi-

[4] C. Wright Mills, *The Power Elite* (New York: Oxford University Press, 1956).

[5] (Palo Alto, Calif.: Stanford University Press, 1961).

cal relationships of a very distinctive kind became associated with such policy processes. Next, regulative policies are also characterized by high specificity of impact but very immediate involvement of command or the coercive element. In such an instance the relationship between the state and the individual is very different from that which is established in the distributive area, and therefore, it must follow that political relationships among all persons who have regulatory policies in common could not possibly be altogether the same as those relationships that would emerge with distributive policies. Redistributive policies are in a sense a quantum step away from both of those, in the sense that the impact of the policy is not upon or through individuals but indirectly through their environment. Yet, redistributions do involve command or coercion in the more immediate sense, like regulation. This gives us logically a third combination of the underlying dimension of policy.

There is obviously a fourth dimension, considering that we have logically cross-tabulated remoteness and immediacy of command against specificity and generality of impact. That fourth cell is comprised of policy in which coercion is relatively remote and the impact works through the environment of conduct rather than directly upon the individual. These I refer to as "constituent" policies. This is not a "tion" word, but I became committed to this notion in dealing with the political parties before I realized that it was logically a part of the original policy analysis scheme. (I developed this in *The American Party Systems*.)[6] Constituent policies are second-order policies. They are the structural elements, the "rules of the game" within which policies are made and other policies are implied. Thus a great deal of coercion is ultimately involved, but less directly by these policies than by the policies that flow later as a result of these policies. The constituent structures that set up and maintain our "private sector" are such policies. Procedural rules of Congress are such policies. Civil liberties and criminal immunities are such policies, in the sense that they set restraints upon what it is that governments can make policies about. Also most of the policies that were made dur-

---

[6] Theodore J. Lowi, "Party, Policy, and Constitution in America," in William Nisbet Chambers and Walter Dean Burnham (Eds.), *The American Party System* (New York: Oxford University Press, 1967), pp. 238–276.

ing the "Constitutional period" of the 1790s are basically constituent policies. Finally, the "non-decisions" that Baratz and Bachrach talk about are such policies.

In any case, that closes off my system. The logical analysis, involving the cross-tabulation of the two unavoidable characteristics of all policies, provided me with my sense that I have exhausted all the possibilities. The categories are logically exclusive, although in the real world there will be some bleeding across categories. There has not been much of that in my own work, but this is an operational problem that may never be entirely overcome. In *Arenas of Power,* in any case, I will do my best to avoid the instances of bleeding at the edges because I will be trying to establish a principle of analysis and a basis for a theory. It would be ridiculous to deal with hard cases before being able to handle the clearest cases of categorization. It should be remembered that despite these problems, the dimensions I am talking about possess both a logical and historical character beyond the convenience of the analyst. That is a great deal to have. The proof of the pudding cannot be tested until it is cooked, and that involves the processing and analysis of great masses of data that deal with every possible aspect of political life.

I am sorry to dwell so long on the language and logic of the analysis, but it is necessary and useful, because most of the specific empirical hypotheses tend to follow pretty clearly from all of this. I have found after discussing it for many hours with my students that, whether they agree with me or not, they find it relatively easy to operate through the logical steps, either toward further elaboration of the legal analysis or toward further elaboration of the empirical possibilities and consequences. And this is what I wanted to establish here. I only wanted to convey the principles of analysis. This is more important to me than my particular resolution of it and the three- or fourfold scheme.

To summarize and conclude, let me give a couple of statements that constitute the logical relations in my own mind that move from the scheme of public policy—the jurisprudential level— through to the prediction of public policy processes and political relationships. Once delineated it will seem to be not very far removed from what I was grasping at in the original New York effort. Properly catalogued, policies are the functions of the state. Policies are in a very important sense the indices of things that we cannot observe directly. We cannot observe functions or the state, but we can look at outputs and analyze backwards towards the source. My categories are taken to be the actual functions of the state. These are ongoing and relatively permanent features of the state, even though individual policies may be added or subtracted, and issues may arise over different ones at different times. As ongoing processes or functions, these functions set the limits or provide the focus of political activity. If one wants to psychologize about this point, one can say that these functions have a fundamental bearing upon the perspectives, attitudes, and motivations of individuals as they enter the political realm.

Next, if people act according to their perspectives and motivations, which I insist have been shaped by these ongoing functions, they will end up relating to other individuals in a predictable way—predictable because the source of perspectives and motivations is set in the activities and functions of the state. Therefore, we can know more about the political process from the public policy variable—properly catalogued—than from any other single variable. To put it another way, we will be able to account for more of the variance in the political process with this factor than with any other factor or factors.

Let me commend it to you in one additional way. Even if the public policy variable were not so powerful a predictor, we should want to consider it because it comes so much closer to a *political* theory than almost any other predictive factor. This means that we might be able to develop a politics of politics, a *pure* politics, rather than continuing to depend upon the sociology or a psychology of politics for our theory. I am not attacking those perspectives. I am merely saying that it is also possible to treat government as something more than an epiphenomenon of the social or psychological process.

Beyond this logic of the inquiry come the actual empirical steps. These I have only implied and in some instances alluded to during the course of this treatment, but I will not try to do anything more than that. Suffice it to say that data already collected go a long way toward dealing in a single language with variations in the political structures and processes of the most important institutional units of the system. The empirical work deals with the structure and the interrelationships within and among interest groups. It also deals with the general institution of Congress and its varying but predictable relation with the executive branch and with outside interests. Further, the data deal, and in many ways most successfully, with internal variations among the working parts of Congress, particularly with regard to the relationship between the committees and the floor. Data just coming in show consistent, although somewhat less clear, variations among administrative agencies, both as to their structures and as to their political relationships with their clientele. Variations in statistical distributions of data ranging from average Q values of role-call votes to scale analysis of the amending process (as a measure of committee-floor relationships), and gamma and other analyses of organizational characteristics of bureaucratic personnel have been confirming the hypotheses that in turn confirm the theoretical approach. Naturally I have been in a state of high excitement for a long time as these data come in.[7] I am very pleased to add to this inventory of data the rich and important body of policy-making case studies. From the beginning of the production of case studies after World War II, people were always asking the question: How do we generalize from the case studies? The answer always was: Have a theory! It is only with theory that one can break away from the uniqueness of single cases. Having a theory even as rough and preliminary as mine has converted this mass of case studies into data. We have been "interviewing" these case studies and have turned up repetitive but highly variable characteristics among them. So far we have completed the analysis of thirty-five lengthy case studies, whose authors report variations in the importance of different actors and units that strongly confirm—i.e., could have been predicted by—my scheme.

[7] A dissertation completed after the presentation of this lecture by James L. Grant, The University of Chicago, on variations in administrative structures, has resolved any doubts I once had as to the susceptibility of bureaucratic structures to this kind of analysis. Mr. Grant's dissertation constitutes a significant departure from the Weberian ideal-typical approach by being able to posit several models of administrations rather than a single one. More important for me, three of his statistical clusters constitute models that are highly correlated with the three policy areas and the administrative agencies that fit within each.

6 PICTURING ELECTIONS ABROAD: A STUDY IN FINNISH POLITICS

Pertti Pesonen
University of Tampere

1. The Background

The political scientist living in the 1970s might be amazed or amused to learn that there were once researchers who ran double- and triple-punched IBM cards through a counter-sorter; who ran out of the machine room to calculate their own Chi squares and product-moment correlations, not to mention their percentage distributions; and who possessed a slide rule to make some preliminary sense of their material (which had not even been obtained from a data file). In other words, some political scientists were so curious that they could not wait a decade or two for modern computers to be invented, developed, programmed, and made accessible to students in most countries.

However, historians advise us to reconstruct the past as the contemporaries experienced it, without the bias of today's additional wisdom. Thus the proper background

---

This is the first publication of Pertti Pesonen's essay. All rights reserved. Permission to reprint must be obtained from the publisher and the author.

Pertti Pesonen, *An Election in Finland: Party Activities and Voter Reactions* (New Haven: Yale University Press, 1968).

of an account of a research project launched in 1958 would be the intellectual environment of the 1950s. And recollections of that era seem to bring to mind a mood of unusual liveliness and optimism. Although we, the political scientists, had lived "too long and too one-sidedly on the heavy diet of laws and constitutions, . . . empirical research was currently the most vigorous branch of political science"; . . . a discipline which had "reached that level of development on which realism and the dynamic processes of government and politics are emphasized."[1] More specifically, four aspects of that situation constituted the focal background for the particular Finnish election study to be discussed in this paper.

The first one was the rise of behavioralism, still a new albeit widely inspiring approach to the study of politics. It was as late as the Paris World Congress of the IPSA in 1961 that Robert A. Dahl presented the first "epitaph" to the movement, which he then considered successful enough to have been broadly accepted and thus to have lost its need for identity.[2] The issue was further debated in the 1960s. But although behavioral research had already proceeded along several frontiers by the mid-fifties, many an observer tended almost to equate behavioralism with research on voting and elections. That field was perhaps the most successful and certainly the most typical representative of the behavioral approach at the time.

Secondly, the general acceptability of the survey method in electorate research had become obvious. Its utility and the comparability of its findings were also illustrated by the first attempts actually to summarize the results of recent research. I am thinking especially of the appendix called "Summary of Findings from Similar Election Studies" published in 1954 in *Voting* by Berelson, Lazarsfeld, and McPhee.[3] This was a listing of 209 low-level correlations reported in fourteen publications and based on five American and two British panel interview surveys of voting

---

[1] Quotations are from the opening speech by James Kerr Pollock in the Fourth World Congress of the IPSA, Rome, 1958. Their wording may be inaccurate because they are translated from Finnish back to English (Pollock, "Valtiotiede atomikaudella," in *Politiikka*, 1959).

[2] Robert A. Dahl, "The Behavioral Approach," *American Political Science Review*, 55 (1961), 763–772.

[3] Bernard R. Berelson, Paul F. Lazarsfeld, and William N. McPhee, *Voting: A Study of Opinion Formation in a Presidential Campaign* (Chicago: University of Chicago Press, 1954).

behavior. In the same year, the *Handbook of Social Psychology* presented a more synthetic attempt to summarize knowledge of voting behavior.[4] Five years later, *American Voting Behavior* provided a general forum for twenty-two evaluations from various specialized points of view.[5] These and several related publications of the 1950s have, of course, maintained their place in the reading lists of courses and seminars in today's universities.

Thirdly, having experienced the new developments of the 1960s we now take for granted the idea of comparative or cross-national empirical research. But in the 1950s such research emerged in political science at a very slow pace.

And finally, the actual use of mass interviews was confined to a limited region of the world. American public opinion had been polled since the 1930s, and opinion surveys had spread into an increasing number of countries during the 1940s and 1950s. But those were still few, and even in some countries where public opinion research had been introduced party political preferences were hardly touched upon. There seemed to be good reasons for such caution in continental Europe because of the widely shared or at least presumed popular suspicions of uninvited interviewers who intrude into the private world of individual political attitudes.

Because books and journals know no national boundaries, Finnish political scientists (or, literally, Finns engaged in the knowledge of the state) were informed about the developments in their discipline. Behavioralism began in Finnish political science no later than it did in the United States. But small resources and meager manpower delayed its start in actual practice. For example, the first two studies on voting behavior to be reported at book length appeared in 1956. Both used ecological and other recorded data. One dealt with voting turnout and tested the so-called cross-pressure hypothesis with aggregate data available on the country's fifty-five municipalities,[6] and the other

---

[4] Seymour M. Lipset, Paul F. Lazarsfeld, Allen H. Barton, and Juan Linz, "The Psychology of Voting: An Analysis of Political Behavior," in Gardner Lindzey (Ed.), *Handbook of Social Psychology, Volume II* (Cambridge, Mass.: Addison-Wesley, 1954), chapter 30.

[5] Eugene Burdick and Arthur J. Brodbeck (Eds.), *American Voting Behavior* (Glencoe, Ill.: Free Press, 1959).

[6] Erik Allardt, *Social struktur och politisk aktivitet* (Helsingfors: Soderstrom, 1956).

analyzed the geography of Communist support in two adjacent constituencies.[7]

2. The First Step

Party activities and the behavior of the electorate in the parliamentary election of 1958 are the main focus of *An Election in Finland*. But quite obviously the work would have been impossible without the preceding study commenced in late 1955.[8] Therefore, when asked why I undertook the election study of 1958, I might simply answer that I did it primarily because my first panel study of voting behavior had proven itself possible and worthwhile and because it would animate further research, preferably on a larger scale. But such an answer would evade the actual question. A sensible 'causal chain' of motivation would originate at an earlier point when I acquired the desire to do research on the Finnish electorate.

As I have attempted to point out, the prevailing mood in political science or at least among "radicals" in the field favored empirical research. In addition to the general situation, it is also easy to single out one book that provided essential inspiration for me as it did for many others: *People's Choice* by Lazarsfeld and others of Columbia University. Its field work was done in Erie County, Ohio, in connection with the 1940 presidential election, and it was published originally in 1944, in a second edition in 1948.[9] This study of the vote decision deserves the distinction of being called a classic in political science. Of special value was its demonstration of the utility of the panel interview technique, a methodological innovation.

---

[7] Jaakko Nousiainen, *Kommunismi Kuopion laanissa* (Joensuu: Pohjois-Karjalan Kirjapaino, 1956).

[8] Pertti Pesonen, *Valitsijamiesvaalien ylioppilasaanestajat* (Helsinki: Tammi, 1958); summarized briefly in English, "The Voting Behavior of Finnish Students," *Democracy in Finland* (Helsinki: The Finnish Political Science Association, 1960), pp. 93–104, and more extensively in Swedish, "Studenternas valjarbeteende vid elektorsvalet 1956," in Jan-Magnus Jansson (Ed.), *Studier i finlandsk politik* (Falkenberg: Scandinavian University Book, 1968), pp. 245–290.

[9] Paul F. Lazarsfeld, Bernard R. Berelson, and Hazel Gaudet, *The People's Choice*, 2nd Ed. (New York: Columbia University Press, 1948).

That was a sound idea. The importance of dynamic social processes was emphasized in current scientific discussion. As the investigators now interviewed the same respondents several times, they could follow the vote decisions in the making and detect both the constants and the changes within the time span observed, in this case from May to November. The successful research technique was by no means the only inspiration the book offered. Many findings were fresh and reorienting, and the authors wrote about their research "adventure" with catching enthusiasm. The opening of a path in electorate research was a greater service than the writing of one book in itself.

Naturally, the panel surveys and other interesting foreign literature provided stimuli which met an already existing substantive interest in elections and voting behavior. A considerable need was felt to gain increasing understanding of democratic elections, and research on the electorate might have made valuable advances even without the particular sequence of panel surveys. In such an environment my personal interest in voting was also affected by a job experience, an affiliation with the youth organization of a political party. The most famous critique of research on voting behavior in the 1950s was that it tended to "take the politics out of politics." Having observed how party organizations function during election times, I was thrilled by the politics and politicking of elections, as well as by the self-reliance with which some experienced party men conducted campaigns both wisely and foolishly.

The idea of doing research on the voting behavior of the Finnish electorate seemed to me both exciting and hopelessly unrealistic. Excitement was a product of curiosity. It was known now that earlier scholarly thinking had maintained serious misconceptions about the electorate, and it was known that American and British research tended to produce a cumulation of mutually consistent new information. So far you could not speak of any broad theory, hardly even of any "middle range" theories of voting behavior. Nevertheless, available research findings supported and supplemented each other. Would this be true about a largely different political setting also, or would the dissimilarities of the systems shade off the applicability of foreign knowledge of voting behavior? For example, would vote decisions made in multiparty systems with proportional representation develop very differently than they do in two-party systems with plurality elections? Would the size of the country create differences? Furthermore, would existing knowledge of the motivation of the vote hold good only in stable party systems? If there were research evidence to support negative answers to these and related questions, then the voters would indeed behave in a comparable fashion in different types of political systems; a rich and obviously growing body of information would help one to understand Finnish elections, too; and knowledge could be applied directly to the formation of additional hypotheses in different environments.

My interest in such problems in fact proved fruitful. However distant they had seemed, the desire to do research helped me to seize an unexpected opportunity in the autumn of 1955. The editors of the *Ylioppilaslehti,* the weekly newspaper of the University of Helsinki student body, asked me whether I would do a survey of the political opinions of Finnish students. They had an urgent journalistic reason: the paper wanted to publish an analysis of the students' political world before the approaching national election of January 16–17, 1956. The Electoral College was to be elected then; on February 15th this body in its turn was to elect the successor of President J. K. Paasikivi (1946–1956). All six political parties had nominated their own presidential candidate. The election was of great interest, and so were the hitherto unknown political leanings of the students.

I promised to conduct the study, provided that I could design a questionnaire which went beyond the immediate needs of the newspaper and, especially, that I could later collect additional data through a reinterview of the original sample of students. We agreed on these points. What followed took place under high pressure. The easiest part was the sampling, because names could be drawn at random from the student catalogues of the University of Helsinki, the Institute of Technology, and the Finnish School of Business Administration (a separate sample was drawn, for comparisons, at the Teachers' Training College in Jyvaskyla). Because the average age of the students was fairly high at that time, only about twenty percent of the names were dropped because they had not reached the voting age. The lack of adequate financial resources was compensated for by semi-volunteer field work, performed by students who were quickly trained for it. During the first week of December, 430 interviews were completed;

this was ninety percent of the original sample. Between the January election and the eve of the election of the President in February, 410 students were reinterviewed.

This study had three aims. Two of them, a comparison of the students with the Finnish electorate at large and a description of interesting aspects of the students' opinions and political behavior, were somewhat secondary from the point of view of future research. But the third aspect of the study was intended to provide a direct link forward. This was the attempt to compare the results of American and British studies of electorate behavior with a group of Finnish voters. I summarized the relevant result of eight previous studies and formed a systematic list of fifty-six findings (of those, thirteen had been obtained in one study, whereas nine were consistent results of six or more studies). This summary concerned information about political participation, the changes in vote intentions, party identification, and the impact of cross-pressures. Generally the analysis supported the conclusion that the behavior of a group of Finnish electors conformed to earlier knowledge on the electorates of two bigger Western democracies. Various forms of interest and participation tended toward unidimensionality; the intensity of party identification seemed an important predictor of behavior; and the students subject to exceptional cross-pressures showed uncertainty in their political behavior. An exciting basic comparison concerned the frequency of changes in intentions: of the students, sixty-seven percent had made their final decision on how to vote before the first interview, eleven percent did not vote, sixteen percent changed candidates, and six percent "crystallized" their choice after the first interview. Consequently, the floating vote in the Finnish multiparty system was no greater than in the electorates of two party systems.

The study on how the Finnish students behaved in the presidential election was published in 1958. It produced some new factual ground for discussions about Finnish elections. And I believe it was essential for the planning and execution of a larger project. It brought experience and self-confidence to scientific thinking, and, besides, it helped to cultivate such native curiosity in the electorate as made the idea of further survey research more acceptable and less "risky" than the case might have been otherwise.

3. The Framework

Noticing the increased scholarly interest in elections, the Board of the Finnish Political Science Association in 1957 began considering the possibilities of organizing a comprehensive research project to deal with voting and campaigning. Not surprisingly, however, funds were not obtained to finance the large team work the Association has hoped for. It was a fortunate coincidence which pushed electorate research forward. The Finnish Cultural Foundation adopted a new policy of supporting individual scholars with three consecutive annual grants. Its "long-term scholarships"—an idea we now take for granted also from the governmental research councils—were granted for the first time in February 1958. Because the Parliament of Finland was due to be elected on July 6-7 of that year, my application for electorate research was so timely that I had the honor of being among those who got the support in the first round. Thus, I made plans and preparations for the new study while still giving finishing touches to the publication of the "first step." Despite the Foundation's very good intentions, the field work and other direct expenses took up a large part of the personal grant. But those were the days of unpragmatic attitudes toward scientific activity: confidence in oneself and public recognition, not livelihood, provided the main energy to keep research going.

The book came out a lot later. It includes a passage entitled "The Present Research Problem." Under that title I listed eight aspects to be emphasized in the investigation. Five of those carried on directly the objectives of the survey of students:

> 2. Voting decisions include a decision to participate and the choice of one of the competing parties. . . . the aims of the study demand information on the time of and the possible changes in the voting decisions of the citizens.
> 4. It is possible to summarize earlier research findings on the political behavior of small groups with two statements. (a) Small groups tend to create uniform attitudes toward politics. . . . (b) . . . The communication advances in two steps, so that opinion leaders mediate the content of mass media to other members of their small groups.
> 5. . . . (a) there is a general tendency to adopt the position of the

> party in individual program matters, . . . (b) the more closely citizens identify with the party the more intensely they want to be informed of the stands taken by their party and the more nearly their opinions conform to the opinions of their party.
> 6. . . . When the present study was begun, it was reasonable to presume that once again many findings would not differ from the earlier ones. Comparison with other voting studies is, therefore, one of the objects of this study. . . .
> 7. An attempt has been made to devote special attention to the correlation of party identification and political activity and to the so-called cross-pressure hypothesis. . . .

Obviously the basic framework of such items repeats, more or less, the thinking behind my "first step." Also, I took the comparative approach for granted, making no more attempts to summarize in detail previous research findings relevant to this study.

On the other hand, the new study promised to draw "a general picture of a parliamentary election in Finland." This intention had been influenced undoubtedly by the interest in broad outlines which had penetrated the earlier sketching in the Political Science Association. Indeed I wanted to find out and present "how it all happens" and what might have constituted notable peculiarities in the election upon which this study focused:

> 8. . . . it may be possible to present specific aspects of the 1958 election which can be interpreted as the effect of the political situation on voting behavior and on the results of the election.

Even the most descriptive aims presuppose some frames of reference to guide the author through the presentation. In this case, the analysis was not linked with any master theory of voting and elections. But I presume three models of a very general nature served an especially useful purpose in the designing phase of the study as well as in the detailed analysis and in drawing up the "general picture."

First of all, a conceptual differentiation between the campaign and the election on the one hand, and the "normal" political process on the other, seemed to clarify thinking throughout the project. The whole idea might be illustrated with a simple line or time axis. Most of that line would describe the flow of the 'normal' political process. That is the actual label I used in the book, and I also talked about the "normal" political behavior of the electors.

Included in that concept were their political attitudes, their interest in politics and, significantly, their precampaign predispositions to vote in some given way in future elections.

Election days have their place on such a line. In the American system they occur at regular and predictable intervals. Events are certain in Finland, too, as far as Presidential and local elections are concerned, while the timing of coming parliamentary elections involves an element of uncertainty. In Britain the specific dates of elections and by-elections cannot be foreseen with any confidence at all. In all systems the time axis then converts back to the 'normal' process after the elections, and the days immediately preceding the election belong naturally to the election campaign, that temporary phase during which the "gladiators" exert their efforts, striving to influence the outcome of the election.

The least certain point of this model is that where the campaign replaces "normalcy." It is obvious that the thought of future elections casts some shadow on the political process all the time. Political parties also specifically prepare themselves for the campaign (and possibly suffer from their campaign debts afterwards). But an election campaign has its typical aspects, such as its openness and the high concentration of effort for electoral purposes. Thus the duration of a campaign should be easily observable. The British case creates no problem: the brief race begins after the Queen announces the dissolution of the House of Commons. In Finland some content analysis of newspapers was available in 1958, and it pointed out how campaign material had been packed into a surprisingly short period, considerably shorter than the forty days' time from the legal deadline for nominations to the polling days. In order to design my study I needed to guess when the campaign would be under way. The first wave of interviews had to be placed not too far from the voting, yet far enough to occur definitely while the political system still functioned "normally." Such data would concern the 'normal' predispositions of the electorate without leaving much room for other intervening influences than those connected with the campaign. The second wave of interviews would then provide information about campaign experiences and the impact of the campaign. The preelection field work was actually done about eight weeks before the election. Considerable analysis was made later of the political content of the newspapers, in part in order to ascertain that the campaign segment of the imagined time axis had not influenced the preelection interviews.

Of the two additional models one came to mind, I confess, after I had been analyzing the material for a long while. The other one, I also confess, I was not able to utilize to the extent I should have and had been hoping to do. The newcomer was the political system as a communication network, and the yielder was the center-periphery dimension.

On a lonely evening it occurred to me that a speech I had heard a couple of months earlier was very relevant to the attempts to "draw a general picture." The talk had been given in Finland in 1961 by an American guest lecturer, professor Lester W. Milbrath, and the particular point that proved so helpful had been his model of communication lines in a political system, later published in *The Washington Lobbyists*.[10] It led me to "A Model of Decision-Making and Communication Channels in a Democratic Political System," which included the official power relations from the people through the authorities to official decisions, the multiplicity of the channels of communication between the system's interacting components, and the directions of the effect of the authoritative decisions.

The channels of communication may be used for the purpose of influencing some other components of the system, and obviously the importance of such channels varies not only among different political systems but also in any given system at different times. The idea of intrasystem dynamics linked my "time axis" and "communication" models with each other. When one assumes that communication tends to be directed towards those who make authoritative decisions, its "normal" objects are the "high-ups" in the system. An election provides the people with a rare opportunity to make an official decision of importance. Consequently, the transfer from the "normal" to the electoral process should manifest itself in the system through a relative change of the flow of communication from the "higher" decision makers towards the people; such a change should occur in the quality as well as the quantity of political mass communication.

Of the two interlinked models, only the normal/electoral time axis idea influenced the design of the study, and it was also the

[10] (Chicago: Rand McNally, 1963), pp. 180–182.

more prominent one in the introductory listing of the research problems:

> 1. The 1958 campaign can be defined as that communication directed by the political powers toward the citizens which specifically aimed at influencing the voting decisions realized in July 1958. . . . In order to define the approximate duration of an election campaign, when the party organizations completed their preparations and moved to open campaign activities will be noted. Also, changes in the volume of campaign material and other political material will be studied. . . .
> 3. . . . To find out factors which influenced the 1958 voting behavior, three time periods will be studied. The object is: (a) to classify the population just before the campaign according to political interest and attitude toward parties; (b) to observe the influence of earlier experiences on that interest and party affiliation; and (c) to study how precampaign differences . . . in turn predict exposure to the election campaign and possibly participation in the election. . . .

By the time the summary of my results had attained actuality, the interlinkage of the two models had proven its usefulness:

> The theoretical background of the study led also to another hypothesis about trends in the content of the material. If the political system undergoes a real change as the attention of political powers. . . . turns from other decision makers toward the people, . . . changes could be expected in the relative emphasis put on different issues. A content analysis indicated that such changes did occur. . . . Speculations on campaign tactics helped to interpret many of the findings.

My third model or frame of reference, the center-periphery dimension, was also useful throughout the project. It had both geographical and organizational applications, each in turn leading to thoughts about diffusion and control. Therefore this model did not give way because of any fruitlessness, but simply due to my lack of energy and lack of means to utilize it to full advantage.

The geographical consideration was important when I chose which regions would be investigated in detail. I did not want to concentrate on either extreme of the center-periphery dimension. The analysis was then confined to Tampere, Finland's second largest city, separated from Helsinki by 110 miles and by two constituencies. The city of Tampere was in turn the center of its district (Northern Hame Consistuency). A large but peripheral rural commune in the same constituency was also surveyed. The thought of a pervasive center-periphery dimension helped me to interpret many survey findings, and it led to comparative analyses of the contents of the national and the provincial party press.

I was unable to analyze the functioning of the campaign organizations in accordance with my original intentions. I had been interested in "vertical linkage," not from the point of view of power relationships within the parties but as channels through which plans and platforms reach the grass roots of campaign activity. In this connection, the related considerations of the differentiation of the various degrees of participation among party memberships and, especially, among the electorate at large, were quite clarifying. The concern was not with party organizations as such; rather, I reviewed the conversion of the "normal" parties to campaign organizations. I had intended to find out how their "inmost circles animate and guide the outer circles."[11] In order to realize the intention it would have been necessary to collect many more data from party archives and through interviews of party functionaries.

A natural consequence of the newness of Finnish electorate research was the open possibility of making choices in the field. This possibility aroused, in addition to substantive interests, temptations to experiment with research methods. My concern was not with new methods of analysis as much as with the search for previously unused sources of primary information. This side of the task brought its own share to the excitement of putting the operation in motion.

4. The Work

The powers of one man, even one equipped with a fuller purse, would have been inadequate to organize and execute the field work. My good fortune was a helpful environment. I am especially grateful for the activities of some personnel of the city government offices and for the help which a group of young friends gave

---

[11] Maurice Duverger, *Political Parties*, 2nd English Ed. (London: Methuen, 1959), p. 91.

when they arranged the field work in Korpilahti commune. Anticipations of the reactions of interviewees worried me greatly; to ease their possible suspicions I was allowed to speak on a local radio program, and the project was given favorable press coverage just before the field work was launched. Because "local patriotism" is a live factor in Finnish communities I believe it was useful to stress publicly how significant it was that the city of Tampere was to be the very ground for a new type of research project. Local helpfulness included also an access to the district offices of political parties and the availability of material from the local newspapers, as well as the cooperation of many public authorities.

Those who make political interview surveys in the United States may not notice some of their relative advantages. I am not even thinking of comparisons between the U.S. and various developing countries. I allude to such advantages as experience and favorably reacting public, in addition to what seem like fair chances of finding adequate financial support. Many attitude measures and the phrasing of questionnaires are well tested in the U.S., and many survey organizations can readily provide field staffs there. One knows how to collect data and often what it is one wants to know. Secondly, the American public was early accustomed, if not to being actually interviewed, at least to thinking that the pollsters might call on them. The aura of open personal discussions about politics also seems helpful.

The local concentration of the Finnish study contributed to the organization of my field work, and I was fortunate to find people who had previously done interviewing for a sociologist in the same city. It was useful, even necessary, that they enjoyed the work (and did not charge much for it). A good portion of the interviewers were municipal social workers who were by profession used to talking with strange persons. Nevertheless, because the fear of a high rate of refusals was very salient in my mind then, easy rapport seemed an important consideration when the questionnaire was designed and pretested. Party identification was among those items for which I felt I had to make compromises between the sharpest measuring instruments and an easy cooperation of the interviewees. As it turned out, sixteen interviewees (2.8 percent) in May and eight others in July refused cooperation, and four percent of those interviewed refused to reveal their partisan preference. This compares well with the refusals in 1959 among those national samples which were drawn for the Five-Nation study (from ten percent in Germany to sixteen percent in the U.K.).[12] Although interviewees who may refuse to cooperate continue to deserve attention in Finland, encouraging experiences and the growing number of surveys on political attitudes have lessened their salience in recent study designs.

Sampling is easy in Finland, as in other countries with permanent population registers. My random samples of 583 in Tampere and 101 in Korpilahti were taken directly from the (automatically prepared) registers of voters. Because these "poll books" of July 1958 were based on the residences as of January 1, 1957, a part of the city sample had to be traced to a new address; thirty-one had moved beyond reach either abroad or to an unknown residence. A total of 501 interviews were completed in the city. In the sparsely populated rural commune only four persons were not interviewed (one was dead, another one disqualified from voting, one was too sick, and one refused).

At this point I might confess that I was suspicious of generalizations based on the "soft data" of a smallish number of interview responses. Gradually I began to feel easier, however, after the findings started making sense and showing internal consistency. The original suspicion provided one motive that made me experiment with documented "hard data" on the behavior of individuals. A few such "hard" sources complemented the actual interview schedules, and additional recorded data were obtained about other persons in order to do small separate investigations which could be compared with the survey findings.

Participation in the election belongs among Finland's "hard" variables if one makes use of the archived voting registers of the election boards after the voting. Such a "poll book" contains the name (and some personal data) of each enfranchised citizen living in the voting area (ward), and every voter's name is marked by the board to prevent double voting. The "poll books" of Tampere's fifty-five voting districts revealed that twelve nonvoters had reported in the July interview as having voted and

---

[12] Gabriel A. Almond and Sidney Verba, *The Civic Culture: Political Attitudes and Democracy in Five Nations* (Princeton, N.J.: Princeton University Press, 1963), pp. 509–521.

one actual voter had reported abstention. Thus, the interviews had "softened" the participation variable by three percent, and corresponding "hardening" corrections were made in the coding. Years later, when I was bothered by the aging of my survey data, it occurred to me that the same method made it possible to lengthen the observed "time axis" of the sample of voters. The voting registers of 1962 provided comparable information on participation in the Presidential election of January 15–16 and the parliamentary election of February 4–5, 1962. I was really glad to modernize my card desk by punching in that additional information.

Naturally one can obtain similar information for any interesting group of enfranchised people. First one needs to find the addresses to determine each person's voting district, and second one notes which people have and which have not been marked as voters by the local election boards. I included in the project such an analysis of two somewhat overlapping local groups: the 448 chairmen and secretaries of Tampere's political associations (names were obtained from the register of associations, kept by the Ministry of Justice), and those 1,765 inhabitants of the city (also their spouses) who had participated in the nominations by signing some candidate's petition (names were obtained from the central election board). Political party was, of course, another available variable in these cases. To help in another experiment, some local election boards agreed to improve their "process-produced" data; they also marked in the register the day and the time of day each voter cast his ballot. Another source of very "hard" data concerning the samples of interviewees were the local assessment boards, which released for the study a statement of the taxable income of the interviewees and their spouses for 1957 and, later, for 1958.

Naturally, I did not work alone. I had assistants collecting information: interviewing, going through documents, and observing campaign events. Man- and womanpower was necessary during the analysis, too, to code, punch, tabulate, and test the interview material and to classify and measure the centimeters of newspaper contents. Nevertheless, the researcher's close participation in the daily work was essential, especially since I moved the data analysis operation twice from the basement of the University of Helsinki to the old basement of the Institute for Social Research in Ann

Arbor, Michigan. Due to the fairly small number of respondents it was also feasible to return several times to the original interview schedules in order to get new looks at the open-ended responses; even a trunkful of questionnaires spent the year 1962 in New Hampshire and Michigan. The several handy aspects of both the Institute of Political Science at Helsinki and the ISR in Ann Arbor included the proximity of the punching machine to the counter-sorter (useful when replacing damaged cards), and the fact that nobody chased me out of the machine room in the later hours.

I wonder whether my working habits were planned and structured enough to be presentable for any other purpose than penance. Writing and data analysis progressed hand in hand. Newly-gained knowledge often provoked new problems and courses of detailed analysis, and new concepts emerged during the analysis. For example, when I began to analyze the flow of communication it seemed sensible to me to replace my intention of comparing the two traditional types, opinion leaders and followers, by the thought of comparing three groupings: opinion leaders, ordinary discussers, and outsiders. New literature also provoked new ideas. Among other things it pointed to the utility of investing special effort in comparisons between strong and weak party identifiers as to their opinions and characteristics. On the other hand, it is also true that basically the framework and the general outline of the book did not change very much while it was written. In accordance with the original plan, the book has an introduction, four chapters on "normal" politics, two chapters on the campaigning interlude (its framework and content), then finally the two chapters on voting itself (participation and choices), and the finale.

The factors that generally pushed the work forward included the desire to know more, the desire to digest a consistent structure out of a large body of heterogeneous facts, the encouragement given by some fine colleagues, and the deadlines. The deadlines were the product of invitations to present papers for the International and the Finnish Political Science Association and for other audiences of sane judgment. Should I generally compare the various points of my effort, it is obvious that the most strenuous work was the thinking. Nothing could be more irritating and more inspiring than having somebody like Angus Campbell repeatedly ask you "Why?"

5. The Joy

An enterprise in empirical social research seems to me very comparable with an exploring expedition. It may emphasize methodology like Kon-Tiki and Ra II, or it may make use of something like Amundsen's dog team in order to enter an unknown territory. It is an adventure, and it is risky. Things might go wrong for the social scientist even in collecting primary information. Other hazards, too, could keep worthy goals beyond reach. But new knowledge is a payoff that well outweighs the risks.

The output of research can be communicated to others via speech and publication. But its evaluation is not likely to be the same everywhere. And the personal satisfaction a researcher gets from his work may be too subjective to communicate at all.

The better part of my subjective joys in doing the Finnish election study were the discoveries that assured me little by little that I seemed to be doing something worthwhile. They might be summarized as belonging to six different types: (1) individual findings could be fitted into consistent patterns; (2) survey evidence was supported by the "hard" data; (3) the conclusions were not too far off the existing knowledge familiar to me; (4) I figured out some new interpretations (5) new hypotheses for future research also came to mind; and (6) I traced some unique phenomena that may be of historic interest.

Because the book communicates my findings, I shall not repeat them here. Perhaps I am permitted, however, to illustrate each subjectively "joyful" category with one example: (1) Indifference towards a "normal" news broadcast and non-voting in an election were typical items in one general pattern running from "normal" inactivity to a low exposure to various campaign events, a delayed voting decision, and a late attendance at the polling place; (2) The pre- and postelection questionnaires of 1958 grouped the electors into classes which turned out in significantly different proportions in the elections of 1962; (3) The strength of party identification again predicted both interest and opinions; (4) Non-voting could be explained as the negative difference of an individual's motivation to vote and his external restraints to voting; (5) The prevailing "wind" of party fortunes may determine at the grass-roots level the demand of opinion leaders speaking for each party, and a locally established party machine may compensate for a temporary loss of opinion leaderhip; (6) The red/white cleavage in Finnish electorate behavior seemed to have broken down for the first time during the 1958 election campaign.

One's memory may tend to select only the favorable recollections, because it seems to me now that even writing, analytic and especially descriptive, is a sort of pleasure in itself. And I should not like to give the impression that scholarship offers no earthly pleasures; I had many of those, such as two grants to do research in Michigan, the pleasure of cooperating with outstanding men and women, and some kind recognition of my work. Yet the deepest gratification comes from the fulfilment of a large research task through the finding of relevant facts and their ordering into one consistent whole.

The most joyful day of a typical research project, I presume, is the one when its major publication appears from the press. I was fortunate to have two such days. The Finnish book came out in 1965 and the English version in 1968. In 1967 I told a visiting professor from California who taught journalism at Tampere and specialized in news writing that my new book will deal with the 1958 election. He said, "That's ancient."

7 **POLITICS, ECONOMICS AND THE PUBLIC: LOOKING BACK**

Thomas R. Dye
Florida State University

Systematic Policy Analysis: Developing a Subfield

Public policy is not a new concern of political science; the earliest writings in our discipline reveal an interest in the policies pursued by governments, the impact of these policies, and the environmental conditions associated with different kinds of policies. But the approach to public policy I set forth in *Politics, Economics, and the Public*[1] —an approach reflected in a great deal of subsequent research literature—can be clearly distinguished from much of the earlier writing on public policy. It is an approach which I would label "systematic policy analysis."

Systematic policy analysis involves:

1. A primary concern with explanation rather than prescription. Policy recommendations—if they are made at all—are subordinate to description, analysis, and understanding. There is an

This is the first publication of Thomas R. Dye's essay. All rights reserved. Permission to reprint must be obtained from the publisher and the author.

[1] (Chicago: Rand McNally, 1966.)

implicit value judgment that understanding is a prerequisite prescription and that understanding is best achieved through systematic analysis, rather than rhetoric or polemics.
2. The systematic comparison of the policies of different communities, states, government agencies, and nation-states. There is clear commitment to comparative analysis, in contrast to case studies. Whatever the unit of analysis—cities, states, government agencies, nation-states—they are viewed in the comparative fashion.
3. A rigorous search for the determinants and consequences of public policies. This search involves a commitment to scientific standards of inference; sophisticated quantitative techniques may be helpful in establishing inference, but they are not always essential. Policy analysts are far-reaching in their search for factors which might influence policies; they have investigated the impact of economic, social, cultural, and historical forces, as well as political and governmental variables.
4. The effort to develop and test general propositions about the causes and consequences of public policy and to accumulate reliable research findings of theoretical relevance. Much of the recent systematic policy research has relied, explicitly or implicitly, on a systems-analytic framework, but there is no reason why other systematic models could not be employed. The important point is that the research is not concerned with the explanation of specific policy decisions but with the development of general propositions.

Systematic policy studies, particularly at the state and community levels, have expanded very rapidly in recent years. Perhaps the appeal of systematic policy analysis is that it enables social scientists to address themselves to the important policy questions facing American society without abandoning their commitment to scientific method. It enables social scientists to attack "relevant" policy issues with systematic enquiry rather than rhetoric, polemics, or activism. It might be labeled the thinking man's response to the demand that social science become more "relevant" to the problems of our society.

Insofar as *Politics, Economics, and the Public* pointed younger scholars in the direction of systematic analysis, it served an important purpose. Its findings challenged many traditional notions about the policy impact of some popular political variables—party competition, voter participation, Democratic and Republican control of state government, and malapportionment. Specifically, it suggested that these political variables were not as important as levels of economic development in determining public expenditures and services among the fifty states. These findings attracted considerable attention from students of state politics, who had long been nurtured on the *a priori* reasoning and case studies of Key, Lockard, Fenton, and others.[2] Perhaps these findings disturbed scholars who felt more comfortable with the reassuring notion of pluralist democracy that "politics count."

But the findings themselves—regarded almost as commonplace by economists[3]—were not really as important as the mode of inquiry which had been fashioned. A number of scholars were stimulated to systematically reexamine traditional wisdom in the state politics field, a field which had not been hitherto renowned for its comparative, systematic orientation.

The result was an outpouring of systematic social science research which employed rigorous and comparative methods of test propositions about the determinants of public policies, particularly at the state and local levels.[4] New and more sophisticated methodological techniques were introduced;[5] some causal modeling was developed;[6] additional political variables were tested for their

[2] V. O. Key, Jr., *American State Politics* (New York: Knopf, 1956), and *Southern Politics* (New York: Knopf, 1951), Duane Lockard, *New England State Politics* (Princeton, N.J.: Princeton University Press, 1959), and John Fenton, *Midwest Politics* (New York: Holt, 1966), and *Politics in the Border States* (New Orleans: Hauser, 1957).

[3] See, for example, Solomon Fabricant, *The Trend of Government Activity in the United States Since 1900* (New York: National Bureau of Economic Research, 1952), Glenn Fisher, "Interstate Variation in State and Local Government Expenditures," *National Tax Journal*, 17 (March 1964), 57–73, Seymour Sachs and Robert Harris, "The Determinants of State and Local Government Expenditures and Intergovernmental Flow of Funds," *ibid.*, 75–85.

[4] The early works include Richard E. Dawson and James A. Robinson, "Interparty Competition, Economic Variables and Welfare Politics in the American States," *Journal of Politics*, 25 (May 1963), 265–289, Richard Hofferbert, "The Relation between Public Policy and Some Structural and Environmental Variables in the American States," *American Political Science Review*, 60 (March 1966), 73–82; Thomas R. Dye, "Malapportionment and Public Policy in the States," *Journal of Politics*, 27 (February 1965), 586–601, Herbert Jacob, "The Consequences of Malapportionment: A Note of Caution," *Social Forces*, 48 (1964), 261.

[5] Ira Sharkansky and Richard Hofferbert, "Dimensions of State Politics, Economics and Public Policy," *American Political Science Review*, 63 (September 1969), 867–879, and Thomas R. Dye, "Income Inequality and American State Politics," *ibid.*, 157–162.

[6] Charles F. Cnudde and Donald J. McCrone, "Party Competition and Welfare Policies in the American States," *ibid.*, 858–866.

policy impact;[7] some policy outputs other than levels of public expenditures and service were examined;[8] changes over time were described and analyzed;[9] research findings were modified, and exceptions to general propositions were described;[10] the impact of public policy on the environment was investigated;[11] some more discerning theoretical notions about public policy were developed;[12] propositions developed at the state level were tested at the municipal level;[13] and so on.[14]

In short, a whole subfield of discipline grew to maturity in a very short period of time. Scholars did not always agree on conceptualization or on the utility of each other's work. But they

[7] Ira Sharkansky, "Agency Requests Gubernatorial Support and Budget in State Legislatures," *American Political Science Review*, 62 (December 1968), 1220–1231, and Thomas R. Dye, "Executive Power and Public Policy in the States," *Western Political Quarterly*, 22 (December 1969), 926–939.

[8] Bryan R. Fry and Richard Winters, "The Politics of Redistribution" *American Political Science Review*, 64 (June 1970), Jack Walker, "The Diffusion of Innovations among the American States," *American Political Science Review*, 63 (September 1969), 867–879, and Thomas R. Dye, "Inequality and Civil Rights Policy in the States," *Journal of Politics*, 31 (November 1969), 1080–1097.

[9] Richard Hofferbert, "Ecological Development and Policy Change," *Midwest Journal of Political Science*, 10 (November 1966), 464–483.

[10] Sharkansky and Hofferbert, "Dimensions of State Politics, Economics, and Public Policy," and Cnudde and Donald J. McCrone, "Party Competition and Welfare Policies in the American States."

[11] Ira Sharkansky, "Government Expenditures and Public Services in the American States," *American Political Science Review*, 61 (December 1967), 1074–1075.

[12] Ira Sharkansky, "Environment, Policy, Output and Input: Problems of Theory and Method in the Analysis of Public Policy," in Ira Sharkansky (Ed.), *Policy Analysis in Political Science* (Chicago: Markham, 1970).

[13] Lewis A. Freeman, Jr., "An Analysis of Public Policies in Cities," *Journal of Politics*, 29 (February 1967), Robert L. Lineberry and Edmund P. Fowler, "Reformism and Public Policy in Cities," *American Political Science Review*, 61 (September 1967), 701–716, Heinz Eulau and Robert Eyestone, "Policy Maps of City Councils and Policy Outcomes," *American Political Science Review*, 62 (March 1968), 124–143, and Thomas R. Dye, "Governmental Structure, Urban Environment, and Educational Policy," *Midwest Journal of Political Science*, 11 (August 1967), 353–380.

[14] Of course, not all of this literature has been good. See, for example, John Crittenden, "Dimensions of Modernization in the American States," *American Political Science Review*, 61 (December 1967), 982–1002, Alan G. Pulsipher and James L. Weatherby, "Malapportionment, Party Competition, and the Functional Distribution of Government Expenditures," *American Political Science Review*, 62 (December 1968), 1207–1220.

were able to build upon each other's research efforts. They agreed on the premise of a systematic, comparative mode of inquiry. They were able to talk to each other, to use each other's research findings, and to actually engage in a collective scientific enterprise. It was a really exciting experience, and not a very common one in the social sciences. I consider myself fortunate to have been part of this subfield and to be associated with the many fine scholars who have contributed to it.

The Limited Utility of Systems Theory

Some years ago, David Easton commented on the disutility of political theory in empirical research.[15] His comments were generally acknowledged to portray accurately the gap between theory and research in political science. He later devoted a great deal of scholarly effort toward overcoming the discrepancy between theory and research.[16] His important work on systems theory was a notable contribution to our discipline, and it brought Professor Easton well-deserved professional distinction. Yet despite Professor Easton's truly meritorious efforts, the systems analytic framework possesses only limited utility in guiding empirical research in public policy.

Let me try to describe the ways in which systems theory was helpful and the ways in which it was not.

By postulating three major categories of phenomena—environmental inputs, political system characteristics, and policy outputs—systems theory encourages the researcher to distinguish between types of variables. This simple framework provides a means of ordering reality. It assists in designating what phenomena are to be considered independent and dependent variables: environmental conditions and political system characteristics are considered independent variables in the explanation of public policy, and public policy is considered an independent variable in assessing feedback effects on the environment and the political

---

[15] David Easton, *The Political System* (New York: Knopf, 1953).
[16] David Easton, "An Approach to the Analysis of Political Systems," *World Politics*, 9 (1957), 383–400, *A Framework for Political Analysis* (New York: Prentice-Hall, 1965), and *A Systems Analysis of Political Life* (New York: Wiley, 1965).

system. In the real world, data do not come with labels attached—"inputs," "system characteristics," or "outputs." Systems theory is helpful for suggesting categories and labels for real-world data. For example, data can be obtained from the real world on "median family income," "percentages of legislative seats won by Democrats," and "per pupil educational expenditures." But it is only in the context of systems theory that these data become neatly categorized as environmental inputs, political system characteristics, and policy outcomes. Some other theory might designate the real-world data in some other way. Of course there is no way of knowing whether systems theory provides the best of all possible ways of ordering reality. We simply wait until something more useful and more intellectually satisfying comes along.

In some ways, systems theory is not helpful, even as a classification scheme, since it really does not help much in deciding whether some variables should be classified as inputs, system characteristics, or outputs. For example, after the publication of *Politics, Economics, and the Public*, at least one study was produced which classified the division of state-local responsibility (the percentage of total state-local spending attributed to state rather than local government) as a political system characteristic rather than as a policy outcome as in my book.[17] As a political system characteristic, the division of state-local responsibility correlated independently with policy outcomes better than party competition, voter participation, partisanship, and malapportionment. This enabled the author "to contrast" his finding about the strength of his political system characteristic with my earlier findings about these other political system characteristics. There is nothing really wrong with this, but it creates confusion among the readers of this literature if they do not read it very carefully. This kind of confusion could be avoided if systems theory provided better guidelines in classifying variables as environment, system, or policy.

Systems theory also suggests linkages between the environment and the political system, the political system and public policy,

---

[17] Ira Sharkansky, *Spending in the American States* (Chicago: Rand McNally, 1968).

and the environment and public policy, as well as feedback linkages. In *Politics, Economics, and the Public,* I commented on the utility of the systems framework in positing these linkages:

> Linkages *A* and *B* suggest that socioeconomic variables are inputs which shape the political system and that the character of the political system in turn determines policy outcomes. Those linkages represent the most common notions about the relationship between socioeconomic inputs, political system variables, and policy outcomes. They suggest that system variables have an important independent effect on policy outcomes by mediating between socioeconomic conditions and these outcomes. Linkage *C,* on the other hand, suggests that socioeconomic variables effect public policy directly, without being mediated by system variables. . . .
> Already the task of model building has succeeded in directing attention to an important problem in the explanation of policy outcomes. In exploring the relationships between socioeconomic variables, political system characteristics, and policy outcomes, we must ask whether or not differences in policy outcomes are *independently* related to system characteristics. Do system characteristics mediate between socioeconomic inputs and policy outcomes (as suggested by linkages *A* and *B*), or are policy outcomes determined without regard to system characteristics (as suggested by linkage *C*)?[18]

However, even though systems theory suggests certain linkages, it does *not* designate *which* environmental variables or *which* political system characteristics affect public policy in what way or why. An infinite variety of environmental conditions or political system characteristics might conceivably influence public policy. Systems theory provides no real help in the identification of these variables or characteristics. One must search for additional theoretical guidance in selecting environmental variables and political system characteristics for study. Because of its failure to specify causal linkages, systems theory is really something less than a genuine theory of politics. It is not much more than a classification scheme for variables.

In *Politics, Economics, and the Public,* I was obliged to turn to economic development theory to justify the selection of my

---

[18] Pp. 4–5.

environmental variables—income, education, urbanization, and industrialization.

> Economic theory provides solid justification for postulating that economic development influences political system characteristics and policy outcomes. Industrialization, whether in a planned or unplanned society, is said to result in increased specialization in demands for coordination. Coordination in a free enterprise economy is provided by the market mechanism and by corporate bureaucracies, but a great deal is also provided by government. The coordination demanded in our industrial society always involves certain inescapable difficulties; expansion of some industries and contraction of others, overestimates and underestimates of economic conditions, and errors of judgment resulting in economic imbalances. In response to these dislocations, collective remedial action tends to increase, and added responsibilities are placed upon government. In addition, urbanization is understood to lead to a variety of social problems which are presumed to be amenable to collective action. This too implies added governmental responsibilities. Migration from rural to urban areas in response to the development of industry, the decline of agriculture, and the general search for economic opportunity by individuals and businesses also create governmental responsibilities. Economic development also involves expansion at the state and local levels of education, transportation, and welfare services, which are largely responsibilities of governments, as a result of dislocations not only adjustment of state policies in these areas but also adjustment of the government tax and revenue systems which must finance all of these new responsibilities.[19]

Nor was systems theory much help in selecting political characteristics for analysis. In selecting system characteristics, I simply turned to the existing literature on state politics to see which political variables attracted the greatest attention of scholars in the field. This meant relying on the traditional literature of state politics, which focused so much attention on party competition, voter participation, party control of state government, and legislative malapportionment. Numerous passages in the traditional literature on state politics suggested that these system characteristics had important impact on public policy. Later, of course, my critics would chide me for ever believing that these aggregate characteristics of state political systems would have

[19] Pp. 7–8.

any great impact on levels of taxing, spending, and service in the states. Later commentators would suggest that these rough measures of the political system "do not represent the whole of the political system, not perhaps even its most significant elements,"[20] and of course they would also suggest that other policy outcomes besides levels of taxing and spending and service be investigated. But *at the time* the existing literature clearly asserted that these particular system characteristics did indeed affect levels of taxing, spending, and service.[21] It could hardly be said that I was attacking a straw man. As a matter of fact, I really expected that most of the ideas about the policy impact of party competition, voter participation, and malapportionment would be confirmed in systematic analysis. I was really surprised when I began to read the computer print-outs.

The selection of policy outputs was really a matter of the availability of measures of public policy on a state-by-state basis. Unlike economics, political science does not have a developed data collection system which gives us much choice in the selection of public policy variables. Political scientists record election returns and public expenditures and very little else. Getting reliable measures of consumer protection, civil rights legislation, insurance regulation, labor management relations, public school curricula, or any other policies not directly reflected in public expenditures, for each of the fifty states, is very difficult. Getting measures of the intrastate distribution of government burdens and benefits among groups and classes of people, in each of the fifty states, is almost impossible. So most (but not all) of the policy outputs in *Politics, Economics and the Public* were measures of the *level* of government taxing, spending, and service. These variables were largely the product of the availability of comparative information on public policy in the states.

Thus, systems theory had little to do with the selection of en-

[20] Herbert Jacob and Michael Lipsky, "Outputs, Structure, and Policy: An Assessment of Changes in the Study of State and Local Politics," *Journal of Politics*, 30 (May 1968), 515.

[21] Key, Jr., *American State Politics*, pp. 76–77, Duane Lockard, *The Politics of State and Local Government* (New York: Macmillan, 1963), p. 319, Charles Adrian, *State and Local Governments* (New York: McGraw-Hill, 1960), pp. 306–307, Malcolm Jewell, *The State Legislature* (New York: Random, 1962), pp. 30–33; and Daniel Grant and H. C. Nixon, *State and Local Government in America* (Boston: Allyn and Bacon, 1963), pp. 204–205.

vironmental variables, political system characteristics, or policy outcomes. Systems theory did little more than classify variables and suggest simple linkages. Sometimes I think I might have been able to do this without ever having read Easton.

Confusing Systematic and Incremental Models

Some years ago Charles Lindbloom observed that public policy develops incrementally.[22] Decision makers do *not* annually review the range of existing and proposed policies, identify societal goals, research the benefits and costs of alternative policies in achieving these goals, rank preferences for each alternative policy, and make a selection on the basis of all relative information. Constraints of time, intelligence, and cost prevent decision makers from identifying the full range of policy alternatives and their consequences. Constraints of politics prevent the establishment of long-range societal goals and clear preferences among policies. So rather than a complete review of all aspects of programs, policies, and budgets each year, decision makers generally accept the legitimacy of established programs and agree to continue previous levels of expenditures. They reduce their task by considering only *increments* of change proposed for next year in programs, policies, and budgets. This incremental decision making tends to be short-range, pragmatic, and non-ideological. It also provides for flexibility in response to conflicting political demands. When increments rather than major changes are at stake, conflicting interests can participate in the political process without posing major threats to each other. Moreover, annual statements of goals and priorities would lead to considerable instability in public policy.

This descriptive model of the policy-making process found in the writings of Lindbloom, Wildavsky, and Sharkansky is widely known as "incrementalism."[23] Its utility in understanding the

---

[22] Charles Lindbloom, "The Science of Muddling Through," *Public Administration Review*, 19 (Spring 1959), 79–88, and *The Intelligence of Democracy* (New York: Free Press, 1966).

[23] Lindbloom, *Public Administration Review, op. cit.*, Aaron Wildavsky, *Politics of the Budgetary Process* (Boston: Little, Brown, 1964), and Sharkansky *Spending in the American States.*

policy-making process can hardly be overestimated. Anyone who has any experience with state budget making can testify to its relevance. And there is comparative systematic evidence in support of incremental decision making. For example, the single factor that shows the closest relationship to state government expenditures in a current year is the level of expenditures in the recent past. Indeed, expenditure and service levels in the states in a current year correlate quite closely with expenditure levels in the states many decades ago. Doubtlessly, current expenditure and service levels reflect past habits, accommodations, and the conservative orientation of government budget procedures. There is no question that past decisions do have an important independent effect on current decisions; and this fact helps to explain the relationship between past and previous expenditure levels.

Yet, it is important to realize that the incremental model does not conflict with the systemic model described earlier. Both explanatory models can be asserted simultaneously. To say that public policies this year are related to public policies last year does not contradict the statement that public policies this year *and* last year are a product of environmental forces and system characteristics. One can "explain" public policy today by reference to its relationship with policy in the previous year, or one can "explain" public policy by reference to the environmental forces impinging upon a specific type of political system. Both explanations are logically correct; they do not contradict each other.

Unfortunately, Ira Sharkansky offers the correlation between current and past expenditures as a refutation of the systemic model.[24] Actually, there is no contradiction between the finding that expenditures, both past and present, are shaped by environmental resources and political system characteristics and the finding that current expenditures are shaped by previous expenditures. Sharkansky notes that current state government expenditures are *more* closely tied to previous state government expenditures than to any other socioeconomic political variable. This is, of course, true. The problem is that he asserts that this finding "contrasts" with those showing the effect of environmental and systemic forces. But actually the correlation between

[24] Sharkansky, *Spending in the American States,* and "Economic and Political Correlates of State Government Expenditures," *Midwest Journal of Political Science,* 11 (May 1967), 173–192.

past expenditures and present expenditures is shaped by the same environmental resources and political system characteristics. For example, New York and Mississippi were at opposite ends of the rank ordering of the states on levels of public expenditures in the 1960s and the 1890s. During the same periods, these states were also at the opposite ends of rank-ordering of the states on environmental resources. Their environmental resources shaped their relative expenditures in both 1960 and 1890, so, of course, there is a correlation between expenditures in these two time periods.

It is logically incorrect to put previous expenditures together with current environmental conditions in a regression problem on current expenditures. This is because previous expenditures *embody* the effect of the environmental resources against which they are matched within the regression problem. On the basis of partial correlation coefficients in a multiple regression equation with both previous expenditures and current environmental resources, Sharkansky concluded that, "The impact of previous expenditures over current expenditures—most noticeable in a multiple regression and partial correlation analysis with other independent variables—. . . indicates the great extent to which government expenditures depend upon intragovernmental stimuli rather than on economic, political, or social stimuli from their environment."[25] Of course, such a conclusion is based upon a logical confusion between systemic and incremental models. Economists were quick to note the logical confusion: Robert Harlow writes about Sharkansky's work: "Since . . . [environmental forces] were operative for 1961 as well, and since these factors are not likely to be radically different over the two year time span encompassed by the study, they are in a sense represented by, or contained in, the previous expenditure variable. . . . Using the previous expenditure variable tells us only that there are differences because there were differences."[26]

Incrementalism refers primarily to the process of policy determination. It emphasizes the tendency of decision makers to focus their attention upon marginal changes in public policy, on in-

[25] Ira Sharkansky, "Some More Thoughts About the Determinants of Government Expenditures," *National Tax Journal*, (June 1967), p. 179.

[26] Robert L. Harlow, "Sharkansky on State Expenditures: A Comment," *National Tax Journal*, 21 (June 1968), 215–216.

creases and decreases in the funding of current programs, and to accept the present policies, programs, and expenditures as a base. Of course, past decisions may have an important *independent* effect on current decisions, and this fact helps to explain the relationship between past and previous policies. Because the same environmental and systemic forces at work shaping current policy were also at work in shaping past policies, the relationship between current and past policies is explained. Systemic and incremental explanations do not "contrast" with each other. They are both important contributions to our understanding of public policy.

The Units of Analysis Hang-Up

One of the problems of political science today is that it continues to define its subfields by the units of analysis studied—individuals, local governments, state governments, governmental institutions, or nation-states—rather than by the nature of the political phenomena being studied. We generally offer courses in municipal government, state government, national government, voter behavior, Congress, courts, presidency, Asian governments, African governments, etc.—as if the problems, concepts, methods, and findings of all of these units of analysis were different. Courses which integrate relevant systematic research from various units of analysis in order to deal with significant political phenomena—for example, political violence, conflict management, political integration, determinants of public policy, the impact of public policy, etc.—are rare.

Systematic policy analysis should not be considered a development in the field of *state* politics. States are merely convenient units of analysis for systematic testing of propositions about the causes and consequences of public policy. In *Politics, Economics, and the Public* I commented on the utility of the American states as units of analysis:

> The American states provide an excellent opportunity for applying comparative analysis in non-experimental research. These fifty political systems share a common institutional framework and cultural milieu. All states operate under written constitutions which divide authority between executive, legislative, and judicial

branches. The structure and operations of these branches are quite similar from state to state. All states function within the common framework of the American federal system. All states share a national language, national symbols, and national history. In short, important institutional and cultural factors may be treated as constants for analytical purposes.

This background of institutional and cultural uniformity in the American states makes it easier to isolate casual factors in our analysis of public policy outcomes. Comparative analysis of national political systems is made very difficult because of the many great institutional and cultural differences among national societies; it is difficult to isolate the reasons for variations in system characteristics or policy outcomes where vast differences exist in geography, climate, language, economy, history, religion, and so on. In contrast, when one focuses upon the American states many important independent variables are held constant, and the explanatory power of a single set of variables can be observed.[27]

However, any unit of government which makes authoritative allocations of societal values can be studied in much the same fashion as the American states have been studied. In fact, if we are to develop a viable theory of public policy, we *must* undertake comparative, systematic testing propositions at all levels of analysis—communities, states, governmental agencies, nation-states—and we must do so at different periods of time.

Certainly the recent research on municipal public policy demonstrates that systematic policy analysis need not be limited to the states. A landmark in systematic policy research at the municipal level is Robert L. Lineberry's and Edmond P. Fowler's study of the taxing and spending policies of 200 American cities.[28] These researchers contrasted policies of politically reformed cities (cities with management governments, at-large constituencies, and non-partisan elections) with those of politically unreformed cities (cities with mayor-council governments, ward constituencies, partisan elections). They found that reformed cities spend and tax less than unreformed cities. But more importantly, they found that unreformed cities were more responsive in their public policies to the class, racial, ethnic, and religious composition of their populations than reformed cities. Thus, Lineberry and Fowler identified an important policy impact of a political system

[27] Pp. 11–12.
[28] Lineberry and Fowler, "Reformism and Public Policy in Cities."

characteristic—*responsiveness*. Of equal importance in the systematic study of municipal policies is the comprehensive work of Eulau and Eyestone on the linkages between public policy, urban environment, resource capability, and the goals, perceptions, and policy positions of city councilmen in ninety West Coast cities.[29] The "policy maps" of city councilmen—that is, their perceptions of public problems, recommendations for actions, and hopes and expectations concerning their city's future—are viewed as independent variables affecting policy as much as environment and resources.

Can propositions derived from systematic analysis of state and municipal policy be tested in a similar fashion at the cross-national level? For example, *Politics, Economics, and the Public* suggested that environmental variables are more influential than political system characteristics in determining levels of public spending and service. Can this proposition be extended to national political systems? Does the character of national political systems substantially affect public services? Or do democratic and non-democratic nations at the same levels of economic development undertake the same levels of government service? One of the very few systematic studies of the relationship between political system variables and domestic policy outcomes among nations is Phillip Cutwright's study of social security programs in seventy-six nations.[30] Interestingly, Cutwright's findings parellel those in *Politics, Economics, and the Public*. In spite of very great differences among nations in ideological orientation and type of system, social security policy outcomes are more closely related to levels of economic development.

The systematic literature on domestic and international conflict participation also falls within the general framework of policy analysis. I did not have the opportunity to read much of this literature until after the publication of *Politics, Economics, and the Public*, but I felt very much at home with the concepts and methodology of this research. Although this literature has been concerned almost exclusively with one type of policy output

[29] Eulau and Eyestone, "Policy Maps of City Councils and Policy Outcomes."

[30] Phillip Cutwright, "Political Structure, Economic Development, and National Social Security Programs," *American Journal of Sociology*, 70 (1965), 537–550.

—involvement in conflict situations—the methodology could easily be extended to other types of policy outcomes. Of course, the great obstacle to cross-national research on public policy is the availability of reliable and comparable measures of policy output. But the idea of systematically comparing the domestic policies of a large number of nation-states is an exciting one.

Overcoming Methodological Constipation

Too frequently, formal methodology gets in the way of significant social science research. The methodologically constipated researcher can never bring himself to produce worthwhile findings because he fails to understand the instrumental nature of methodology. It is nonsense to insist that empirical measures always be exact equivalents of the concepts they represent, or to require that the data fit all of the assumptions of the statistical tests employed, or to refuse to make explanatory inferences because research operations are not precisely equivalent to the hypothesized linkages. Insistence upon methodological purity can only result in research constipation.

I am well aware that such advice runs counter to the direction of graduate school training, where the validity of measures, the fit of the data, and the limitations on inference are emphasized. And this is the way it should be, since professional training of researchers should sensitize them to methodological problems. The vast majority of students entering graduate school come with an excess of rhetoric, intuition, and anecdotal information, and very little understanding of the scientific method. But after the last seminar paper in "methodology" has been turned in to the instructor and the student turns to the real nitty-gritty of social science research, it is essential that he set aside some of the methodological inhibitions which have been pounded into him in graduate school. Only by so doing will he have any chance of saying something worthwhile about government or politics.

It should be recognized that there is a serious gap between the language of research and the language of explanation. This gap can never be bridged in a completely satisfactory manner. In describing linkages between dependent and independent variables, explanatory language uses words like "determines," "accounts for," "produces," "results in," and "explains." Yet statistical correlations can at best tell us only how close the association is between variations in dependent and independent variables. It is quite obvious that the causal language of explanation is not the same as the relational or associative language of statistics. No explanatory model can ever be fully demonstrated empirically. All we can do is produce research findings which are either consistent or inconsistent with our explanations. It is nonsense to insist that our research operations be completely symmetrical with explanatory statements, or to refuse to make explanatory inferences because research operations are not precisely equivalent to our explanations. In working with explanatory models, it is always necessary to make use of a whole series of untestable, simplifying assumptions. Even when a model yields correct empirical predictions, this does not mean the model itself has been empirically verified. But unless we permit ourselves to make simple assumptions, it will never be possible to generalize beyond the single or unique political event. There is no point in banning causal language or refusing to make simplifying assumptions. We ought to be able to move freely from operational to explanatory language and back again as necessary, largely on the basis of convention. And unless we make the kinds of assumptions that an explanatory model requires, we shall never be able to explain political life.

My work has convinced me that data will never be completely consistent with social science concepts, at least not in the near future. If we wait until we have data which is the exact equivalent of our concepts we will never get on with the job of research. Methodological purity would require us to say that "median family income" refers to the median figure received by the census taker when he asks respondents what their family income was last year. Viewed in this fashion the measure is useless. So we make the assumption that median family income can be employed as an index of a larger phenomenon—namely, economic well-being. Instead of viewing "per pupil expenditures" as the quotient one obtains by dividing pupil attendance figures by educational expenditures, we employ the measure as an index of financial support of education. Thus, in the interest of developing and testing general explanatory models, we make great inferential leaps from data to concepts and back again. All that we can reasonably expect of the researcher is that he use the best available data, that is, data which most closely approximates the concepts which it is supposed to represent.

Social science data rarely fits all of the assumptions of common statistical tests. Rarely does social science data fit the normal curve. And there is no reason to believe that relationships in the real world are always linear. But the development of social science would be seriously inhibited if we were to insist that all of our data fit all of the assumptions of statistical tests. I am not arguing that we ignore these problems; I am merely saying that we should handle them as efficaciously as possible and then get on with the more important business of making explanatory inferences.

Recently, factor analysis has come into widespread use in the effort to study underlying "dimensions" of the American states. Long lists of independent variables have been reduced to several "dimensions" via factor analysis. These dimensions have been labeled "industrialization," "cultural enrichment," "metro-urbanism," "integrative message exchange," "scope of government," "agrarian society," "professionalism—local reliance," "competition—turnout," "welfare—education," "highways—natural resources," etc.[31] In contrast, *Politics, Economics and the Public* employs a limited number of specific independent variables —median family income, percentage of the population living in urban areas, percentage of the work force in non-agricultural employment, median school year completed by the adult population.

Factor analysis is flashy in terms of methodological sophistication, but has the use of factor analytic dimensions provided us with any better conceptualization of our independent or dependent variables? I seriously doubt that these "dimensions" are better representations of the relevant forces in the environment, significant characteristics of the political system, or the important dimensions of public policy than straightforward measures of directly observed phenomena are. There is nothing *wrong* with factor analysis; I just do not believe that it has contributed much to an understanding of the forces that are at work in the shaping of public policy. The labels assigned to factor analytic factors do

---

[31] See Sharkansky and Hofferbert, "Dimensions of State Politics, Economics, and Public Policy," and Crittenden, "Dimensions of Modernization in the American States."

not add to conceptual clarification, and, in fact, frequently contribute to ambiguity. Moreover, the factors seldom explain much more of the variance in public policy than a single independent variable such as per capita income! Finally, the independent measure can be directly linked to the phenomena which it represents, and this contributes to the clarity of our explanatory model. But factor scores are second-order conceptualization; one must first inquire into the weightings of various measures in each factor and then attempt to develop explanatory propositions.

It would be helpful if researchers in a particular field of policy analysis would endeavor to employ similar measures of the same phenomena wherever possible. Of course it must be recognized that many times there are impelling reasons for using new measures or different ones than those which have been tried in the past. But frequently new and different measures are used for no good reason at all, and the result is that whatever replicative value a study may possess is lost in measurement differences. This is another reason why specific measures are to be preferred over factor analytic dimensions. Unless there are good reasons for doing otherwise, we ought to try to employ the same measures of phenomena employed by earlier researchers so that replication can contribute to the scientific enterprise.

One of the problems confronted in practically all social science research is that of "multi-collinearity." Multi-collinearity refers to the existence of correlation between two or more independent variables and the difficulty in assessing the relative impact of intercorrelated variables on independent variables. Of course, it is nonsense to insist that social science research be devoid of the multi-collinearity problem. As soon as a researcher includes both income and education among his independent variables, he has "multi-collinearity." The question is not whether there is multi-collinearity among independent variables, but rather how this phenomenon is handled in the analysis and whether it makes any difference relative to the propositions under investigation.

My own experience is that partial correlation coefficients are not terribly reliable in identifying the strength of the relationship between an independent variable and a dependent variable when the control variable is highly intercorrelated with the independent variable. Partial coefficients behave quite unexpectedly sometimes. By this I mean they can jump from positive to negative or from one magnitude to another, when there is little theoretical reason for them to do so. It was my own research experiences with partial coefficients which led me to this conclusion. However, I later read in Blalock the following:

> Stated in most simple terms, whenever the correlation between two or more independent variables is high, the sampling error of the partial slopes and partial correlations will be quite large. As a result there will be a number of different combinations of regression coefficients, and hence partial correlations, which give almost equally good fittings to the empirical data. In any given case, the method of least squares will usually yield unique solutions, but with slight modifications of the magnitude that could easily be due to sampling or measurement error, one might obtain estimates which differ considerably from the original set.[32]

If the independent variables are not highly intercorrelated, then the partials seem to be reliable. But I would not become overly excited about partial coefficients for intercorrelated independent variables.

My purpose in these comments on methodology is to foster the view that methodology is the instrument of explanation. Our objective is explanation, not elegance of technique. The serious social scientist will make the best use of available data in testing explanatory propositions. He will be honest in pointing out the weakness of his data and the inelegancies of his methodology. But he will not shy away from explanatory inferences. Explanation is the objective.

A note of caution: many researchers, unfortunately, feel obliged to dress up their modest research findings in imposing theoretical attire. Not every research effort can provide complete proof of a major theoretical system in political science. Yet a great deal of research *claims* to be a proof or disproof of a grand theory of politics. (Doubtlessly, outlandish claims to theoretical significance are encouraged by the shortage of journal space in political science; researchers seeking a publication outlet feel they must make claims to compete for limited space.) Policy analysts would probably be better advised at this point to concentrate attention on middle-

---

[32] Hubert M. Blalock, Jr., "Correlated Independent Variables: The Problem of Multicollinearity," *Social Forces*, 42 (December 1963), 233, and *Causal Influences from Nonexperimental Research* (Chapel Hill, N.C.: University of North Carolina Press, 1964), pp. 87–91.

range propositions linking environment, politics, and public policy. Of course, it is important to point out whether or not one's research findings are consistent or inconsistent with prevailing models of politics. And it is helpful to point out whether they are consistent with previous research. But I would like to see us accumulate a great deal more in the way of comparable research findings before we claim proof or disproof of any major theories of political life.

Mucking around in the Data

Research does not proceed in a step-by-step fashion; at least, mine does not. Research activities—conceptualizing and model building, formulating hypotheses, searching the literature, selecting variables and measures, collecting data, coding and punching, selecting statistical tests, running computer programs, analyzing results, designing tables, writing up findings, comparing findings with models and theories—are seldom ordered in the rational sequence I've just presented. Theorizing and model building go on all the time; new hypotheses have an unseemly way of occurring *after* the data has been run; relevant previous research is overlooked until after the results are written up; new measures are discovered, added to the data, and run through the computer at various times; mock-up tables are designed before the data is run, and then new tables are designed after the data is run; a variety of statistical tests are employed, many of which never appear in the final report (once the data has been collected, coded, and punched!). We live in an age of high-speed computers, yet many social scientists approach research as if they were unaware of this fact. They still insist that the selection of each independent variable be justified by elaborate references to theory and previous research. No doubt in an earlier era, when investigative capabilities were limited, there was wisdom in selecting for study only those independent variables which had a high expectation of payoff. Today, though, we can investigate thousands of independent variables on no more than a vague hunch that they might be causally related to our dependent variables. We can go on searching expeditions just to see how many things vary with our dependent variables.

Of course, once relationships are discovered we must explore their nature: Does variation in the independent variable cause variation in the dependent variable, or is it vice versa? Or are both dependent and independent variables caused by some other phenomena, and their correlation really spurious? Or are there reciprocal forces at work—do independent variables cause variation in the dependent variable and dependent variables cause variation in the independent variables simultaneously? Or are dependent and independent variables functional equivalents which both really measure the same thing, and for this reason occur together? Or is the relationship between independent and dependent variables merely a product of measurement error?

Thus, even with modern computer technology to assist us in discovering relationships, we still must think about the meaning of the relationships which are discovered. In fact, the discovery of a relationship is only the first step in developing an explanation. My point is that results which fit the model are accepted, while results which do not fit are reexamined for coding or punching errors or programming flaws, and so on.

We have already commented on the role of theory in the selection of dependent and independent variables. Obviously these selections are going to be guided by implicit or explicit ideas about causal linkages in political life. And of course these selections are going to be influenced by previous research. But the selection of dependent and independent variables must *also* be guided by the *availability of data*.

It is really pointless to propose theories or hypotheses about politics that can never be tested because no data exists which will permit testing. A common criticism of empirical research is that its models and propositions are determined by the availability of data. Of course this is true. There is little to be gained by denying that the availability of data influences every aspect of the research enterprise. But this is how it should be. Models or propositions which lack available empirical referents have little utility. "Mucking around in the data" of social science—that is, becoming familiar with the major sources of social science data—is very important. The knowledge of available data enables the researcher to quickly judge the feasibility of research ideas and propositions. Moreover, a knowledge of social science data sources helps generate research ideas; one's powers of induction are frequently improved by mucking around in the data.

Computer technology enables us to simultaneously investigate a large number of hypotheses. We are able to investigate relationships between thousands of dependent and independent variables in a matter of seconds with computer capabilities to assist us in our thinking. Induction and explanation can develop in the course of interaction between the researcher, the data, and the computer. The research enterprise does not proceed undirectionally from model to hypothesis to variable selection to data collection to statistical testing to analyzing results to revising models. Instead, the research process can proceed in almost any direction—from data to hypothesis, from data to models, from results to new data collection, from results to new hypotheses, and so on.

Coping with the Critics

The most important, and controversial finding set forth in *Politics, Economics, and the Public* was that certain characteristics of the political system—party competition, partisanship, voter participation, malapportionment—were not *as* influential as economic development in explaining levels of public spending and service. With some notable exceptions, most of the policies examined in the book were more closely linked to wealth, industrialization, urbanization, or educational levels in the states, rather than to apportionment practices, party competition, voter turnout levels, or Democratic or Republican control of state government. Political variables were shaped by the socioeconomic environment and often correlated with levels of spending and service, but political variables did not exert much *independent* effect on the policies which were studied. The implication was that political systems function as neutral mechanisms which transform demands arising from the socioeconomic environment and generating levels of public spending and service.

These findings turned out to be very discomforting to many political scientists. Findings which were hardly considered novel by economists seemed to offend professional political scientists. It was almost as if some political scientists believed the discipline had a vested interest in proving that political variables were the most important factors in explaining public policy, and that the discovery that economic or other variables were more important in determining levels of public spending and service than political variables was somehow damaging to the professional interests of political scientists. Perhaps these findings also disturbed scholars who felt more comfortable with the reassuring idea of pluralism —that party competition, voter participation, party affiliation, and apportionment practices are key instruments in policy determination. In short, some of my colleagues reacted as if I had challenged some of the basic tenets of pluralist ideology.

There seemed to be a great deal of scrambling about by scholars ideologically committed to proving that party competition, voter participation, partisanship, and apportionment do indeed influence public policy. Of course, insofar as the findings of *Politics, Economics, and the Public* stimulated comparative systematic research into the policy impact of political variables, then it served an important and valuable purpose. Political institutions, processes, and behaviors may indeed help to determine the effect of politics on policy. This is a question which we must try to answer in our research. But we should not insist that political variables influence policy outcomes when research evidence suggests otherwise simply because our conventional training and wisdom in political science has told us that political variables are important. We cannot reject research findings out of hand simply because they appear to challenge a narrow view of our professional interests, or even worse, because they appear to challenge our ideological commitment to pluralism.

William Keech and James W. Prothro set forth a truly professional view of the relationships between research findings, professional interests, and ideological commitment. In referring to *Politics, Economics, and the Public* these scholars stated:

> This research has produced some findings that have been unsettling for many political scientists. Dye concludes that "the evidence seems conclusive; economic development variables are more influential than political system characteristics in shaping public policy in the states." Some have reacted to these and earlier findings as if political science had a vested interest in political variables being the most important factors in explaining political phenomena, and as if the discovery that economic or other variables are more important than political variables in explaining policy is somehow going to damage the discipline. A more balanced view is that political science derives its importance from its dependent variables, the phenomena it seeks to explain. Thus the important thing to achieve is the most effective and efficient ex-

planation of political variables. If economic or other independent variables explain policy more clearly than political variables, so much the better. The point is that we must seek out the best explanations, not that they must be political.[33]

Constructive scholarly criticism is very basic to the development of a science. Of course we all knew of the importance of criticism in pointing out defective work, e.g., poor conceptualization, invalid measurement, illogical testing procedures, incorrect interpretation of results, and so forth. But constructive criticism of competent research can also make a valuable contribution to science. The contribution occurs when the critic suggests additional dependent variables which might be studied in a similar fashion; when he suggests additional independent variables to be tested for their impact on the dependent variables used in the research; when he suggests additional tests which might clarify the causal linkages under investigation; or when he suggests additional theoretical or conceptual utility of the findings.

For example, James A. Robinson's review of *Politics, Economics, and the Public* suggested that the linkage described therein should be investigated over time in order to better understand the dynamics of public policy determination.[34] Herbert Jacob and Michael Lipsky made several valuable suggestions in their critique of the book[35]: that additional political system variables be examined for their impact on public policy; that public policies other than the *levels* of public spending and service be analyzed; and that we try to learn more about the way in which environmental factors lead to the articulation of demands and support and are communicated to political authorities. Finally, several critics suggested that finding a strong correlation between economic development and public policy does not in itself create understanding of the functioning of political systems. They suggested that we still want to know *how* a political system goes about transferring economic inputs into policy outcomes. In other words, they were suggesting that political scientists still want to know what goes on within the little black

[33] William Keech and James W. Prothro, "American Government," *Journal of Politics*, 30 (May 1968), 438.

[34] James A. Robinson, *American Political Science Review*, 61 (December 1967), 1113–1114.

[35] Herbert Jacob and Michael Lipsky, "Outputs, Structure and Policy," 510–538.

box. The more fair-minded of my critics noted that I had acknowledged many of the limitations of *Politics, Economics, and the Public* in the book itself and that I had made similar suggestions for future research.

Building a science is a collective enterprise. No research effort should be considered a "final thought" or a "finished contribution." Just as the athlete expects his records to be broken, the scholar expects his work to be improved upon. Perhaps the most important measure of scholarly contribution is the extent to which one's work stimulates the efforts of subsequent scholars. The serious scholar does not discourage interpretive challenges, conceptual improvements, more sophisticated methodological techniques, new explanatory variables, or modifications and exceptions to research findings. On the contrary, these developments must be encouraged if the science is to advance. In my judgment, a serious scholar is obliged to send his data to whoever asks for it, to provide whatever informational assistance he can to those working in the same field, and to refrain from suppressing the publication of studies which are at variance with his own.

8 INFLUENCES OF MILIEUX ON THE DEVELOPMENT OF A MODEL AND ITS METHODOLOGY IN INTERNATIONAL RELATIONS: AN AUTOBIOGRAPHICAL ESSAY ABOUT A DECADE OF RESEARCH WITH THE INTER-NATION SIMULATION

Harold Guetzkow
Northwestern University

The development of the Inter-Nation Simulation is the outcome of a great complex of influences, not the least of which was my good fortune to live in a society where resources for scholarly work are available through academic establishments generously undergirded by support from private foundations and from government funds.[1] This es-

---

This essay is reprinted from "A Decade of Life with the Inter-Nation Simulation," by Harold Guetzkow, from *The Process of Model-Building in the Behavioral Sciences*, edited by Ralph M. Stogdill, and is copyright © 1968, 1970, by the Ohio State University Press. All rights reserved.

The writing of this essay was made possible by the author's occupancy of the Gordon Scott Fulcher Chair of Decision Making at Northwestern University, complemented with funds from the Carnegie Corporation of New York. Its contents were presented at The Ohio State University Symposium on *The Process of Model Building in the Behavioral Sciences* on April 20, 1967.

[1] My gratitude is unbounded for a decade of opportunities to pursue international relations research of risk as to "payoff." My seminal stay during 1956–1957 at the Center for Advanced Study in the

say will focus on the decisions emerging from the intellectual and social milieux provided by persons and institutions comprising such environments. The decisions involved in building a simulation emerged from a complex of givens, deriving from my cognitive and social background. My working style, reflecting a need for intellectual structure and an appreciation for team endeavors, reinforced my penchant for allowing the exigencies of the situation to influence the unfolding of intellectual decisions. Even the details of the simulation's design and the particular experiments used in its operation were importantly constrained by these milieux, as they derived from the cultures of methods and substance in which I worked.

Before delineating ways in which the milieux influenced the development of the Inter-Nation Simulation, I will briefly describe this man-program simulation. By assembling two to five persons in a quasi-bureaucratic team, one has "decision makers" for a "nation." By placing varying constraints upon their decision making, the political, economic, and military characteristics of their nation may be differentiated from those of other nations. The decision makers are responsible for both the internal and external affairs of their governments. Through a set of programs some of the consequences of their decisions may be computed; these outputs along with the non-programmed consequences of actions then constitute the bases for decisions taken in the next round of activity. By composing an "international system" of some five to nine such simulated nations, a world in miniature is constructed. Permit some of the participants to serve as representatives in an "international organization"; establish "news media," as well as "world statistical services," so that the direct interactions among the nations are complemented through these sources of information. One then has an operating "international system." A more detailed description of the Inter-Nation Simulation is given in an

---

Behavioral Sciences in Stanford was financed by the Ford Foundation. Exploratory runs of the Inter-Nation Simulation were underwritten in 1957–1959 by funds from the Carnegie Corporation of New York. During 1959–1963 the research was supported by the Behavioral Sciences Division of the U.S. Air Force Office of Scientific Research, Contract No. AF49(638)–742 and Grant No. AF-AFOSR 62–63. During this period special tasks were undertaken for Project Michelson of the Department of the Navy, N123(60530)25875A. After 1964 the work was financed by a contract from the Advanced Research Projects Agency, SD 260, of the U.S. Department of Defense, with funds from the Carnegie Corporation of New York more recently providing for its direction.

article I wrote for *Behavioral Science* in 1959.[2] This article has been reprinted in a number of other places in full and revised versions, as indicated in the reference.

II. The Web of Intellectual Givens

The plan for the development of the Inter-Nation Simulation took its form during a year spent at the Center for Advanced Study in the Behavioral Sciences, 1956–1957. When I arrived in Palo Alto, my thinking as a social scientist was anchored in three commitments: (1) to the generation of knowledge for immediate application, especially with respect to the problems of peace and war; (2) to problem-oriented research which is multi-disciplinary; (3) to the development of an experimental social science, building eclectically in a cumulative way. Consider the implications of each of these commitments for research in international relations:

1. Knowledge for Use

In developing fundamental knowledge to apply to the problems of peace and war, I assumed that my research efforts should encompass many aspects of international relations, for practical problems come in "wholes." The political exercises which Hans Speier talked about at the Center and which were based on work at the RAND Corporation seemed constricted in being crisis-oriented.[3] The tradition of war gaming tended to be tactical in outlook. Yet one might build thereon, despite such narrowness of scope.

2. Multi-Disciplinary Research

If the research were to be problem-oriented, it would need to take help from whatever discipline might contribute. It was taken

---

[2] "A Use of Simulation in the Study of Inter-Nation Relations," *Behavioral Science*, 4 (1959), 183–191. Reprinted as Reprint No. PS-112 in the *Bobbs-Merrill Reprint Series in the Social Sciences* (Indianapolis: Bobbs-Merrill, and in the *Proceedings of the IBM Scientific Computing Symposium on Simulation Models and Gaming* (York, Pa.: Maple, 1966), pp. 249–278.

[3] Joseph M. Goldsen, *The Political Exercise: An Assessment of the Fourth Round* (Santa Monica, Calif.: The RAND Corporation, May 1965).

for granted that my work in international relations would certainly take the individual level into account, leaning heavily upon the contributions of many in decision making; the presence of Richard Snyder at the Center reinforced this orientation.[4] It was clear that the research would utilize our knowledge about groups —be they face-to-face, organizational, or societal in their inclusiveness—given my interests after six years of work with Herbert Simon.[5] A small seminar at the Center at Stanford in 1955 included Charles McClelland;[6] the vigor of his presentations showing the relevance of systems theory reinforced my willingness to use whatever capabilities were available from within all the social sciences.

3. Cumulative Social Science

It was a foregone conclusion that I would build eclectically upon what had gone before and would be integrative with respect to the work of others in international affairs. I found it easy at the Center to lean upon other seminar members who were interested in international relations, namely Karl Deutsch[7] and Wilbur Schramm.[8] With the Stanford University library at hand, it was possible to delve deeply into the writings of others, including the contributions that Raymond Cattell already had made to the study of the dimensions of nations.[9]

---

[4] Richard C. Snyder, Henry W. Bruck, and Burton Sapin, *Foreign Policy Decision Making: An Approach to the Study of International Relations* (New York: Free Press, 1962), pp. 14–185.

[5] James G. March and Herbert A. Simon with Harold Guetzkow, *Organizations* (New York: Wiley, 1958).

[6] Charles A. McClelland, "Applications of General System Theory in International Relations," *Main Currents in Modern Thought*, 12, 2 (November 1955), pp. 27–34.

[7] Karl Deutsch, Sidney A. Burrell, Robert A. Kann, Maurice Lee, Jr., Martin Lichterman, Raymond E. Lindgren, Francis L. Loewenheim, and Richard W. Van Wagenen, *Political Community and the North Atlantic Area: International Organization in the Light of Historical Experience* (Princeton, N.J.: Princeton University Press, 1957).

[8] Wilbur Schramm (Ed.), *The Process and Effect of Mass Communication* (Urbana, Ill.: University of Illinois Press, 1955).

[9] Raymond Cattell, H. Breul, and H. Parker Hartmann, "An Attempt at a More Refined Definition of the Cultural Dimensions of Syntality in Modern Nations," *American Sociological Review*, 17 (1951), 408–421.

These were the "initial conditions" of my milieux. These background commitments were reinforced by my peers at the Center. The alternative of researching broadly within empirical materials *per se* in the tradition of the behavioral scientist seemed impractical at the time, considering problems of access to affairs of nation-states. The development of a political-economic-military simulation involving both men and programs appealed to me as an experimental vehicle which might have a scope adequate to meet my interests in application. Here was a medium in which a broadly engaged social scientist might sketch, dipping eclectically into the various disciplines as the study of policy problems might require. With notes jumbled in my briefcase I left the Center in the summer of 1957 to begin a new life in the study of inter-national relations at Northwestern University.

In the early years in Northwestern's Program of Graduate Training and Research in International Relations, the influences of my past milieux were reflected in our simulation building in the styles that characterized my "thoughtways" and "workways": (1) My disposition was (and is) to want to order things with some rigor. (2) My predilection was (and is) to work in teams. These styles had impact upon the construction of the Inter-Nation Simulation.

1. Systematic, Rigorous Work

It was my habit to build by first specifying the entities with which I would work, then by characterizing these entities in terms of their attributes through the development of variables, and finally in attempting to build "islands of theory" by interrelating some of these variables with others.[10] It was my pattern to tolerate gaps within my work, especially when the going became rough.

These proclivities influenced my work during the formation of the Inter-Nation Simulation. We built upon what others had delineated as the "actors" within international affairs—the decision makers, their foreign offices, and the international organizations—all interrelated in an international complex. We might have

[10] Harold Guetzkow, "Long-Range Research in International Relations," *The American Perspective*, 4, 4 (Fall 1950), 421–440.

gone on almost endlessly in the enumeration of variables characterizing these "actors." But if one were content with a limited number of variables drawn from each of the important domains, it seemed more likely that the researcher could get on with the construction. Certainly the political, economic, and military factors were prime, if one were building upon what others had indicated. With reluctance I omitted in this first approximation such aspects as "culture." In the attempt to link variables to one another, it was difficult to find solid work upon which to build, given the state of theory about international relations in the mid-fifties.[11] Thus, relations among variables were sketched in a most abbreviated fashion in the Inter-Nation Simulation, omitting important "chunks," such as the interrelations between regional and universal international organizations.

In my past searches for adequacy as an experimenter I had been accustomed to moving freely back and forth from field to laboratory and from laboratory to field. At Michigan, Donald G. Marquis and Roger W. Heyns and I[12] had gone from the laboratory study of face-to-face discussion groups to observation in the field of ongoing conference groups embedded in organizations making life-affecting decisions (see "A Bibliography from Conference Research," pp. 240–241 in Collins and Guetzkow, 1964).[13] At Carnegie Tech we had examined organizational hypotheses in our Controller's Study, both on the natural site and within our laboratory.[14] Thus, it now was important to attempt to construct a laboratory within which international phenomena might be studied, so that again both field and laboratory work might contribute to theory development. In addition, a simulation which might be operated with many replications seemed a useful tool for managing experimental intervention, so as to permit one to study the consequences of new factors.

---

[11] Richard Synder, "Toward Greater Order in the Study of International Relations," *World Politics*, 7 (April 1955), 461–478.

[12] Donald Marquis, Harold Guetzkow, and Roger W. Heyns, "A Social Psychological Study of the Decision Making Conference," in Harold Guetzkow (Ed.), *Groups, Leadership and Men* (Pittsburg: Carnegie, 1951), pp. 55–67.

[13] Barry E. Collins and Harold Guetzkow, *A Social Psychology of Group Processes for Decision Making* (New York: Wiley, 1964).

[14] Herbert A. Simon, Harold Guetzkow, George Kozmetsky, and Gordon Tyndall, *Centralization v. Decentralization in Organizing the Controller's Department* (New York: Controllership Foundation, 1954).

2. Team Research

It was imperative to work with teams, inasmuch as the development and operation of the Inter-Nation Simulation was a task beyond my personal competence, given my knowledge, energy, and time constraints. Throughout the coming decade my proclivity for working with others led to the formation of a variety of face-to-face groups. These included a "superteam" in the form of the International Relations Program itself at Northwestern, "subteams" through which I executed the Inter-Nation Simulation, and "sideteams" which served to stimulate and challenge my efforts as others went in alternative directions.

III. Simulation Development

Within the aforementioned intellectual and social milieux, the Inter-Nation Simulation took shape. In the first year or two, decisions were made with respect to the Inter-Nation Simulation's (1) format and (2) contents. These decisions held with some firmness throughout the decade.

1. Format

In many ways the decision to use a mixed simulation involving both men and programs was easy. Yet this decision proved to be a significant one, in that it allowed a degree of rigor which is not present in the relatively unprogrammed political-economic-military exercise.[15] Further, it avoided the problems of the limits of our capability in attempting an all-computer construction, both financial and with regard to the state of our knowledge of the computer arts.[16] As a social psychologist, I wanted to avoid attempts by the participants at role playing which seem to be endemic to the politi-

---

[15] Lincoln Bloomfield and Barton Whaley, "The Political Military Exercise: A Progress Report," *Orbis*, 8, 4 (Winter 1965), 854–870.

[16] Morton Gorden, "Burdens for the Designer of a Computer Simulation of International Relations: The Case of TEMPER," in Davis B. Babrow (Ed.), *Proceedings of the Computers and the Policy-making Community Institute* (Englewood Cliffs, N.J.: Prentice-Hall, 1967).

cal-economic-military exercise. How could the usual participant in the laboratory exercise—the high school senior or the college sophomore—imagine himself to be a decision maker of another nationality operating within the international scene? As an organization theorist, I wanted to provide a set of constraints upon decision making which were somewhat stable and objective, therein contrasting with the use of "umpires" whose human judgments about an ongoing situation are fed into war games in an *ad hoc* way. Having our decision makers constrained by consequences derived from programs as well as from the reactions of component parts in other nations in the international system, it seemed possible to have a laboratory which might avoid these difficulties by incorporating both men and machines into a simulation format. The use of quasi-abstract nations leads decision makers to occupy roles which are induced by the ongoing situation, and thus they do not need to "play act" strange nationalities. With preordained programs there is no need for human "umpires" constituting a control team.

This decision with respect to the mix between men and programs coincided with another decision: the "nation" aspects of the simulation were to be programmed in the main, while the "internation" aspects were to be left more or less free. Given the state of international theory in the late fifties, there was little more that one might do, inasmuch as what was called "international relations" was largely speculation about foreign policy making.[17] Then, once the nations were operating as entities, the evolution of their interaction might be relatively unconstrained by programmatic features of the model. In this way it was hoped that the simulation construction might be of heuristic value, producing phenomena of an international character which would suggest new solutions to some of the problems extant in international affairs. Further, this delineation of "programmed" versus "free" aspects of the simulation coincided with well-agreed-upon notions that the internal features of a nation-state, such as "national interest," were important determinants of its external behavior, and vice versa—although fewer scholars subscribe to the point of view that the external environment of the nation importantly influences its domestic processes.

[17] Snyder, "Toward Greater Order in the Study of International Relations."

Thus, the decisions with respect to format also derived from the intellectual and social milieux in which I worked in the late fifties. My multi-disciplined expectations as an experimental social psychologist and organizational theorist were satisfied through a man-machine simulation which allowed humans to operate within a constrained decision environment. The state of the computer arts in the late fifties precluded an all-encompassing construction, which my pragmatic commitment dictated; one then settled for a man-computer mix, for at least such a simulation was somewhat broader than the manual exercise focusing upon crisis. Given the fact that our knowledge of domestic affairs was more firmly grounded than our knowledge of international affairs, the social scientist could build eclectic programs for the nation with more adequacy than for the international system. As matters look in retrospect, these conditions of milieux explain why the Inter-Nation Simulation was constructed in the format of a man-program simulation.

2. Contents

In developing the contents of our simulation I joined in an *ad hoc* team with Robert Noel and Denis Sullivan in a set of pilot runs in which political, economic, and military aspects of the simulation were meshed together on the basis of intuition. By working within the three domains, we hoped to avoid a construction which would be "politics"-dominated. In order to get the construction working, expediency was the order of the day. However, I do not think that we ever permitted our "theoretical objectives to be swamped by practical necessities."[18] When we ran into a dead end, we attempted at times to circumvent the difficulty through omission, as we did during our troubled times while developing an international public opinion component.[19] At other times we rationalized our way out of them, as in our decision that we would have no geographical component inasmuch as our simu-

---

[18] Guetzkow, "A Use of Simulation in the Study of Inter-Nation Relations," 183.

[19] Robert C. Noel, "Evolution of the Inter-Nation Simulation," in Harold Guetzkow, Chadwick F. Alger, Richard A. Brody, Robert Noel, and Richard Synder, *Simulation in International Relations: Developments for Research and Teaching* (Englewood Cliffs, N.J.: Prentice-Hall, 1963), p. 99.

lation was abstract and strategic in nature, with the consequences of geography being implicit in such devices as the comparative advantages of trade and in differential damage rates with respect to military operations.[20]

Sullivan was immersed in the textbook literature of international relations, disentangling relationships which might be included in our simulation.[21] Noel, with his background of economics, was preparing for a more thorough treatment of some features of our construction.[22] My role was largely one of effecting integrations and serving as an inhibitor for much which might be incorporated, so that the simulation would remain workable. By conducting pilot runs, we constantly checked whether the simulation bogged down when it was in operation, either because it was beyond the managerial capabilities of a staff or impossible for the participants to learn within reasonable time limits. A detailed chronology of three of these runs is presented by Noel elsewhere.[23]

Members of the "superteam"—the International Relations Program at Northwestern—provided a milieu from which it was difficult to escape. Colleague Chadwick Alger continually reminded us of the importance of international organizations, so that our simulation would not be a simple interstate system. In the end, we but loosely incorporated an international organization as part of the Inter-Nation Simulation.[24] Colleague Snyder barraged us with variables to be included, as we attempted to winnow the many candidates for inclusion as programmed variables. For example, we aborted the early attempt to implement motivational directives, as delineated in the 1954 monograph by Snyder, Henry W. Bruck, and Burton Sapin;[25] our posited "national goals" tended to limit the operation of the situational factors.[26] On the other hand, it proved

[20] *Ibid.*, p. 148.

[21] Denis G. Sullivan, "Towards an Inventory of Major Propositions Contained in Contemporary Textbooks in International Relations" (Northwestern University, Department of Political Science, unpublished Ph.D. dissertation, 1963).

[22] Robert C. Noel, "A Simplified Political-Economic System Simulation," (Northwestern University, Department of Political Science, unpublished Ph.D. dissertation, 1963).

[23] Guetzkow *et al.*, *Simulation in International Relations*, p. 73.

[24] *Ibid.*, pp. 145–147.

[25] Snyder *et al.*, *Foreign Policy Decision Making*.

[26] Guetzkow *et al.*, *Simulation in International Relations*, p. 73.

feasible by physically separating the participants to avoid some "small groups" effects, representing instead a quasi-bureaucratic structure in "Communication and Information" processes, as outlined by Snyder, Bruck, and Sapin.[27] In the end, we sought to placate our critics as to whether or not we had included the variables in which they had especial interest by designating "prototype" variables which were supposedly representative of a gamut of political measures or economic processes or military capabilities.[28] In this way we were able to keep the entire construction within bounds. The use of prototypes served to increase the level of abstractness of our model.[29] This orientation meshed with our attempt to posture the entities as typical nations—large and small, developed and developing, aggressive and cooperative[30]—so that, as our decision makers took their positions within these components of the simulation, they might avoid "role playing," reacting instead directly to the imposed realities of their national situations.

Throughout the development of our simulation we presented our definitions of the variables used and our equations programming their interrelationships to *ad hoc* groups within our International Relations Program. It was a salutary experience to defend one's choices—even though in the case of the relationships among the variables we operated largely without empirical foundations. Throughout the work our skills in verbal analysis were tested; at times, we found mathematics a useful complementary tool in developing our formulations, as has been explained in some detail elsewhere.[31]

At the time it seemed the factor analyses of Cattell were not adequately established to be utilized as an important guide in our variable selection. Yet, such a procedure would have enabled us

---

[27] Snyder *et al.*, *Foreign Policy Decision Making*.

[28] Guetzkow, "A Use of Simulation in the Study of Inter-Nation Relations."

[29] Guetzkow, "A Use of Simulation in International Relations," *Proceedings of the IBM Scientific Computing Symposium on Simulation Models and Gaming*, p. 253.

[30] Guetzkow *et al.*, *Simulation in International Relations*, pp. 138–139.

[31] Harold Guetzkow, "Some Uses of Mathematics in Simulations of International Relations," in John M. Claunch (Ed.), *Mathematical Applications in Political Science* (Dallas: The Arnold Foundation, Southern Methodist University, 1965), pp. 21–40.

to have cut through the plethora of variables, choosing those which were more unitary in conception. However, we were again stimulated to want improvement with respect to this part of our work, whence came the spin-off of the Dimensionality of Nations project at a later date, in collaboration with a "sideteam" consisting of Rudolph Rummel and Jack Sawyer.[32] In retrospect it is provocative to report that we had accepted Hans Morgenthau's popular theory with respect to the national security function[33] but had rejected Cattell's work. Yet the former exhibited no more empirical substantiation in the work of Lewis F. Richardson[34] than had been obtained by the factor analyses of the latter.[35] Do these decisions indicate we were willing to give more weight to the eminence of a sage than to the weight of his empirical evidence, as we brought our intuitions to bear in selecting variables and formulating the relationships among them? Perhaps it might have been wiser to have also used Cattell's factors as variables, rather than the intuitively-constructed "prototypes" actually employed in the formulation of the Inter-Nation Simulation.

Before proceeding to an examination of the nature of the model itself considered from a meta-theoretical point of view, let me recapitulate. The working "subteam" which constructed the simulation, along with the "sideteams" and the "superteam" of the International Relations Program in which this "subteam" was enmeshed, provided rich substantive milieux. The variables and relationships used in composing the man-machine simulation of the international system, known as the Inter-Nation Simulation, were selected within these milieux largely in terms of intuition, as sharpened by the socio-intellectual pressure of our peers. A vague sensing of a ceiling to the complexity which would be practicable played an important role in forcing consolidation and omission of various features of the simulation, especially as the

[32] Rudolph Rummel, Jack Sawyer, Raymond Tanter, and Harold Guetzkow, *Dimensions of Nations* (forthcoming).

[33] Guetzkow, "A Use of Simulation in International Relations," *Proceedings of the IBM Scientific Computing Symposium on Simulation Models and Gaming*, p. 256.

[34] Lewis Richardson, in Nicolas Rashevsky and Ernesto Trucco (Eds.), *Arms and Insecurity: A Mathematical Study of the Causes and Origins of War* (London: Stevens and Sons, 1960).

[35] Cattell, et al., "*An Attempt at a More Refined Definition of the Cultural Dimensions of Syntality in Modern Nations.*"

limits of feasibility were checked out in pilot runs. As Noel has indicated, the evolution of the simulation certainly was of a "prescientific character."[36]

Now consider what had occurred from a meta-theoretical viewpoint. It became increasingly clear, as we went from pilot run to pilot run in 1957 through 1959, that our participants were not serving as human subjects within an experimental situation, as it had been my custom to regard those who took part in the experiments at Michigan and Carnegie Tech. This laboratory situation was different, in that our human participants were acting as surrogates rather than as experimental subjects in their own right. In the development of our national entities it was our intention to use abstract representations, so that all participants, regardless of nationality, could man any of the nations and act in terms of the simulated environment within which they would find themselves. Likewise, in our formulations of variables through the use of prototypes, a more abstract simulation was being developed. In fact, had the work in simulated thinking been further along it might have seemed useful then to have employed all-computer components as decision makers within our Inter-Nation Simulation. Instead, it was practical to use human beings as "black box" surrogates. Thus, our simulation was not really a laboratory counterpart of field behaviors. As it gradually developed, the Inter-Nation Simulation was rather a theoretical construction complemented by the verbal and mathematical formulations.

Awareness of this state of affairs was perhaps the most important "decision" which befell us in the decade in which I have lived with the Inter-Nation Simulation. It is an orientation far from that accepted by many. Although admitting their own work is theoretical, some all-computer simulation people often are unwilling to accept the notion that humans and groups can serve as components within an operating model, despite my attempt to ease their discomfort by calling such components "black boxes," in the jargon of the systems engineers. And, on the other side, my colleagues in social psychology sometimes insist that I am simply operating noisy, poorly controlled experiments in which too many variables are being permitted to move simultaneously in providing a simulated environment for our subjects.

---

[36] Guetzkow, et al., *Simulation in International Relations*, pp. 101–102.

IV. Realizations of the Inter-Nation Simulation

Inasmuch as the Inter-Nation Simulation is a man-program model, involving humans as surrogate decision makers and manually-computed or machine-computer programs in intimate interface, along with a structure of materials in ordinary language (through couriered messages and mass communication media), work with the model consists in its realizations, so that the initial starting conditions plus its contents are operated to yield consequences or outputs. Once the pilot work was done, it was feasible to utilize the simulation as an operating model in a somewhat systematic way. The bulk of our energy has been devoted to its utilization in the exploration of a large variety of phenomena within international affairs.

Simulations differ centrally from other theory constructions in the fact that they operate from initial conditions, unfolding consequences which their builders have not been able to explicate through verbal or mathematical manipulations. Once the pilot work has been completed, utilization of the simulation in quasi-experimental ways is of critical import.[37] In retrospect, employment of the Inter-Nation Simulation seems somewhat orderly; in actuality, its evolution has been a conjunction of researchers and contents happening to be available at the moment. Even though it is now possible to indicate that in our use of the simulation an attempt was made to explore its value in the replication of a past, in the duplication of a present, and in the projections of a future, our choice of experimental problems was somewhat fortuitous.

Had it not been for Richard Brody's concern with the proliferation of nuclear capabilities, it is doubtful that this attempt to understand the "Nth-Country Problem" would have been first on our experimental agenda. It is fortunate, also, that Michael Driver, then at Princeton University, was willing to collaborate in the work, so that multi-leveled characteristics could be studied. Driver worked on the problem of the impact of personality, finding that those with a complex cognitive style use force less often than those with

---

[37] Donald Campbell and J. C. Stanley, "Experimental and Quasi-Experimental Designs for Research on Teaching," in N. L. Gage (Ed.), *Handbook of Research on Teaching* (Chicago: Rand McNally, 1962).

a simple, more concrete orientation.[38] Brody was concerned with systemic processes, finding that when nuclear capability spread, alliances tend to fragment.[39] This "subteam" worked with remarkable autonomy, as I stood by rationalizing their research.

The exploration of the crisis during the summer of 1914 leading to World War I was undertaken by the Hermanns because of the availability of support for summer work from Project Michelson and because of the existence of a corpus of data which could be used in tailoring the simulation to fit the historical situation.[40] Once again a multi-level approach could be used, inasmuch as Margaret Hermann was able to work with the personality materials while Charles Hermann worked at a more systemic level with the political contents of the crisis.[41] In this work our attempt to disguise the situation in abstraction for our participants failed; it turned out that about half of our decision makers recognized that we were simulating the preevents of World War I. Through colleague James Robinson's mentoring of our International Relations Program, the Hermann team soon became a "sideteam" as they mounted a frontal attack upon such crisis behaviors through the Inter-Nation Simulation format after making considerable revision of its contents.[42] Their work exhibits the importance of a multifactor approach, in that crisis behaviors were induced, in the

[38] Michael J. Driver, "A Cognitive Structure Analysis of Aggression, Stress, and Personality in an Inter-Nation Simulation (Lafayette, Ind.: Herman C. Krannert Graduate Schools of Industrial Administration, Purdue University, Institute of Research in the Behavioral, Economic, and Management Sciences, Institute Paper No. 97, January 1966).

[39] Richard A. Brody, "Some Systemic Effects of the Spread of Nuclear-Weapons Technology: A Study Through Simulation of a Multi-Nuclear Future," *The Journal of Conflict Resolution*, 7, 4 (December 1963), 663–753.

[40] Dina Zinnes, Robert North, and Howard Koch, Jr., "Capability, Threat, and the Outbreak of War," in James N. Rosenau (Ed.), *International Politics and Foreign Policy: A Reader in Research and Theory* (New York: Free Press, 1961), pp. 469–482.

[41] Charles F. Hermann and Margaret G. Hermann, "An Attempt to Stimulate the Outbreak of World War I," *American Political Science Review*, 61, 2 (June 1967), 400–416.

[42] Charles F. Hermann, "Crises in Foreign-Policy Making: A Stimulation of International Politics" (Northwestern University, Department of Political Science, unpublished Ph.D. dissertation, 1965), and Margaret G. Hermann, "Stress, Self-Esteem, and Defensiveness in an Inter-Nation Simulation," (Northwestern University, Department of Political Science, unpublished Ph.D. dissertation, 1965).

main, only when there was a perceived concomitant occurrence of their three components of crisis: an (1) unanticipated (2) endangering of important national interests with (3) pressure for immediate decision.

The increasing importance given by my peers to validity considerations in experimental work stimulated further work in the comparison of the Inter-Nation Simulation with empirical materials obtained from political, economic, and military studies of international affairs—the reference system. Recognition of the need for validation combined with our interest in doing something in a contemporary way. When the "subteam" of Dorothy Meier and Arthur Stickgold undertook a series of runs moving forward from 1964 to a year or two into the future, the design of a past-present-future exploration across time was achieved. Because our decision makers are surrogates for actors in the international scene, it seemed appropriate, also, to check the compatibility of high school versus college versus professional participants. With rare skill and a precious willingness on the part of Quaker Harold Snyder of the Washington Seminar to aid in our recruitment, Meier and Stickgold were able to operate the simulation with foreign diplomats from the international community in Washington serving as decision makers, as well as with our customary participants—high school and college students.

As we proceeded with these realizations representing past, present, and future situations, the same simulation model was being used by others throughout the United States and in a few places in Europe and Asia. In our Northwestern "shop," modifications of the model were constantly being made, although none seemed to be of major scope, therein constituting a series of "step-changes." All these seemed to derive from the same sources used in composing the original formulation—from intuitive assessments of incongruities (as in Meier's and Stickgold's[43] use of a budgeting process in order to dampen fluctuations in the allocations made of Basic Capabilities) or through attempted matching of the simulation with empirical findings (as in adjustment of parameters to approximate conditions during the summer of 1914 by the Hermanns.[44] As findings poured in from other researchers, it was

[43] Dorothy L. Meier and Arthur Stickgold, "Progress Report: Analysis Procedures," (St. Louis, Mo.: Washington University, 1965).

[44] Hermann and Hermann, "An Attempt to Stimulate the Outbreak of World War I."

possible to make a summary assessment of the extent to which the simulation model was describing the world reference system it was designed to represent. On the basis of some twenty-three studies, Guetzkow noted that approximately one-third of the fifty-five comparisons between simulation and reference materials made within these researches revealed "Much" correspondence, another one-third revealed "Some," while in thirteen instances the simulations failed to produce (or produced but weakly) the phenomena of the "real world."[45] Only four times did a simulation model produce an outcome which was an opposite or an inversion of a finding from the international reference system.

Thus, in our experimental realizations of the Inter-Nation Simulation in operation, we were guided by attempts to match empirical data, either existing or to be created, all at a level which was not too concrete, so that applications of our research would not be restricted to particulars.

V. Reflecting on the Retrospections

The development of the Inter-Nation Simulation has been influenced powerfully by the intellectual and social milieux. On the eve of the decision to constuct a simulation, past intellectual and value commitments served as a web of givens. The state of our knowledge in the last half of the fifties provided constraints. Working habits and intellectual styles proved throughout the decade to be important determinants of how the construction of a man-program simulation of the international system would be implemented, both in its pilot stages as well as in its experimental phases. The particularities seem rather fortuitous: the "objective" social scientist being buffeted by the interests of research personnel, by the availability of research materials for construction of contents, and by the strong influences of peers and other research teams in the environment.

It is gratifying to note that in providing grand opportunities for the building of the simulation model in all its variations, the milieu provided by our sponsors—the foundations and the U.S.

---

[45] Harold Guetzkow, "Some Correspondences Between Simulations and 'Realities' in International Relations," in Morton A. Kaplan (Ed.), *New Approaches to International Relations* (New York: St. Martin's, 1969).

government—was salutary, helping to ensure that our work was focused and productive, as we from time to time presented reports of past work and justifications for future activity to these monitors. Yet building a model of such a grand—almost preposterous—design has had repercussions on the builder. In the process of developing within the intellectual milieu of a multi-disciplined approach, I became a "marginal" scholar, little understood by many members of the very disciplines which served as seed beds. My attempt to embody the substance and methods of the behavioral sciences in the development of a simulation model of inter-national affairs has led me into constructions which seem suspect and alien to some in today's policy community. Ten years of life with the Inter-Nation Simulation have been most demanding, I confess. After experiencing the pangs involved in confronting the problems of peace and war through the use of a simulation which is perhaps "too big" and "too soon," a number of my younger colleagues became disillusioned and have fallen by the wayside. Seeing our travail, most of my older colleagues have kept their distance—perhaps with wisdom.

The call for a retrospective essay came at an appropriate time, inasmuch as in the very academic year of our symposium on *The Process of Model Building in the Behavioral Sciences* at The Ohio State University, an associate from overseas, Paul Smoker, constructed and operated a new simulation model, the "International Processes Simulation,"[46] representing a compromise between an incremental and a step-change. Building upon many of the products of our collaborators, including Richard Chadwick,[47] Charles Elder,[48] Robert Pendley,[49] John MacRae,[50] and

[46] Paul Smoker, "International Processes Simulation," (Evanston, Ill.: Northwestern University, Simulated International Processes project, 1968).

[47] Richard W. Chadwick, "Developments in a Partial Theory of International Behavior: A Test and Extension of the Inter-Nation Simulation Theory" (Northwestern University, Department of Political Science, unpublished Ph.D. dissertation, 1966).

[48] Charles Elder and Robert Pendley, "An Analysis of Consumption Standards and Validation Satisfactions in the Inter-Nation Simulation in Terms of Contemporary Economic Theory and Data" (Evanston, Ill.: Northwestern University, Department of Political Science, 1966).

[49] Robert Pendley and Charles Elder, "An Analysis of Office-Holding in the Inter-Nation Simulation in Terms of Contemporary Political Theory and Data on the Stability of Regimes and Governments" (Evanston, Ill.: Northwestern University, Department of Political Science, November 1966).

[50] John MacRae and Paul Smoker, "A Vietnam Simulation: A Report on

Dina A. Zinnes,[51] as well as on his own work,[52] Smoker has developed a greatly enriched simulation model. But even now, Smoker has found it necessary to continue working in the man-program format, although the operation has been complemented by an on-line, time-shared computer for rapid feedback to the decision-makers participating in the simulation. Without the decade of work that was done on the Inter-Nation Simulation, this move to the International Processes Simulation would have been impossible.

At the present time there seem to be two central barriers to the rapid building of more satisfactory simulation models of the international system. It is imperative to have computer-aided instruction facilities available for man-program simulations. A PLATO-like[53] or System-Development-Corporation-like set of interconnected consoles for the decision makers, interlaced to a central computer, is necessary to ensure a less "noisy" operation. Such an arrangement would permit more adequate instruction of the participants as they learn the intricacies of their offices, would forestall mechanical errors in the course of the operation of a run, and would permit rapid analyses of the outputs upon completion of each realization.[54] Secondly, it is imperative to create a "bank" of componential computer programs, so that various researchers need not start from scratch, as radical reorientations are developed in the formulations of other simulations.[55] Yet, the

---

the Canadian/English Joint Project," *Journal of Peace Research*, 4, 1 (1967), 1–25.

[51] Dina A. Zinnes, "A Comparison of Hostile Behavior of Decision-Makers in Simulation and Historical Data," *World Politics*, 18, 3 (April 1966), 474–502.

[52] Paul Smoker, "Trade, Defense, and the Richardson Theory of Arms Races: A Seven Nation Study," *Journal of Peace Research*, 2, 2 (1965), 161–176, and Paul Smoker, "Nation-State Escalation and International Integration," *Journal of Peace Research*, 4, 1 (1967), 61–75.

[53] Donald Bitzer, Elizabeth R. Lyman, and John Easley, Jr., "The Uses of PLATO: A Computer-Controlled Teaching System," *Audiovisual Instruction*, 2, 1 (January 1966), 16–21.

[54] Harold Guetzkow, with Donald L. Bitzer and Bruce Hicks, "A General Strategy in the Incremental Development of IPS through PLATO" (Evanston, Ill.: Northwestern University, Simulated International Processes project, September 1965).

[55] Harold Guetzkow, "Simulations in the Consolidation and Utilization of Knowledge about International Relations," in Dean G. Pruitt and Richard C. Snyder (Eds.), *Theory and Research on the Causes of War* (Englewood Cliffs, N.J.: Prentice-Hall, 1969).

development of such programs in turn depends upon two states of the art—the use of all-computer simulation in the social sciences generally[56] and the consolidation of an empirical base in reference materials in the international system.[57] Just as in the past decade in the development of the Inter-Nation Simulation we were importantly dependent upon our social and intellectual milieux, so in the decade ahead—when, I anticipate, forward strides will completely dwarf past efforts—we once again will be influenced mightily by those milieux, as we build the next generation of simulation models about peace and war.

[56] Harold Guetzkow (Ed.), *Simulation in Social Science: Readings* (Englewood Cliffs, N.J.: Prentice-Hall, 1962), pp. 82–94.

[57] J. David Singer (Ed.), "Quantitative International Politics: Insights and Evidence in World Politics," *International Yearbook of Political Behavior Research*, 6 (New York: Free Press, 1967).

9 THE LEGISLATIVE SYSTEM AND AFTER: ON CLOSING THE MICRO-MACRO GAP

Heinz Eulau
Stanford University

The publication in 1962 of *The Legislative System* by John C. Wahlke and his associates was something of an event. The book was "noticed," and the research it reported had some impact on the subsequent course of legislative study. Different readers, of course, noticed different things. The authors themselves were impressed by the fact that, after seven years of collaborative turmoil, they had come up with a collaborative product.[1] My own initial feeling was that its genuinely and systematically comparative approach was what most distinguished the State Legislative Research Project.[2] The younger researchers who

---

This is the first publication of Heinz Eulau's essay. All rights reserved. Permission to reprint must be obtained from the publisher and the author.

Much of this article was written in connection with the work of the City Council Research Project, sponsored by the Institute of Political Studies, Stanford University, and supported by grants from the National Science Foundation.

[1] John C. Wahlke, Heinz Eulau, William Buchanan, and LeRoy C. Ferguson, "The Annals of Research: A Case of Collaboration in Comparative Study of Legislative Behavior," *The American Behavioral Scientist*, 4 (May 1961), 3–9.

[2] Heinz Eulau, "Comparative Political Analysis: A Methodological Note," *Midwest Journal of Political Science*, 6 (November 1962), 397–407.

came to model their own work along the lines pioneered in *The Legislative System* seemed most impressed by the Project's use of role analysis and the categories of role orientation that had been developed and used to understand legislative behavior and functions.[3]

More recently another aspect of the work has come to attention. In their lucid Introduction to *Micro-politics: Individual and Group Level Concepts,* John H. Kessel and his collaborators, referring to *The Legislative System,* found it:

> worth noting . . . that by beginning on the microlevel, the four political scientists were able to knit concepts together so as to arrive at a quite distinctive understanding of the legislative system. They found that the legislatures, although quite similar in their formal structures and processes, differed significantly in their behavior patterns.[4]

They are quite right. Part V of *The Legislative System* was an attempt to "construct" the legislature as a *whole* out of its component parts, at least those empirical parts that were available for construction. Much of the effort in this direction was more conceptual than empirical for the simple reason that many links for complete empirical construction were missing. While I think that what we wrote made sense, the notion that we could fill in the missing links by conceptually treating the legislature as a subsystem of the legislative system was somewhat facile. But "system" was in the air. It had partly guided us in designing the research at the outset, even before Easton, Parsons, and Kaplan had popularized the idea in reference to politics. We therefore gratefully acknowledged their work in a footnote.[5] Today, with the benefit of hindsight, I wish we had never succumbed to system notions, for they now strike me as not only facile but

---

[3] Roger H. Davison, *The Role of the Congressman* (New York: Pegasus, 1969), or Allan Kornberg, *Canadian Legislative Behavior* (New York: Holt, 1967). An important continuation is Harmon Zeigler and Michael Baer, *Lobbying: Interaction and Influence in American State Legislatures* (Belmont, Calif.: Wadsworth, 1969), which introduces an empirical "significant other" into role analysis.

[4] John H. Kessel, George F. Cole, and Robert G. Seddig, *Micro-politics: Individual and Group Level Concepts* (New York: Holt, 1970), pp. 12–13.

[5] John C. Wahlke, Heinz Eulau, William Buchanan, and Leroy C. Ferguson, *The Legislative System: Explorations in Legislative Behavior* (New York: Wiley, 1962), p. 380, fn. 11.

theoretically empty as well. The "role structures" that we developed were empirically viable enough, but I think we could have done more with the material.

What we were after—and system concepts really did not help us much in this—was a method of coping with the exasperating problem of how to use data collected from and about *individuals* to say something about the collective body of individuals as a *unit* or whole. We wanted our concept of the unit to be just as "real" as what we had learned about the parts composing it. In short, we were searching for a closure of what I later called the "micro-macro gap."[6] It seemed to me then, as it does now, that linking social units of different size and, therefore, of possibly different structural character, is the most important methodological problem of political science.[7]

But before such linkage is possible, it is necessary to transform data collected on different levels of analysis in such a way that empirical confusion of levels is avoided. Additionally, there is the task of comparing wholes in terms of their component parts, for political science is eminently concerned with units larger than the individual. But wholes are difficult to observe as wholes. I touched upon the problem at a round-table discussion held in 1965:

> How does one observe whole systems? Well, I would say that, at the present time, it is impossible to observe whole systems. I think that one can make statements about whole systems, large systems, but that one cannot observe them. This is precisely the reason why one has to move on the individual level. This is the meaning, it seems to me, of what is called the behavioral movement in political science—that one has to move from the level of the individual to the level of the system.[8]

---

[6] I first discussed this in an article, "Segments of Political Science Most Susceptible to Behavioristic Treatment," in James C. Charlesworth (Ed.), *The Limits of Behavioralism in Political Science* (Philadelphia: American Academy of Political and Social Science, 1962), pp. 44–45, reprinted in James C. Charlesworth (Ed.), *Contemporary Political Analysis* (New York: Free Press, 1967), pp. 46–47. See also "Macro-Micro Dilemmas," in Heinz Eulau, *The Behavioral Persuasion in Politics* (New York: Random, 1963), pp. 123–127.

[7] "Introduction: On Units and Levels of Analysis," in Heinz Eulau, *Micro-Macro Political Analysis* (Chicago: Aldine, 1969), pp. 1–19.

[8] In James C. Charlesworth (Ed.), *A Design for Political Science: Scope, Objectives and Methods* (Philadelphia: American Academy of Political and Social Science, 1966), p. 207.

This is what we tried to do, however fancifully and fumblingly, in *The Legislative System*. But, as far as I know, scholars who subsequently took off from *The Legislative System* did not pay heed to this effort; rightly, perhaps, because the procedures employed were simplistic and dependent more on a diagrammatic than on a genuinely analytic technique.

But enough of hindsight. Looking forward, the payoff was not in the royalties received (hardly worth a farthing) but in the direction that my research took after publication. Not only did the theoretical and methodological problems of "micro-macro analysis" come to fascinate me, but I concluded from the experience with research on a small number of fairly large legislative bodies that the problems involved could be more effectively tackled by studying a large number of small institutionalized groups. So the City Council Research Project was born in 1962, with Kenneth Prewitt, now of the University of Chicago, serving as midwife.[9]

Now, as I begin to compare the results obtained in the research on state legislatures with the results of the city council study, what strikes me most is an observation which is largely speculative, but which, I think, could be substantiated if one were to take the trouble of doing so: The smaller the unit of action about which propositions are made, the more rigorous seems to be the type of analysis that ensues; and the larger the unit, the more discursive the analysis is likely to be. In other words, propositions about individual behavior are subjected to the most rigorous tests; propositions about the behavior of small groups (like courts or committees) come next; and so on until we reach the nation as the unit. Here writing is most discursive and relevant hypotheses seem to elude rigorous proof. If this observation is correct, it has obvious implications for comparison of large-scale units—say political parties, legislative bodies, bureaucracies, or entire nations.

---

[9] The City Council Research Project is a study of eighty-two local legislative bodies in the San Francisco Bay region. The data collected from and about individual councilmen have been used by some of my students in Ph.D. dissertations, some of which are in process of publication, and in a number of articles. The major analysis, by Prewitt and myself, is being conducted exclusively at the group level of analysis. Three articles published so far give an indication of preliminary results obtained by group-level analysis: Heinz Eulau and Robert Eyestone, ''Policy Maps of City Councils and Policy Out-

The Micro-Macro Problem

My concern is whether or not propositions about the behavior or action of large political units are in principle amenable to rigorous empirical analysis. Before proceeding I must specify what I mean by a "large" unit. Whether a unit is considered large or small depends on the standpoint of the observer. What from one standpoint may appear to be a small unit, say a legislative subcommittee in the Congress if compared with its parent committee, may appear to be a large unit from the standpoint of its individual members. In other words, size is not absolute.

Propositions in political science typically consist of elements whose referents are collective actors. Take, for instance, the proposition that nations with multi-party systems experience more cabinet instability than nations with two-party systems. The truth or falsity of this proposition is not at issue. At issue is the nature of the elements in the proposition and their empirical referents. In this example, the object units of analysis—the "things" whose behavior is to be explained—are nations, and their behavior is to be explained in terms of the relationship between two variables: first, "party system," and second, "cabinet stability."

What is actually to be compared, then, is not "national behavior" but the relationship between two properties or variables of nations. To make the comparison and test the relationship expressed in the proposition, "party system"—a property of the nation—has to be reduced to another set of units, namely, parties: what we observe and count is the distribution of parties in the nation. Although the proposition may have given the impression that "party system" is some global or integral property of the nation, it is in fact a distributive-structural property. Similarly, cabinet instability as a property of the unit nation has to be re-

---

comes: A Developmental Analysis," *American Political Science Review*, 62 (March 1968), 124–143, Kenneth Prewitt and Heinz Eulau, "Political Matrix and Political Representation: Prolegomenon to a New Departure from an Old Problem," *American Political Science Review*, 63 (June 1969), 427–441, and Heinz Eulau, "The Informal Organization of Decisional Structures in Small Legislative Bodies," *Midwest Journal of Political Science*, 13 (August 1969), 341–366.

duced to the comings and goings of individual ministers over time. Thus, cabinet stability or instability is measured by ascertaining, through summation, the turnover rate of the men who come and go, the length of their stay in office, and so on.

In fact, then, the only way in which the original hypothesis can be rigorously tested is by reducing the object unit "nation" to some component smaller unit—in the case of the property "cabinet instability," to individual persons. Only after we have reduced the unit "nation" to "parties" and "ministers" can we construct the properties of the larger units in which we are interested and compare them in order to test the hypothesis that multi-party system and cabinet instability are related.

I have chosen an example that is simple and obvious because its simplicity and obviousness disguise the profound methodological problem that is involved. Obviously, one must count parties and minister turnovers to determine the nature of a "party system" or "cabinet stability." But what is involved is not only a process of reduction but also of construction. The whole is constructed out of its parts.

Yet, I would argue, we have not self-consciously faced the issue of reduction. For if reduction is a viable procedure, there is no reason to stop short, as in the earlier example, with units like parties. For these units are also "large" and in turn decomposable. Rather, once the reductionist route is taken, there is no reason for not taking it all the way—that is, reducing macrophenomena like nations, parties, or cabinets, to their smallest analytic and empirical units. Yet, few students of comparative national politics have taken the leap from the nation as the object unit of analysis to the individual as the subject unit of analysis. This, it seems to me, is the main reason for the relative lack of rigor in the testing of propositions about national behavior.

Political science has produced very sophisticated propositions about the relationships of properties of political units—stability, legitimacy, authority, integration, development, power, and so on. But these propositions are not tested rigorously over many units because relevant data have not been generated. Although aggregate statistics have served as empirical indicators of social-structural (independent) variables and other quantifiable data as decisional-output (dependent) variables, valid and reliable indicators of political process variables are difficult to come by in the study of large collectivities.[10] When such indicators were generated, the data were highly suspect.[11] In other words, the issue of reduction —the problem of reducing macro-phenomena to the level of individual behavior and using data collected from or about individuals to construct the properties of collective units of action —has not been solved.

When reduction has been made, as in *The Legislative System* or other studies using survey research, analysis has proceeded on the level of the individual, and statements about the behavior of collective actors were in the nature of inferences from individual behavior. These inferences—involving the "individualistic" or "compositional" fallacy—are dangerous and possibly misleading. Reduction, it appears, is only a first step, and though it is necessary to generate data that can be rigorously treated, it is not sufficient to test propositions about the behavior of units that are larger than the individual actor. Another step is required: the whole must be reconstructed from the parts. If construction does not occur, it is possible only to test propositions about the behavior of individuals *in* larger units, but not about the behavior *of* larger units. Yet, most propositions of politics are not propositions about individuals but about collective actors —on the very good assumption that collective units are, in fact, *real* political actors.

Let me develop the theme in a different way. Insofar as political research has been "behavioral," in the sense that it is based on the individual person as the unit of analysis, it has dealt with the behavior of individuals in collectivities and not with the behavior of collectivities. What is found are similarities or differences in the behavior of individual members of collectivities like nations, bureaucracies, or legislatures. This is easy enough. More difficult is the identification of the factors that make for these similarities or differences. Explanation is sought in extraneous social-structural or speculative "cultural" conditions that are introduced *post hoc* and not part of the data set itself. What is involved is

[10] See Richard L. Merritt and Stein Rokkan (Eds.), *Comparing Nations: The Use of Quantitative Data in Cross-National Research* (New Haven: Yale University Press, 1966), and Mattei Dogan and Stein Rokkan (Eds.), *Quantitative Ecological Analysis in the Social Sciences* (Cambridge, Mass.: M.I.T. Press, 1969).

[11] As, *par excellence*, in Arthur S. Banks and Robert B. Textor, *A Cross-Polity Survey* (Cambridge, Mass.: M.I.T. Press, 1963).

a shift in level of analysis: concepts or indicators of concepts that refer to macro-phenomena are used to explain individual behavior. Or, as the case may be, individual behavior is used to explain macro-phenomena by way of inference.

If the empirical unit of analysis is the individual, research on large units must come to grips with two further problems: first, as already mentioned, the problem of how units on different levels of analysis are "linked" and second, how a unit on one level of analysis has an "impact" on (causes) the behavior of a unit on another level. Both are important problems of analysis, but I shall not deal with them here. For my concern is with the testing of propositions about the behavior of collectivities *in their own right*. For these propositions can only be tested at these units' *own* level and cannot be tested at the level of subunits or individual members. Such testing cannot rely on inferences from subunit or member behavior but involves the construction of unit properties out of their behavior.

One consequence of dealing with the problem of reduction and construction has been the false distinction between "behavioral" and "structural" variables. But what is involved is a level of analysis problem, and, if it is a problem, some solution must be sought. In fact, of course, structural variables are behavioral variables writ "large." And if they are of this nature, I see no reason why the properties of large units should not be constructed out of data gathered at the lowest feasible level of analysis. Data at this level can be manipulated in more or less elegant ways—as frequency distributions, proportions, rates, and other parametric measures. And they can forcefully bring to our attention the fact that the global ("structural" or "functional") language common at the macro level disguises much of the variance in the behavior of collective actors that occurs at the micro level of individual behavior. Unless the properties of collective actors are obtained through reduction and construction, analysis of large units will inevitably remain literary, discursive, and speculative.

I shall, from this point on, ignore the issue of reduction. There is much controversy in this matter between "reductionists" and "holists"—those who believe that scientific advance is predicated on reduction and those who hold that in social relations there are units which, because they act as wholes, should be treated as wholes and, therefore, must not or cannot be reduced to parts. I shall ignore this controversy because I am sympathetic to both sides. I believe that, as is the case with many dualisms, the whole-part dualism is a pseudo-problem that has no empirical merit.[12] Instead, I suggest a pragmatic guideline that does not require commitment to either an intransigent reductionist or holistic position. The guideline is simple: *reduce if you can and if it makes theoretical sense; do not reduce if you cannot and when it makes no sense.* In other words, use as a starting point the data that are available or the data that can be generated, regardless of the level on which the analysis is to be conducted. But in conducting the analysis, keep in mind that it can only be conducted on one level of analysis. In other words, keep in mind that correlation is possible only between units on the same level of organizational complexity. If, however, data are available from units at other levels, they must be *transformed* to make them manipulable at the level of the units whose behavior is to be compared and explained.

In general, data are available at three levels of analysis: first, at the unit's own level; that is, we have direct knowledge about some property of the unit; for instance, we know a nation's size, boundaries, or formal constitution. Second, at the level of subunits or members, for instance, we may have knowledge of the opinions, attitudes, or expectations of a legislature's members. And third, at the level of the unit's environment, for instance, we may have information about the character of a party organization's surroundings—whether it is located in a large or small city, in a densely populated slum area or a sparsely populated suburb, in a region with many natural resources or with few natural resources, and so on. If this is the case, the methodological problem is how such data from different levels can be made manageable at the level of the units whose behavior is to be compared and explained.

The Nature of Unit Properties

In order to tackle the problem of data transformation (i.e., bringing data from different levels onto the unit's own level), let

[12] See Heinz Eulau, ''The Maddening Methods of Harold D. Lasswell,'' *Journal of Politics*, 30 (February 1968), 3–24, where I discuss this at length.

us assume for a moment that transformation is in fact possible. If it is possible, we must have a clear picture of the properties of the units to be treated.

Comparison involves relationships among unit properties at their own level of complexity or comparison of interlevel relationships (as when we wish to compare the impact that leaders have on groups). Thus, clarification is all the more necessary for two reasons: first, properties of collective actors and properties of their members must not be confused and false inferences must not be made from one level of analysis to another; and second, the data base of the properties to be compared must be unambiguous; for different unit properties can be ascertained on different levels and can be constructed by different transformation techniques. Put differently, conceptual clarification of unit properties is necessary because it affects the practical operations performed on data gathered on different levels of organizational complexity. It affects *what* data are transformed, *how* the data are transformed, and *why* the transformed data are interpreted as they are.

There has been some attention to this in the sociological literature; however, as is so often the case in the social sciences, the nomenclature has not been identical. In general, variables identified at the unit's own level are called its global, integral, or syntality properties; variables stemming from subunits or members and transformed into unit variables are called population, aggregative, or analytical properties; variables characterizing the environment and transformed into unit variables are called structural or contextual properties.[13] For reasons that will become clear later on, I shall suggest two other properties that are called "relational" and "structural" properties. Table 1 presents these properties, with the nomenclature used by other scholars and by Eulau-Prewitt.

Because I think that methodological matters are best discussed in the context of empirical research, I shall draw on my current

[13] The two most useful references to the "Lazarsfeld school" or micro-macro analysis are Paul F. Lazarsfeld and Herbert Menzel, "On the Relation between Individual and Collective Properties," in Amitai Etzioni (Ed.), *Complex Organizations* (New York: Holt, 1965), pp. 422–440, and Hanan C. Selvin and Warren O. Hagstrom, "The Empirical Classification of Formal Groups," in Theolore M. Newcomb and Everett K. Wilson (Eds.), *College Peer Groups* (Chicago: Aldine, 1966), pp. 162–189.

TABLE 1

Nomenclature of Unit Properties

Property is constructed from information about:	Nomenclature of Sociologists	Nomenclature of Eulau-Prewitt
Unit Itself	Integral Global Syntality	Integral
Members (Subunits)	Population Aggregative Analytical	Distributive
		Relational Structural
Environment	Contextual Structural	Contextual

research for illustrations. Thus, I must briefly refer to the units with which I am concerned. I am interested in the behavior of small legislative councils because I believe that they are important decision-making units in democratic politics. But more importantly I am interested in these groups because I believe that the methodological problems of social science can best be tackled in research arenas in which data are available and can be fruitfully manipulated. It seems to me that we cannot solve the complex methodological problems of comparative analysis at the level of relatively small-scale phenomena. But, as has been argued, the distinction between what is to be considered "large" or "small" is a matter of observational standpoint. While the legislative groups with which I am dealing are "small" from the perspective of national parliaments or assemblies, they are "large" from the perspective of the members who compose them. And national assemblies are "small" from the perspective of the nation which they serve. Both relatively large or small legislative groups have in common the representative function: whether large or small, they are in fact acting *for* even larger units or aggregates.

Research on small legislative groups of from five to nine members has a number of methodological advantages. First, the smaller the group, the easier is it to observe the interaction. Second, as the methodological problem is that of reduction and construction, the choice of small, formal groups facilitates both the identification of the group's members and the collection of the same kinds of data from or about each member. Third, in small, face-to-face groups the information from each individual can be used in two ways: (a) as "respondent" data—that is, as information about the respondent himself; and (b) as "informant" data about either other individuals in the group or the group as a whole. Fourth, informant data collected from individuals in a small, face-to-face group are probably more reliable than data collected in a large group: there can be a strong presumption that the respondent as informant in fact describes reality, and the information given by one can be easily checked for reliability against the information given by another member of the group. Finally, the number of small legislative groups is large: while there are only one Congress and fifty state legislatures, there are hundreds of committees. In our research we happen to deal with eighty-two city councils. These still are not enough cases for more than bivariate analysis, although, if linear assumptions are met, it is enough for at least some multi-variate comparisons.

Integral Properties

A group's integral properties are attributes or characterizations that pertain only to the group as a whole. They are properties which cannot be decomposed or reduced to properties of its members. They are, in short, properties that can be conceived as "belonging" only to the group as a whole and not to its parts.

Integral properties are of various kinds. Some of them are descriptive attributes, such as a group's "age" (longevity or period of existence as distinguished from the "median age" of its members which, we will see, is a distributive property); its "wealth" (the amount of money in its treasury as distinguished from the individual wealth of its members); its language (as distinguished from dialects or idioms of subgroups or individual members); its size (number of members) or "boundaries" (which may be territorial in the case of a unit that occupies space, as a city or nation, or which may be functional, as when there is a formal division of labor between two governmental agencies).

A second set of integral properties are a group's organizational attributes—such as its "constitution" or "laws." Included here are such aspects of a group as its criteria for membership, the procedures by which members are inducted or officers chosen, the conditions of continued membership, the specification of positions, and so on. These properties are usually enumerated in documents that are themselves, in a literal sense, properties of the group. These documents may be adopted by the group under given decision rules—say, majority voting—which are also integral properties.

A third kind of integral property is a group's "external relations." For instance, the number or kinds of links that exist between the council as a whole and organizations in the community are integral to the group as a whole. The relationship may be one of domination, subordination, or equality—modes of relationship that define a group property. Similarly, such terms as "authority," "legitimacy," or "officiality" refer to integral properties of governmental units that set them off from other groups and that depend for validation on external support of the group as a whole.

A final set of integral properties relates to the group's action or performance as a whole, notably its decisions and policies. Although concepts like decision or policy are difficult to define, they refer to empirical indicators such as legislative statutes, court opinions, or fiscal expenditures. Such outputs are properties of the group and not properties of its members. Knowing the group's decisions or policies is independent of knowing any one member's policy views. As integral properties, decisions, policies, and other outputs arise or emerge out of member interactions, but they are different from the properties that individual members may possess.

The fact that a group has integral properties does not mean, of course, that it cannot be reduced with respect to others, such as distributive, relational or structural properties. But it is important to point out that such constructed or reconstructed properties, though inevitable or necessary, are not sufficient to make the unit "whole." For instance, interaction—a relational property—defines a group, but unless the "interaction set" observed is also characterized by integral properties, it can hardly be conceived as a group that is itself capable of action.

Distributive Properties

A group is composed of subunits or members with their own integral and non-divisible properties. For instance, all members of a group are individually characterized by age, race, income, or educational achievement. Each member has these attributes quite independent of any other member or of the group to which he belongs. Hence it is possible to ascertain these attributes from each member without having information about the group as a whole or about his relationships with other members.

At the level of the group, these properties of members can be conceived of as distributive properties. Because a group can be decomposed or reduced to its individual members with respect to members' own integral properties, these properties of the members can be transformed into properties of the unit. Put differently, because members' own integral properties are attributes of *all* group members, they constitute distributive properties of the group. They are "spread" throughout the group or distributed among the group.

Distributions have the quality of being subject to mathematical computations. A group's distributive property is, therefore, always a property upon which some mathematical or statistical operation has been performed. For instance, we can speak of a group's "median age"—as when we say that it is a "young group" or an "old group." We can speak of a group's "racial composition"—as when we say that is "all white," "all black," or "racially mixed." Or we can characterize a group as "highly educated" or "poorly educated." These characterizations of the group are possible because member properties can be transformed into group properties through some kind of computation.

Age, race, income, and education are not the only attributes of members that can be transformed into distributive properties of the group. It is possible to discover members' individual attitudes, perceptions, beliefs, orientations, identifications, demands, expectations, values, or other "psychological" characteristics and treat them at the group level as distributive properties of a collective. Although these characteristics of the members may not be unrelated to their membership in the group—in the sense that "group belongingness" may influence the attitudes or perceptions, and so on, that members hold—it is possible to characterize the group in terms of the distribution of such member characteristics. For instance, a group may be said to be "like-minded" in a matter of policy if a specified proportion—a bare majority, or a two-thirds majority, or a larger percentage—"share" the "same" view. Or a group's reaction to an external event may be treated as a distributive property if member reactions have been ascertained and transformed.

In short, a group's distributive properties are the result of reducing the group to subunits or members and then constructing group properties out of member characteristics through some kind of mathematical manipulation.

Relational Properties

A group is, by definition, a set of members who interact with each other and who stand in specifiable relationships to each other. It is this quality that distinguishes a unit that is a group from a unit that is an "aggregate." While a unit that is an aggregate—say, a population in a given census tract or voting precinct, or all persons in a population of a certain occupation or ethnic background—may be characterized by distributive properties, it does not possess what we shall term "relational properties." Relational properties are group characteristics that arise out of interactions between and relationships among members of a social unit.

The building blocks of relational properties are the relationships that occur among group members as a result of interaction. In other words, relational properties are constructs that characterize the group or unit as a whole, but they are not derived either from member characteristics or from the unit's integral properties. A group's relational properties can be ascertained only through observations of interactions or relations existing *among* members, or from information about such relationships. For instance, if all of a group's members are found to be tied to each other by strong bonds of friendship—they consider each other friends, they get along well with each other, they frequently see each other in the pursuit of common interests—the group as a whole seems to be characterized by a property that we may call "cohesion." On the other hand, if the interactions are characterized by disagreements, competition for status, mutual disregard, and so on, the relational property of the group may be called "tension." Similarly, if members in their interactions disagree on issues but engage in interpersonal practices or strategies that involve compromise, bargaining, or other forms of exchange, then the group as a whole may be characterized in these terms.

There are also "informal" organizational characteristics that are best thought of as relational properties. For instance, what are called "group norms" or sometimes "rules of the game"—conventional or traditional "ways of doing things"—are relational properties. These kinds of property are not so much attributes as emergents from group interactions. They are difficult to observe as is evident in the vagueness of some of the concepts that refer to them, such as culture, ethos, style, or atmosphere. A city council's "ethos," for instance, is more than the aggregation of its members' individual orientations to action. One may have to rely on members' interpretations of how the council as a whole copes with its decision-making tasks, but one cannot predict its "ethos" from the values that individual members may hold. If we say that a council's ethos is "political" or "pragmatic" or "paternal," we refer to a relational property of the group.

Relational properties, then, are distinguished from integral properties in that they are minimally reducible to dyadic relationships, that is, to interactions between two members. They are distinguished from distributive properties in that they are not arithmetic products of individual member characteristics but of intermember relationships. However, relational properties as such cannot tell us anything specific about particular patterns of interaction that may occur in the group. Such patterns, we shall suggest, represent "structural properties." In other words, relational properties are undifferentiated qualities that characterize the group as a whole. This is not to say that these qualities cannot be measured. Metrics such as the Rice "index of cohesion" or the Proctor-Loomis "index of expansiveness" are sociometric devices to summarize a group's relational properties.

Structural Properties

If both the interactions and relationships existing in a group assume forms or patterns in which the positions of members *vis-*

à-vis each other can be ascertained, we speak of "structural properties." For instance, if there is an identifiable "leader" who occupies a position of primacy in a group, the resulting relationship is a structural property of the group.

More precisely, a group is not simply a set of interacting members, but the interactions tend to be uniform and regular, constituting structures of more or less stability. These structures can take many forms. For instance, the group's status system or stratification may resemble a pyramid, a diamond, or a flat box. Or its communication net may resemble a line, a fork, or a wheel. In other words, structures are aspects of behavioral patterns or relationships that can be divorced from time yet which, of course, are also subject to change through time. A structure is, in this sense, a snapshot of the unit's behavioral processes. It "catches" the positions and statuses occupied by the members of the group. These positions and statuses define the flow of transactions and interactions in the group as a whole.

If the patterns are lasting and become formally recognized, they may become, over time, characteristics of the unit that appear to be quite independent of the members and their behavior, as when we speak of the group's "organizational chart." The chart is, of course, only a symbol that stands for or represents the unit's structure: having a chart (or charter that specifies positions, relationships among positions, and forms of prescribed behavior) is a defining characteristic of a group that has become "institutionalized." There may also exist "informal" structures that are more flexible and subject to change as particular members move into and out of positions or statuses and redefine their mutual relationships. This informal organization of the group is a structural property that may or may not be congruent with its formal organization or constitution.

The tendency to reify concepts, especially if the concepts refer to relatively stable social phenomena such as the behavioral patterns and interactions in a group, leads to confusion in the use of the notion of "structure." For instance, such institutionalized groups as the family, the factory, or the government are often referred to as "structures." But structures are not "things" like stones are things; they are qualities or properties of things, like the roundness or flatness of a stone. If we denote a thing by its properties, we confuse the thing with its properties. Structure cannot refer to a thing like a group but only to some property of the group.

By structural properties, then, we refer to specifiable linkages and organizational patterns among group members, so that we can speak of a group's decision-making structure or status system. We may also observe patterned relationships between subgroups and the group as a whole. For instance, there may be a high rate of interaction between some group members but not others, making for two different sets of members, with comparatively little interaction between the members of each set. "Cliquishness," as the phenomenon may be called, is a *relational* property of the group. But if one clique is noted to dominate the other more or less regularly, a *structural* property has been identified, and the group as a whole may be called "clique dominated."

Structural properties are emergents. This is not to say that such structural properties like the status order, the net of communication, or the leadership structure are any less "real" than distributive or integral properties. They only differ in the ways in which they must be ascertained, usually involving more complex modes of data transformation than is the case with other properties.

Contextual Properties

Contextual properties are induced from a group's environmental characteristics. The context or environment may be another "higher level" unit—such as a committee in a legislature, a legislature in a government, or a government in a nation—or it may be what we conventionally think of as environment—say, an "urban environment" as against a "rural environment," or a "lower-class environment" as against a "middle-class environment." Contextual properties, then, are generated by a group's inclusion or location within a higher level of social organization. In other words, any group below the level of a hypothetical "superunit" can be described contextually. A contextual property has the same value for all groups or group members located in the same environment. For instance, a city council, all of its committees, and all of its members have the property "rurality" to the same degree if the council is located in a "rural city."

Contextual properties, then, are induced from a group's context or environment. The data transformation procedure involved is simple and straightforward; it does not require particular new ways of constructing the relevant indicators. Nor is there any prejudgment that the context has an impact on the group. It may or may not have. This is a matter for empirical verification.

Contextual properties may themselves be distributive, structural, or integral properties of the context or environment. For instance, a city council may be located in a city with a city charter (an integral property), a "power elite" (a structural property), and a heterogeneous population (a distributive property). It partakes of these various properties of the city that constitute its environment. However, one must not mistake such contextual properties with the unit's properties that are generated at its own level or stem from lower level units. For instance, being located in a working class suburb does not mean that a council is composed only or necessarily of working-class men. It may well have the distributive property "middle-class."

Contextual properties may serve as independent or control variables. For instance, in the proposition that "urban councils are more likely to allocate substantial funds for planning than do rural councils," the contextual property serves as the independent variable in a bivariate analysis. On the other hand, in the proposition that "strong leadership in a council and unanimity in decision-making are more likely to be related in working-class than in middle-class cities," the contextual property "class character of city" serves as a control variable in a multivariate analysis. What contextual properties one wishes to attribute to a group depends, of course, on the theoretical objective one has in mind.

The Transformation of Unit Data

Conceptually, we have seen, unit or group properties can be classified as follows: (1) properties that are immanent in the unit and that cannot be reduced to a lower level of organizational complexity—integral properties; (2) properties that are member properties and, because they are distributed throughout the group, belong to the group—distributive properties; (3) properties that arise out of the interactions and relationships among group members—relational properties; (4) properties that represent statistical or behavioral patterns among the group's distributive or relational properties—structural properties; and (5) properties that describe the unit's physical or social environment and are attributed to the unit—contextual properties. These distinctions are important for theoretical and analytic reasons, but they are especially important for methodological reasons. The different "natures" of unit properties clearly call for different methodological assumptions and procedures.

If, as is the case with distributive, relational, and structural properties, reduction of the unit to subunits or members is possible, there is in principle no reason for not pursuing it as far as possible. For instance, a state legislature can be decomposed into houses, the houses into committees, the committees into subcommittees, the subcommittees into members; or the houses can be decomposed into party delegations, the delegations into regional subdelegations, the subdelegations into cliques, and the cliques into members. All of these units have their own properties on their own level of organizational complexity. They cannot, therefore, be manipulated at will but are subject to the limitations imposed on a given unit by the nature of its properties.

It may be, of course, that data on subunits or members are not available. For instance, if the unit of interest is a voting precinct, one can describe its distributive properties and possibly some structural properties, but one cannot reduce the unit and then work with aggregate or global indicators of its behavior. In particular, one can say nothing about its relational properties that can only be constructed out of data from or about relationships among individual members. Similarly, while in principle data about integral or contextual properties should be directly available, they may in fact not be available. In that case, although these properties cannot be derived from data about subunits or members, it may be possible to construct them from member information. For instance, group norms are integral properties; yet, it may be impossible to apprehend them directly. Thus, it may be necessary to construct them from indirect information that group members can give. On the other hand, direct data about a unit's environment may not be available. Hence contextual properties may have to be constructed out of information given by group members. One may wish to know, for instance, whether a city council is located in a community characterized by an active group life. Ideally, one might wish to go into the community and determine, through observation or survey research, whether private associations are active, how many are active, or whether the members of these associations are active within the group. But if, as in the city council research, one deals with many units and direct information is not available because of limited research resources, it may be necessary to rely on well-placed informants for relevant data.

If, as may be necessary, a group's members not only serve as respondents but also as informants, the information they give may be of varying reliability. For instance, informant data concerning the city council's norms or external relations are probably more reliable than informant data about contextual properties, such as whether the citizenry is well organized, interested, or active in local affairs. This is simply due to the fact that the individual councilman as informant is in a better position to observe his colleagues than the public at large. There is, of course, a standard justification for accepting an actor's information concerning his environment as reliable data: an environment constitutes a contextual property to the extent that it is perceived; that is, it is the actor's "definition of the situation" that constitutes the socially effective reality. While it is in principle possible to appraise such perceptions of the environment by juxtaposing them with "objective" data of the context if they are available, they may in fact not be available. In that case, one must rely on correlations between the constructs of the context that are derived from informant data and other directly observable contextual properties to support one's acceptance of the former as valid and reliable.

In the study of natural-state groups, be they large or small, the survey is a powerful instrument of data collection because it can simultaneously serve as a source of data that permit the construction of distributive, relational, and structural properties once the group has been reduced to its members; and as a source of informant data that permit the construction of integral and contextual properties. The construction of group properties calls for different technical procedures, depending on the nature of the property in question and the kind of data that are available.

Data transformation is a necessary first step in solving what has been called the micro-macro problem. Bringing data collected on different levels of organization complexity onto a single level of analysis makes it possible to compare comparables and to do so in a more rigorous way than would otherwise be the case. While the procedure is more difficult in larger units, it is applicable in both principle and practice. It is less the technique of transformation and more the lack of data at the level of individual behavior that is the major stumbling block in the way of more rigorous comparative analysis.

10 SOME THOUGHTS ABOUT WHY THE SCIENTIFIC STUDY OF JUDICIAL POLITICS HAS BEEN SO DULL

Theodore L. Becker
New York University

I was informed that a major emphasis of essays in this collection should be the interrelationship between data and theory. As far as my own field is concerned, this focus struck me as being rather dreary. In other words, since the mainstream of the work in the study of judicial processes, judicial politics, judicial behavior (whatever you want to call it) has been so dull and irrelevant, an adventure into the epistemology of that field would be equally, if not more, grim.

Why is this so? Is it something about the nature of the political involvement of the judiciary that is innately devoid of anything other than monastic titillations? I am certain this is not necessarily so, yet the judicial area that has been studied by political scientists seems terribly narrow, and studies of it have lacked vitality.

I might say that I have not been too pleased with my *own* past efforts in political science. So let it be said at the outset that this is as much (if not more) self-confession as it is accusation.

This is the first publication of Theodore L. Becker's essay. All rights reserved. Permission to reprint must be obtained from the publisher and the author.

For instance, there is support for the view that studies of American judicial politics have been monstrously irrelevant to the pressing concerns of our day. In any event, few contemporary writers in the field have troubled themselves to demonstrate where they have social pertinence. Is it enough to shrug off the charge of irrelevance with a simple pronouncement that the scientific enterprise need not, or must not, dote on the fashionable lest it risk requisite academic detachment? I don't think so. Is it truly wise to insist that applications of pure science *must* not engage the working political scientist? I doubt that as well.

I'd like to turn my thoughts on research in this field to a discussion of why the research has added up to such an incredibly bland and unpalatable menu and how I think it could be made far more appetizing and nutritious.

Two major factors that contribute so heavily to this condition are: (1) a complete misunderstanding of what it means to be value-free in a scientific study of politics (and specifically, in the study of courts), and (2) a failure to understand our present proper level of science (in political science in general, and, specifically, in the study of courts). These two flaws in our scholarly personality have allowed us to lapse into a semi-comatose state, and since nobody likes to associate too closely with zombies, we are perilously close to becoming isolated as well as pitied.

Now, on to the first problem, which we might call the irrelevance of the "we-can't-be-objective-in-studying-ourselves" argument. I get tired hearing the cliche that our choice of political science problems—the choice we make when we study something—is value-loaded, biased, and prejudiced. And this charge is frequently leveled; it is no straw man.

In the first place, that particular assertion can be made about natural science and natural scientists as well. *All* original research choice is value-loaded, whether it be in natural science or social science.

The reason men undertake *any* scientific study is simply that someone is curious about a topic. The *reason* a specific person, whether he be a non-scientist, a natural scientist, or a social scientist, is curious about some subject is probably comprised of cultural and personal factors: the kind of society he comes from, what kind of background he has had, the kind of interaction he faced at home, the academic and chance factors that influenced his studies, and so on. I see no more reason to impute "bias" and "non-objectivity" in the research choices of political scientists than to research choices made by biologists. The biologist is equally interested in maintaining living systems. (How many biologists *value* death?) Why does a particular biologist want to study possums, or lemmings, or microbes? In *The Search*, by C. P. Snow, the main character (Miles) decides to study stars because of an interest developed while taking long walks with his father at night.[1] That seems as biased to me as an American political scientist wanting to study Africa because he visited it with his father when he was young. I feel the same argument holds for interpretation of findings as well. Biologists who study cancer *prefer* to find a cure (that is, to kill cancer cells). However, that doesn't mean that they will malinterpret or fudge their data.

This kind of argumentation has been tolerated for too long in our discipline. We seem embarrassed by the fact that what we choose to study *does* manifest a bias. But we shouldn't blush at this; *any* scientist chooses to study that which interests him and that which he values. This kind of value issue hurts us because it inhibits our choice of research topics. We cannot continue to worry about this issue, for, if we do, we will continue to avoid research on many important issues of today which require our attention.

Perhaps a case study of my motives in studying judicial role would help clarify my point as to the irrelevance of the factors influencing my choice of a research topic. First of all, I went into law school solely because my father was a lawyer. Someone had to mind the store. Also, the Korean War was dragging on at the time, and the army had little appeal for me. After graduation from law school, I used some political pull to land a job in the New Jersey Attorney General's office, where I worked for almost eight months. One of my legal chores was to draft memos on complaints by citizens against the State of New Jersey for personal damages caused by alleged negligence of the state employees (e.g., someone fell on a loose rug in the State House). The State had sovereign immunity, and the question was whether or not the State should allow such a claim, out of a sense of justice—as it had no *legal* liability. My job was to scan the claim, then browse through past Attorney Generals' opinions and all available legal

---

[1] C. P. Snow, *The Search* (London: Gollonce, 1934).

precedent and decide whether the law furnished any guidance on the matter. The clearer the law was, the easier my task. In other words, I was playing a role. Sometimes I might have felt more strongly about a claim and I might have resisted the precedent if it was very clearly against my predisposition. However, it was simple for me to hold against my preferences (that is, to recommend against my own predispositions) if that was what the law demanded.

So, these experiences were the source of the hypotheses that motivated my early study on judicial role (precedent orientation). What happened was that much of the work I read on judicial decision making, while I was a graduate student, seemed to omit this factor as being important—and I got curious, because it didn't square with my own experiences. I had and have no vested interest in whether judges follow the judicial role or not. It doesn't matter to me. I was interested in finding out whether, how often, or to what degree a precedent orientation might be a determining factor in a judicial decision, and it seemed to me that a lot of the research being done was unduly pretentious in claiming that, in fact, most or all judicial decision-making was determined by the personal attitudes of judges. It was plain to see that their research was not designed to test the questions in my mind, so that was the purpose behind my original work on judicial role. Does that bias condemn my work to being unscientific? I think not. Should that undertaking classify me into some ideological camp? Absurd.

Now, I am not saying that there are *no* value problems that we have to face as social scientists. I am simply saying that the above-mentioned problems are spurious ones. The genuine value issue is similar to that raised in the recent play *In the Matter of J. Robert Oppenheimer*. This drama portrayed the situation in the middle fifties, where the so-called father of the atomic bomb, J. Robert Oppenheimer, was being questioned as to whether or not he should have his security clearance continued, as very serious questions were being raised about his motivation for opposing the development of the hydrogen bomb. It seems that back in the thirties and forties he had maintained various associations with known Communists.

Oppenheimer's major argument was that the scientific community (in the forties) was highly biased in its decision to study how nuclear energy could be converted into a bomb. At that time, however, American physicists, including Oppenheimer, believed they were involved only in an intellectual problem. But were they value-free in their abstract physical world? Not at all. They bought arguments made to them by President Roosevelt and by the military community that, in fact, there was a great danger to this society, that they should do this military research, and that they should not consider or try to influence how it was to be applied in the long run.

They went about their work with remarkable naivete as to the purpose their research might be put to. Indeed, according to Oppenheimer, they never believed such a bomb would be used. They thought it was simply to be a deterrent—a factor in the equation of the potential balance of terror. The pristine innocence of this belief was shown by its resistance to change in spite of the fact that they spent much of the time figuring out which type of target would be most easily obliterated by atomic bombs, e.g., cities in valleys or on flat terrain or near water.

After the bomb dropped on Hiroshima and Nagasaki, some of the physicists were stunned. Stimulated in part by guilt, several began to ask very serious questions that have persisted until this day as to the role of science in this era. If a man refuses to study physics related to military uses, is he less a physicist?

I have a hunch that the same kind of value freedom that deadened the sense of social responsibility among nuclear physicists thirty years ago still plagues us in political science today. It surely seems to influence what we choose to study in the so-called public law field and the judicial process area. Who really cares about the studies of judicial behavior? Who really cares what factors are not important in relationship to whether a judge makes one kind of decision or another, or about his tendencies in relationship to his background factors, and so forth? What really great social importance inheres in this research? I am sure one can argue that it might have some vague importance, but if you think about the problems of our society today, I don't think you will really find this to be a particularly serious issue worthy of much time and energy. Yet it preoccupies the literature in our journals.

One of the reasons why I put together my anthology on *The*

Impact of Supreme Court Decisions was that I felt it hit at a timely and significant issue in America.[2] As I think about it in retrospect, this is where much research energy should be put because, in fact, the Supreme Court doesn't have nearly as much influence on certain areas of American politics as we all pretend it does. At least this type of research gets closer to a policy analysis which can engage us in honest questioning of the government's record in disbursing social justice. This seems to be an exercise of political science skills far more relevant to some of the major social concerns of the day. By studying processes of compliance to promulgated norms, we can begin to address ourselves to the question of how the Supreme Court can have a greater impact on government officials. If we believe the Court is (or should be) a source of social good and can be an effective source of social change, we must learn how it can be more or less effective in certain situations. Given this knowledge we could offer helpful advice even to the Supreme Court itself, if we thought it desirable. But this is another question. You'll note that there are never any political scientists on the staff of the Supreme Court (except perhaps to do legal kinds of analysis). Small wonder.

Actually, some of the major problems facing the cities have to do with the real political functioning of the entire legal system: police on the beat; judges who are trying cases of political offenders; prison officials' behavior to inmates; and so on. It includes a day-to-day more-than-abuse-of-discretion in interpreting of the law by a variety of administrators (and the judge is only a peculiar type of administrator). What are the ways in which they go well beyond the pale of discretion? What are the ways in which they can go beyond their legal jurisdiction, which they frequently and in fact *systematically* do, in violating the very law they are supposed to be enforcing? *That* is for us to discover.

Looking at the legal system from this perspective—as "official anarchy"—raises a host of concomitant problems. For instance, to the degree that systematic "government anarchy" exists, we must learn how it delegitimizes the system to people who are involved in all kinds of political activism and how "government anarchy"

---

[2] Theodore L. Becker, *The Impact of Supreme Court Decisions* (New York: Oxford University Press, 1969).

affects various segments of the population. Political activists argue that official anarchy is running amok and that the democratic system doesn't work. They argue that ordinary legal channels will not lead to the kind of rapid change that is needed, and that government will, in fact, operate illegally to ensure the *status quo*. By failing to delineate accurately the extent of the failure of our government to obey its own laws, by failing to find out the impact of this phenomenon, and by failing to suggest remedies, we may well be "contemplating our navel" in a time that demands more virile activities.

We, as political scientists, must reorient the scope of our study so we can reach the point where we can begin to be important influences in guiding change in our system and our policies.

We cannot plead scientific objectivity as the reason for our irrelevance; we can only admit our fears and our lack of imagination. Other social sciences have been in the thick of social issues of late, which simply dramatizes our remoteness.

I can't see that in order to avoid being corrupted we must cop out. In fact, I'm saying we must lend serious thought to dropping *in* and addressing the serious problems rupturing our society. Furthermore, in order to be most effective, we do have to produce *good* science, and great care must be taken to accumulate *new* data with *reliable* methods while being especially cautious in maximizing the *validity* of the information we gather.

This call for more and better "science," in a more relevant political science, actually begs an important question. For one of the more serious *causes* of contemporary political science's failure to be relevant is its misconception of its actual level of development. Many political scientists have locked themselves into reality-proof rooms and toyed carelessly with their high-powered tools. If we would admit the primitive stage of scientific development that political science really represents, perhaps we could get down to more socially pertinent research. What we really need at this point are good *words*, that open up new areas and that allow for different observational techniques. The mere fact that we play all kinds of statistical games in our journals, employing the most wonderful formulas and models, is meaningless, because our *data* borders on the insignificant.

At a symposium held at the University of Hawaii in 1968 on T.

Kuhn's *The Structure of Scientific Revolutions*,[3] every single political scientist present felt that the rather vague application of systems theory to political science (David Easton, *et al.*) constituted, in Kuhn's terms, a paradigm. I was amazed. For, according to Kuhn, a paradigm is a single set of concepts that operate in some lawful way one to another, that is *agreed upon* by an entire discipline, and that guides *all* the research in that science (becomes the normal touchstone for all the researchers). Indeed, the quintessence of Kuhn's idea of paradigm is its ability to be "able to guide the whole group's research." Does the concept or model of "systems" have that power in political science? Of course not. Many of us use different concepts—up to now, unrelated to that of system—and even when we use the same words, we operationalize them differently. How can any realistic political scientist believe that we are simply in the process of "mopping up" (the task of post-paradigm scientists)? Of course, I know several political scientists do believe this, but then a lot of generals thought we were "mopping up" in Vietnam as early as 1967.

Another way of demonstrating quite clearly that political science remains in a preparadigm state is to look at the systems characteristic of such a point of scientific underdevelopment. The first of these systems is what Kuhn refers to as an "early fact-gathering," sort of a primitive fruit pickers' stage. ("Early fact-gathering is usually restricted to the wealth of data that lie readily at hand.") That seems to adequately describe what we do in all areas of political science these days. For instance, most of the research on the Supreme Court consists of getting and analyzing only the most readily available data, e.g., Supreme Court decisions, how one justice voted, what another said in an opinion, where they were born, what party they are in, and so forth.

Secondly, we write books. According to Kuhn, in the post-paradigm "normal science" they *don't* write books. They write research articles. They do have textbooks which order the laws of their science in some classification, the relevant experiments, the problems-yet-to-be-solved. But our textbooks are as varied as our research. They aren't based on a paradigm. Moreover, the general public can read our basic text books very easily and can also read

---

[3] Thomas S. Kuhn, *The Structure of Scientific Revolutions* (Chicago: University of Chicago Press, 1962).

many of our research articles. Those they can't read don't seem to me to be really worth reading anyway. The scientific jargon in them is not one we all accept, with certain agreed-upon operationalizations. According to Kuhn, in a preparadigm science, scientists each have their own concepts, and that's the stage we've reached in some of our better books. This is not to say we are not scientists; it is only to correctly locate our early stage of development.

The third symptom is lack of replication. At the paradigm level of science, there is much replication because there is much "mopping up" to do. Everyone has the same definitions and operations for the same concepts. In *Double Helix* (the story of the discovery of DNA) one can obtain a good picture of how the paradigm-level science operates.[4] Papers fly back and forth; everyone knows the different kinds of models that have been tried and failed; they all have similar understandings of the properties of various parts of the model; and there is a good deal of respect between the various people who are competing in the development of this kind of science.

Now, is this analogous to the development of the scientific study of the judicial process? Kuhn makes an analogy between a paradigm and the binding nature of traditional precedent. This is what he means when he states that "a normal science is the articulation and specific application of a set of general rules." By analogy, as far as the study of courts is concerned, I would say that it is barely in an advisory-opinion stage. There is hardly any precedent (conceptual scheme) that has the force of authority to dictate any specific rules, or articulate or compel any particular applications. There are only a set of vague opinions covering no specific area. Each of us gropes around for data. In other words, we are in an early "stage of growth, characterized by 'schools.'" Each school is identified with a specific concept or tool or approach. One is the "statistics-are-the-true-measure-of-science" school. Its motto is, "the fancier the statistic, the clearer the ballistic." About the only value of all this is the storing of some scientific type of data which, in itself, is nothing to be ashamed of. It *could* be a legitimate and important enterprise that is a prerequisite to the ultimate generation of a paradigm. But it probably won't be. Pardon my skepticism.

[4] James D. Watson, *Double Helix* (New York: Atheneum, 1968).

Newton likened the scientific search for knowledge to the action of children picking up pebbles from the beach. That was the stage of science at the pre-paradigm level (which is still science). In other words, the mere fact that we're not at a paradigm level doesn't mean we cannot be doing a scientific type of fact gathering. Nor does it mean we cannot go about disconfirming important hypotheses as well.

What worries me most about those doing scientific work on the courts today is that so many are so deadly serious about their concepts and their techniques. Each seems to have such a tremendous stake in confirming and improving his own pet theories. Our need is twofold. We need to discuss and to reach agreement on what we should look for. We need to discover where the beach is and put a fence around it. Then we need a playful spirit of children who are free to search for pebbles, driftwood, and shells, and who will delight in sharing their discoveries. The only prerequisite for this would be that in fact we should try to use some rigor where possible. We should be trying to quantify data that has not yet been quantified or that seems utterly incapable of quantification and that takes imagination.

I guess I'm positing that the deadly illness of our present enterprise, in scientifically thinking about the political aspects of the legal system, is due largely to the fact that we are wandering aimlessly. People who are lost are bound to be gloomy and in anxious earnest. It is true that in one sense early scientific fact gathering must be random, but this does not mean there is to be a total lack of relevance to what is important, because that would lead the researcher into boredom and alienation. Like any child, he must be given a clear idea of the boundaries in which he is free to roam. Otherwise he may drift too far away and get lost or stumble into the water and drown. He must learn that he must keep himself close to society or he may starve to death.

So we have not defined what we are looking for in this area. The conceptualization has been poor. We grope about without any agreed-upon limits and argue publicly about the ways to go about picking up and describing isolated pebbles and pieces of flotsam. It is not good science, and the data may prove to be of little or no value once we do set our limits and finally set ourselves free to gather fresh, new, and important data. It was a general feeling of frustration about the seemingly isolated and meaningless data gathering that I had done before that forced me into trying to find a theoretical guide. It seemed to me that we in "Public Law" never sat down and asked what it was we all studied in common—its properties, the questions about its properties that could have importance to society. After pondering it for a while, it seemed that we were basically interested in *courts* and their causes and effects. The Court was a government structure, and we were interested in its manifest and latent functions. Thus I arrived at the core of my *Comparative Judicial Politics: The Political Functioning of Courts.*[5]

Now, by setting out what I meant by a court (in other words, judicial structure), I established the prerequisite for making any kind of a structural-functional analysis (seeing whether a court in society makes a difference or not). In other words, what functions is it supposed to have and what functions does it really have? But how can one study what functions are if he never decided (at least at the working-definition level) what the structure was that he should be studying?

So what I did in *Comparative Judicial Politics* was to posit a definition that has a workable grounding, and I tried to apply it as thoroughly as I could to all kinds of theory locked into our literature over the years. This is our beach; it might be barren—but that remains for the combing.

I believe that my own attempt to bound the field as I have will perhaps allow us to advance toward a latter stage in fact-gathering. This will allow us to gain a better feel for playfulness (in terms of developing techniques); and furnish us with a feeling that we're entering an area that could have some significance intellectually, socially, and politically.

For instance, by not coming to grips with the importance of the concept of judicial role, we have failed to come to grips with very major problems. Among other misdirections, we have still failed to heed Jerome Frank's advice and have averted most of our attention from where it counts the most—the trial courts which directly touch the vast bulk of the population of any society. We have not really looked into role conception of trial judges in relation to the police. This is at the heart of judicial independence. I

---

[5] Theodore L. Becker, *Comparative Judicial Politics: The Political Functioning of Courts* (New York: Oxford University Press, 1970).

had an interview in Washington, D.C. recently with a special consultant to the Committee on the Administration of Justice, and we discussed the problem inherent in the fact that judges, when they're dealing with police matters, never really seem to conceive of themselves as being separate from the police. In other words, they feel that they have to dispose of a certain number of cases, and so it serves their purpose to believe that police are basically telling the truth. Thus, if judicial independence makes trials take longer, it may be downgraded in the judges' minds—without their even realizing it. This may be even more exaggerated during special situations like riots, in political cases, or during periods of particular stress. The courts turn into a production line; judges cease to be judges (no independence of perception) and become administrators. What's the judicial role at the trial level like? Why aren't judges more alert to the fact that, indeed, police feel it necessary and important to stretch the truth? Why aren't judges more skeptical of police devices used to circumvent the law, and why don't they account for that in systematic fashion?

We have not really begun to explore the differences between administrative decision making and judicial decision making and weighing whether the difference is worth the cost in the deference we ask our citizens to pay the judiciary. If there isn't much difference between the decision making of a judge and the decision making of an administrator, why do we have to go through all the folderol of dressing them in robes, placing them "on high," and making people rise when they walk into a room? The establishment of a status system should do more for a society than satisfy the egos of the ruling elite. Nor have we seriously considered the cop on the beat as being a judge. Police, after all, are simultaneously judge, jury, and executioner—all in one blow of a billy club. All these are questions relating to the judicial role. None have been posed—nor researched—despite their obvious pertinence to critical issues of our time.

Another problem in our data-gathering stage is that we have not begun to take serious risks in our observations. Aside from staying out of some of the dirtier kinds of situations, we have avoided difficulties inherent in observing the legal system, the courts, and the police as they *really* operate. Systems protect themselves from direct observation, and thus it may become necessary to devise various methods and techniques that would be highly unobtrusive (and perhaps even illegal). Not too long ago, the Chicago University law school people went and tapped the jury room. How shocking! What a terrible thing! Imagine, tapping a jury and disturbing that great institution of twelve men (tried and true), intellectuals all, seriously mulling over the fate of man. Frankly, I don't see anything wrong with bugging jury rooms—whether they know it or not. Back in the good old days of early development of the so-called science of anatomy, people took tremendous risks because they felt that some social good would come out of it. They were the premedical ghouls, who would creep out and dig up freshly interred bodies and then bring them back to the laboratories to dissect them.

There were also people interested in discovering what made the human body tick while alive *despite* the fact that there were a lot of states with anti-vivesection laws. It was pretty important to these people to work out a science that would have a great social value; flaunting those laws was not immoral—though perhaps "unethical." They felt it was important to understand how the body worked when it was alive, not only after it was dead. If one digs up and dissects a corpse, he will not see the process working in a live system. So they broke laws in their states in order to find out something they thought would have greater social significance. If they were only going to study what the lawmen and physicians told them, or make inferences from what people would tell them, or speculate, or guess, we would not have developed a science that was crucial. Similarly, it seems to me that if we're going to find out what makes the legal system tick, as a body, we can't only rely on going to books, measuring the way people vote, looking at the data on their social backgrounds, guessing their personal attitudes, asking the experts in the universities what they think, and so on.

I was impressed by one article I put in my *Impact* reader. It was a report by a group of Yale law students who went to the New Haven police station house and received permission from the police to position themselves twenty-four hours a day for a whole summer. They listened to what the police were doing in interrogation procedures, and they kept various notations in diaries. Pretty soon many policemen didn't even notice them. These law students obtained some very interesting measurements on changes in police behavior. That's an obtrusive measurement. There are ways police stations could be bugged, tapped, to find out what really happens in police stations—and the same would be necessary to discover what really happens in judicial chambers. Why shouldn't top officials in our system allow this—as long as the data is presented statistically? If we're going to find out how the system really operates, it may be necessary to take some risks, though it may be possible to receive authorization. Anyway, if we really believe that what we are doing is important and can have serious social and political consequences, then it seems it would be our duty to do it. We have been simply doing what is very convenient to do and we have reaped juiceless and unnourishing fruits.

In conclusion, I believe that there is a definite demoralysis among those who study the courts and the legal system. There is very little interchange and very little original data coming out of our highly disparate efforts. I've suggested that this has been due to several factors. First, the contemporary thinking has been largely irrelevant to important concerns of the day. As long as we're in this crude preparadigm scientific state, we may as well be guided by the critical contemporary concerns of our society. All sciences make value choice in what they study. It is not inimical to science to be relevant. Second, we have not seriously considered the socio-political ends to which good science might be or should be put. Third, there has been little consideration of the area's boundaries and this has resulted in (1) a widespread intellectual floundering, (2) excessive concern with convenient techniques for data accumulation, (3) a pervasive drabness to the literature, reflecting the lack of zest inherent in collecting data from law libraries and archives, (4) a feeling of social alienation stemming from the failure to do the research necessary to understand the *real* operation of the entire legal system.

Thus we have been doing poor and insignificant science in this area, and we have paid a high personal price for it—all of us. There are as yet no shoulders upon which our future Newton can possibly stand. Our work has lacked appeal for fresh and invigorating minds. It is because we have not reached the advanced stage of curiosity where, as Rod McKuen, we could say: "I pace unfamiliar streets now, attempting new solutions to old problems and the answers seldom come." We have been deadly true to the conservatism of the men we should be studying from a radical perspective. Primitive scientists must be radicals at heart and in mind.

Date Due